Start Where You Are

ALSO BY CHRIS GARDNER

The Pursuit of Happyness

Chris Gardner

with

MIM EICHLER RIVAS

START
Where You Are

LIFE LESSONS
in Getting from Where You Are
to Where You Want to Be

Amistad

An Imprint of HarperCollinsPublishers

HarperCollins books may be purchased for educational, business, or sales promotional use. For information please write: Special Markets Department, HarperCollins Publishers, 10 East 53rd Street, New York, NY 10022.

FIRST EDITION

Library of Congress Cataloging-in-Publication Data has been applied for.

ISBN 978-0-06-153711-0

09 10 11 12 13   OV/RRD   10 9 8 7 6 5 4 3 2 1

To the tens of thousands of you who have reached out to me and said,
"That's great for you, but here's where I am . . ."

To each and every one of you that I have said,
"Start where you are."

And to the loving memory of my mother,
who shines through in every life lesson.

Contents

Author's Note

All of the stories that I have included in *Start Where You Are*'s forty-four life lessons have come from my experience of them in a variety of forms—including private correspondence and personal conversations. In consideration of the privacy of those individuals, some names and identifying circumstances have been changed. Where I have included conversations and dialogue in these recollections, they are not intended to represent word for word documentations but are meant to evoke the spirit in which the exchanges took place and to teach the lesson that was presented at the time. All efforts have been made on my part and that of my co-author to check spellings of names and fact check dates for those who granted permission to have them included. A special thanks to everyone who has blessed me by "sharing the wealth" (see Lesson #29) of how you started where you were and got to where you wanted to be.

Start Where You Are

Overture—C'mon In

I love questions. There was a time in my younger days when I didn't appreciate how powerful questions really were, especially when asked of the right people at the right time. But over the years, the more I got past my own ego, the more willing I was to flex my question-asking muscles, and the more daring I became in putting the answers to use.

For anyone who knows a part of my story—even what you may have read on this book's flap cover—two questions that have been indispensable to me over the years should definitely ring a bell: "What do you do?" and "How do you do that?" At age twenty-eight, as a first-time (soon to be single) parent, I had the good sense to ask those two questions of a San Francisco stockbroker named Bob Bridges. This guy didn't know me from Adam but was willing to let me buy him a cup of coffee and answer my questions. And he went a step further by steering me toward a couple of people he knew, who in turn opened doors that led to my pursuit of an ultimately thriving career on Wall Street. Through all the ups and downs that happened after meeting Bob

Bridges, I never forgot my debt of gratitude to him—even during the toughest pass early on when my toddler son, Christopher Jr., and I became homeless, at the same time that I was working full-time getting my start. There was never any way that I could return a commensurate favor to Bob, but I did make a pledge to myself to pay it forward in the future—by offering meaningful direction that comes from my life lessons to anyone willing to ask for it.

This is to say that as I invite you to c'mon in and browse what's offered on these pages, please know that you and your questions are welcome here. My hunch is you've got some already; you're probably asking, How do I know if this book is something I need? What can I expect to take away from it? And you may also be wondering—why can't Chris Gardner spell "happyness" correctly?

Let me begin with the first question. *Start Where You Are* is a book that has been gathering steam in the back of my mind for many years. Those were the words—"Start Where You Are"—that I wrote down on the top page of a yellow legal pad one day after months of knocking on doors when I was first trying to get just a foothold in the brokerage business. I couldn't seem to catch a break. Maybe you have been in those shoes, too. Well, that basic mantra—to start by using the resources I already had while building toward those I desired—allowed me to hang in there. Since then, whenever difficult circumstances have seemed overwhelming and I didn't know where to begin to take action or how to shift gears, the message in that simple statement has revved me up—just as it has whenever I've been stalled or stuck or a dream has loomed so far in the distance that I began to doubt if it could ever be reached.

When I was fortunate to have the opportunity to publish what became my first book, *The Pursuit of Happyness,* the original idea was to focus on the life lessons I'd pledged to pass on one day. In the beginning, I had inklings that I might not be ready to do that, not without first doing the groundwork of laying out what had happened in my life to inspire those lessons. But whenever anyone suggested that I consider writing a full-length autobiography, I shut down. What, relive the darkness and bare my soul—for everyone and anyone to see, no less? No thanks!

The more I thought about it, however, the more apparent it was that unless I did the hard work of looking back at the grittier chapters of my life, it could easily be turned into the superficial version of the "rags-to-riches" road from homelessness to success, from being literally penniless to having actual wealth. As the CEO of a multimillion-dollar institutional investment firm with millions of stakeholders around the globe, run through three offices staffed by a diverse, amazing team, along with activities I'm passionate about in the areas of public speaking, philanthropy, and personal empowerment, I didn't want my story to be made into a fairy tale. Therefore, in order to tell the real rags-to-riches part—the ability to break the generational cycle of men who abandon the children they father—I had to confront the painful memories of growing up fatherless and the most empowering decision of my life, which I made at age six. That was the promise I made to myself that when I grew up and had children of my own, they would know who I was and that I would be present in their lives.

The result was *The Pursuit of Happyness*—not only the book but also the film version of the same name, which encapsulates one dramatic year amid almost fifty years covered in the memoir. Out of the many incredible gifts that the experience of sharing my story has brought, and continues to bring, is that I now count millions of readers and moviegoers from around the world as part of my new extended family.

No one could have been more amazed than me. Never in my wildest dreams could I have imagined that the story I'd resisted telling would strike the universal chord that it has. The only explanation that has made sense came from Dr. Maya Angelou, one of the most inspiring human beings and beautiful women I've ever met. Long before I had the honor of meeting her in person and was able to ask questions of her, I could remember how as a teenager after reading her memoir, *I*

Know Why the Caged Bird Sings, it seemed that I'd known her all my life and also that she knew me. When Dr. Angelou speaks, everything that rolls off her tongue is connected to ancient wisdom—pure poetry. So, of course, I took note when she observed that the reason people from different walks of life could relate to my experience is that it isn't so much "The Story of Me" but, rather, it's "The Story of Us." Or as she put it—it's the story of "every father who ever had to be a mother, every mother who ever had to be a father, and everybody who ever had a dream and wouldn't quit."

And that same group of people multiplied countless times over—*all of us*—is who *Start Where You Are* has been written for. I've written it to demonstrate that my journey to overcome the odds wasn't mythic but in fact is achievable for each and every one of us. Moreover, I'm writing it in response to all of the questions, concerns, challenges, hopes, fears, and dreams that I've read in the storm of e-mails and letters that have moved and inspired me. And I'm also responding to what I've heard from the thousands upon thousands of people I meet out on the road in my role as "aspirational" speaker—as I prefer to call my second career in public speaking and listening.

In these times of great global change and acute economic challenges, anxiety provoking yet also chock-full of promise and opportunity, there seems to be a growing hunger for answers—for reliable guidance that's being sought with a greater sense of urgency than I've witnessed in a long time. Those four words that I wrote down on my legal pad are meant for each of us who, instead of feeling overwhelmed or discouraged by the volatility, can see our way through. And that includes you.

How do you know if that's so? Well, let's see. If you have a dream and a desire to pursue it with every fiber of your being, but can't move past excuses or circumstances that seem to be standing in your way, there is a life lesson ahead with your name on it. If you are tired of the status quo and are dying to shake up your life, reinvent yourself, and find a pursuit you love doing so much that you can't wait for the sun to come up in the morning, you've come to the right place. If you can't seem to figure out your niche in the crowded marketplace, you need this book. If you are like some of my workaholic, type A peers who have the material trappings of success but long for a sense of true fulfillment, you might be ready for a story or two that I've got to remind you how to dream again. If you've just had the rug pulled out from under you and your loved ones, whether you're facing the loss of a home, a job, or dealing with a health or financial crisis, hope and help from those who've survived the worst and gone on to thrive are here to encourage you.

I often think of the e-mail that came from a man who wrote to tell me of his challenges, how he had given up school and his dream career to care for his father when he was diagnosed with a terminal illness. After his father passed away, this young man wasn't sure where to start. As the years went by, he found employment to make ends meet but had a hard time feeling hopeful about the future. He continued:

> Lately I've been tempted to think that I wasn't given a fair shot at life, but then I give myself credit for doing what I can to get by and remember to appreciate the things I am given. I fight to make it, and feel as if I have knocked out some big troubles in my life. But there is still a lot more I need to do.

Then at the end of the letter he closed by saying, "Well, I don't know if you'll read this but, you know, I feel so much better now that I've written it that I think I might just make it." Sometimes that's all it takes to start life over again. He didn't need a response or to hear anything wise. He just needed to write down for himself where he was and that led to the thought that it was possible to feel better.

So if you're ready to part ways with feeling hopeless or fearful, there are possibilities to be pursued that you may not have considered. You can be empowered not just to feel better but, more important, to pursue your own path to being who you were always meant to be in this world. If you're grappling with changes in your industry, or have concerns about corporate downsizing and job outsourcing, join the discussion about ways to meet the challenges head-on. Like so many folks I've heard from, you might be fired up and raring to go, but need brushing up on fundamentals—perhaps you're returning to the workforce after serving in the military, raising your kids, or overcoming a health crisis. You might also feel that you're not sure what's next for you and hope to find ideas worth pursuing. In all those cases, you're in good company.

On the other hand, if you're looking for that secret, silver bullet that's going to make you millions of dollars overnight or show you how to accomplish effortless weight loss, you can put this book back on the shelf. You won't find magic potions here. No matter how enticing they may seem, promises of quick fixes mostly set us up for failure and do more to deter us than empower us.

What I can promise is that I will share the tools of empowerment with you that have been instrumental to my success—emotional, financial, and spiritual—at every step of my journey. I can promise that your questions will be met with answers that are intended not to coddle but to challenge you. To that end, you'll be meeting some of my mentors, role models, heroes, and antiheroes, an unusual group of teachers who helped me appreciate the lessons that are the heart of this book. I'm talking about the lessons that help shape who we are and who we dare to be—that allow us to see even the darkest days as only temporary, as well as those that shake us out of our comfort zones and inspire us to move onto bolder paths of pursuit.

Some of us tend to think of life lessons as those that can't be learned in books or taught in schools. But I believe in the value of all education—whether it's taught in formal, structured environments or not; via on-the-job training, a Harvard MBA, or street smarts; from ancient history or pop culture; or around the dining room table, in the pews, through direct instruction, or by example. My feeling is—why not let the world be our true classroom? It offers everything we need for attaining our greatest good and highest aspirations, as we'll cover in the six chapters ahead: (1) we'll begin in the present, starting where we are, with universal lessons that can be put to use at once; (2) next we'll go digging in the past and get personal with lessons about ourselves that can transform how we deal with the present and the future; (3) from there, we'll explore classic and evergreen marketplace lessons for success—and for hitting the anvil of hard work your way; (4) building on the basics, we'll focus on peak-moment discoveries for becoming world class at whatever it is at which we aspire to have mastery; (5) we'll then embark on a different kind of soul-searching within ourselves—with lessons that can help us tap what I call our "spiritual genetics"; and (6) we'll wrap up with lessons for happyness available in the good old everyday, starting right where we are, now and forever.

With all of the lessons to be covered, my concern isn't so much where they're found or which ones are more important than others. What matters to me is that lessons learned aren't left on the shelves to gather dust but are taken down, examined, and put to use, whenever they're needed—with takeaways that are applicable immediately and in the future; that is, *get 'em and go!*

How can you best make use of the lessons in this book? By checking them out, taking what's relevant to you, applying them to your life, and leaving the rest. Better yet, my ultimate goal is that they inspire you to discover, claim, and apply the guidance that comes from *your* life and experience—your own life lessons.

And about that misspelling. It is intentional. The "y" in *happyness* was something that I once saw written at my son's day-care center that way—at a time of struggle in my life when I needed to smile. It lightened the load and has ever since. The "y" is also there to represent *you* and *yours* when it comes to defining and pursuing what *it* is in your terms, and what success, growth, fulfillment, and enlightenment mean to you for this life—the only life you've got.

Whenever I'm asked what happyness is to me, my first answer is that it's the ability to look at where I am in the moment, wherever I am, to remember where I came from and how far I've traveled, as a father, a friend, a contributing citizen of the world, and to be able to say—*what a beautiful life this is, I'm so grateful to be here.* More than anything, happyness is being able to appreciate everything and know—*wow, I created this!* And that's the experience I most wish for you.

So, if you're in, let's get started. You know where.

One / Start Where You Are

Live your life so that whenever you lose it, you're ahead.

—WILL ROGERS
Actor, humorist, commentator, entrepreneur

AN INTRODUCTION TO LESSONS #1 TO #10— UNIVERSAL LESSONS FOR PURSUIT

You may not realize it just yet, but by being here on page 9 of this book, no matter how you arrived at this spot or where you aspire to go in the short or long term, you have already started. By reading these words, you've already begun to ask the important questions for any and every pursuit you may choose to undertake. By embracing the possibilities that are yours to be claimed, right now, in this very moment, as promised by those four words—"Start Where You Are"—you have walked through the gates and have begun your journey to the destination of your choosing.

So, before we go one step further, we should celebrate this greatest of occasions and mark this moment as the beginning of your time in the sun.

The power of the present offers each and every one of us that same new beginning. It doesn't matter how young, old, rich, poor, tall, short, or in between you are. You don't have to have lived on the streets or have traveled in high-powered circles. The present throws out a welcome mat as an equal-opportunity invitation to come into your own—in order for you to shine as brightly as you were designed by the forces of the universe to shine.

Here in my early fifties, blessed beyond my dreams, yet with so much more still to learn, I have finally attained a bit of wisdom that almost every life lesson in this book has helped me to grasp. And that is simply that if I look back at everywhere I've been—down every wrong turn, side alleyway, slow detour, or careening in the fast lane at my own peril—every stage of the journey in what has been my life so far was exactly where I needed to be at that time.

I know that applies fully to you as well. Whether you're starting on a brand-new path, or braving new obstacles, or trying to get past excuses and fears that have hindered you in the past, you, too, are where you need to be. What's more, you have every possible resource you can name already at your disposal.

I realize that's not always easy to see, especially when the odds appear to have stacked up like a tsunami coming for you. A moving e-mail from Kimberly in Utah—a "proud mother of five wonderful children" whose husband, the family's main source of financial support, had been let go from his job—spoke to this point so profoundly. No stranger to struggle, Kimberly had worked from the time she was fifteen years old, but chose to stay at home as a full-time mother so that her husband could pursue better opportunities for the family; at the same time she was studying for her degree in criminal justice. But after a car accident left her husband seriously injured and then having to battle a major health crisis, it felt like they were being hit from all sides. Over a period of a few years, they had lost two houses and making the rent was becoming harder every month. Even so, with only nine classes to go for her college degree, Kimberly hadn't forgotten her dream to work as an advocate for those impacted by domestic violence and child abuse. Then again, it had to be tough for Kimberly not to feel overwhelmed:

> I know it is within me to do the things that I would love to do to
> make my mark on the world. But it was a blow for all of us when

my husband lost his job. We are waiting for military orders so that he can go back full-time for the National Guard. He has fought back physically as well for part-time Guard duty. I know we will make it, as we always do somehow. The trials will still come. I will always continue to fight and choose to be happy, regardless of the stress in my life. I do not expect anyone to fix our problems, I want to live life on my terms. I want to do for my family what I can so that they will be my legacy. But on some days, I'm not sure what to do next. Do you have some pointers?

Like the overwhelming majority of folks who write to tell me about their challenges, Kimberly wasn't asking for a handout or a miracle cure. She wasn't complaining because someone had run off with her safety net or because nobody ever left her a trust fund. What she wanted was direction to the tools, assets, and resources that were within her means—which she could access and put to use immediately.

That's exactly what the ten universal life lessons that we're going to cover in this chapter are here to provide for all of us. What Kimberly's example illustrates, even for those of us who aren't dealing with the same kind of harsh reality or with circumstances that feel overwhelming, is that all too often we forget or overlook the abundance of resources that we already have. Much of the time, as you'll see, what we most need is right there at our fingertips—asking to be acknowledged and utilized.

For all that Kimberly feels she doesn't have, what most struck me about her situation was her focus on what she *does* have: her belief that she has it in herself to "do the things I would love to do to make my mark on the world." Starting with that alone, she is ahead of the game, ready to move ahead with resources that will be emphasized in Lessons #1 to #10—as we can see in this preview:

#1 Knowing what **pursuit** of happyness means to her, the first step may be as basic as creating or refining a practical plan to make it happen.

#2 With a reminder of positive choices and actions she's taken throughout her life, this lesson gives pointers for getting back onto the path of **empowerment.**

#3 Another naturally indispensable asset is her own can-do **attitude,** here for the asking when most needed.

#4 As this lesson will reinforce for Kimberly and for everyone, it is often in our times of greatest crisis that we tap our true **ingenuity.**

#5 It's always important to make sure we've engaged our sense of **purpose** that can give us the persistence required for staying on course.

#6 Her concern that she may be at the end of her rope can be a gift—a cue for using the resource of **instigation** that's needed to transform her life.

#7 This lesson is intended to reconnect Kimberly and all of us to **inspiration** we can utilize to face fears and not give up on our dreams or ourselves.

#8 Problem solving and opportunity seeking start by gaining **perspective**—as she has already demonstrated by the awareness expressed in her letter.

#9 A mainstay of success for countless individuals, **"research & development,"** as I refer to the act of asking questions of others, is exactly what Kimberly knows how to do by looking for guidance.

#10 Above all, there is little that can't be overcome for Kimberly or for anyone who chooses to tap the unstoppable force of **passion**—for pursuit and life itself.

As it turned out, when I was able to follow up with Kimberly and her family, she had weathered the crisis—thanks to her ability to recognize and put to use some of these very resources that were at her disposal. What had been most valuable for her, she let me know, was adjusting her attitude by remembering "the cavalry ain't coming"

(Lesson #3) and then choosing to see the challenging circumstances as opportunities to roll up her sleeves and come up with practical solutions. Her recent struggles only made her anticipated success that much sweeter. In short, the experience had helped her discover how capable she and her family members really were.

Indeed, the life lessons for pursuit in this chapter are intended to reinforce and reconnect you with the amazing capabilities that are innately yours. Even though many of us aren't in situations as dire as the one that Kimberly and her family had to face, most of us can relate to those moments of challenge or confusion when we're not sure what our next steps should be. For that reason, I've chosen to start with universal and classic examples in the lessons ahead that have mattered most in directing me to the resources most needed to proceed, all systems go.

Although it's true that I don't know you or where you find yourself today, let me boldly say that you're ready to pursue happyness like never before, just as you are. If you doubt it at this moment, you may feel otherwise after you've taken a look at this first slate of lessons that will steer you toward the true wealth that is already yours—for the asking. You'll find that you actually do have your own safety net of capacities, as well as a trust fund of assets that will never fail you—as long as you get past excuses and make the conscious choice to discover them.

We're talking about resources you've probably used before but may have forgotten or overlooked. Or maybe you've got the knowledge but have never known how to utilize it in a practical way for your specific concerns, hopes, and dreams. These are resources that you don't need anyone to hand to you. They're within you—waiting to be acknowledged and valued. But like anything else that we already have, as I tell my kids, "it's a stomp-down, butt-naked fact" that you'd better use it, or lose it!

There is never a better time and place than right now, right here, for you to make the conscious choice to look more closely at what you already have. The questions you're willing to ask may take you in a direction you haven't yet imagined, as they did me, and further than you might believe possible. But start here so that you can harness the mountain-moving power of the present that the following lessons can help you to do. They all offer applications that are intended to be universally relevant, whether you live in Wichita, Kansas, or in Soweto, South Africa, for use in all seasons, during bear or bull markets, and in all kinds of weather. They're intended to offer guidance for keeping on track with the big questions, to help you keep your power to drive, and to steer you toward your rightful path. They're here at the start to reveal to you the true gift of being where you are. Of course, as the saying goes, that's why they call it "the present."

LESSON #1
Without a Plan, a Dream Is Just a Dream
(the C-5 Complex)
KEYWORD: *Pursuit*

Not too long ago I was invited to Washington, D.C., to speak to a group of veterans on how to pursue happyness.

This was an honor for many reasons. First of all, as a proud navy veteran myself, I knew I'd be in good company. So many times when I've been asked if I ever regretted choosing to enlist rather than going on to college after graduating from high school, I've answered simply and to the point, "Never." Not yet twenty years old at the time, when I sped over to Milwaukee's recruiting office after watching Jack Nicholson as a tough-talking sailor in *The Last Detail*, I admit that my main motivation was to "Join the Navy, See the World" as the poster promised. Though I never left the ground of the good old USA, the navy gave me something more. It allowed me to see the world of possibilities for myself and my future. Not only that, but the navy gave me an education that taught me the fundamentals of pursuing those possibilities—discipline, character, and initiative, all transferable skills that would serve me in every pursuit to come.

Besides the fact that I came away with training as a medic that would have rivaled a degree from a top medical school, the navy provided me with a stepping-stone to civilian life when I took a position overseeing a cutting-edge scientific research laboratory at the Veterans Administration Hospital in San Francisco and at the University of California there. Since then, without question, I count the lessons in the service and at the VA as central to my every success.

The opportunity to speak to the veterans group in Washington, D.C., was also meaningful because it allowed me to honor the army service of my uncles—my mother's brothers who had been father figures to me. Their traditional values—hard work, duty, sacrifice, family, plus the love of adventure—had been part of my upbringing, even though I came of age in a much different era.

All of that said, I have a profound respect for today's veterans and wanted to express my gratitude in a meaningful way. Many in the group who would be in attendance had returned from recent tours of duty in Iraq and Afghanistan, while others had served previously—in different branches of the military during the 1990s and 1980s, as well as in Vietnam and Korea; there were even a few who were veterans of World War II.

Some of these men *and* women were dealing with ongoing medical and psychological issues, either in treatment or on waiting lists at overcrowded VA facilities and overextended support systems. Some of the younger vets had come home to positions at work that had been filled in their absence or that didn't exist anymore. The odds of finding a better job were much less likely than obtaining employment at lower salaries with fewer benefits, or having to hit the pavements to hunt for openings elsewhere. Many were confronting the same mortgage and foreclosure crises, skyrocketing gas and food prices, and other major challenges—including homelessness—impacting an increasing number of Americans.

Current statistics tell us there may be as many as 1 million homeless veterans living in America and that military veterans have come to represent one-third of the adult homeless population in this country. And those estimates are conservative.

As I prepared my remarks, I couldn't help but be outraged by those statistics—not only as a vet myself, but even more so as a citizen of this country. Plain and simple, our veterans of war and of peacetime deserve better. But I suspected that my sense of injustice over their struggles was not the best way to strike up a conversation about how to overcome them. Then again, I didn't want to go in and deliver a rousing pep talk without offering something tangible and even possibly transformational. If I had twenty minutes to share just one story, message, or life lesson, I wanted to choose one that had the potential of making a real difference in their lives.

In the end, I decided rather than arrive with all the answers, I'd start with a question, and maybe, if I paid attention, I'd learn something. That's just what happened.

The question was—what is the single most important ingredient for successful pursuit? In other words, I asked them, when you look at every remarkable story of anyone who ever made possible something that everyone else believed was impossible, what allowed them to succeed where others have failed? Or, if you look at someone who epitomizes the kind of pursuit that inspires you, what does he or she have that you don't?

"You have to start with a dream," said one of the older veterans. There was lots of agreement until someone wisecracked, "I have a dream, but she's married." Then several other veterans talked seriously about their dreams, visions, hopes, and desires. Some dreams were related to having a home, financial security, a different career, a better-paying job, or just a job. Others had to do with wanting an improved lifestyle for their family or a longing to pursue an education in a different field or to continue where they'd left off. There were business venture ideas, investment plans, glamorous dreams of becoming a Hollywood mogul-type, and desires of working to do more to benefit others. Some dreams were more basic: "To feel more hopeful," "Sobriety," "Peace of mind," "To have a better day today than yesterday."

As I listened, it struck me that—as usual—God had put me into a situation to teach me something new. With that, it hit me what the lesson was—that, yes, dreams can inspire and motivate you like nothing else, if you believe that you're capable of making them happen. But if you don't take the necessary steps to make them happen, dreams are just mirages that mess with your head! So, did the recipe for pursuit come down to Thomas Edison's formula that "success is 10 percent inspiration and 90 percent perspiration"? I had to think this one through. If 10 percent is owning your dream—believing you can do it, no matter where you are or the conditions in which you start—is taking action a full 90 percent of the equation? As I reflected on every spine-tingling, master-blaster pursuit story that had ever wowed me, I realized that action alone wasn't the critical part. Just setting off without direction could take you in a circle, or not very far. My conclusion was that the key ingredient, the one thing that marks the difference between those who do and them that don't, is very simply one tangible thing: a plan. Hence: *A dream is just a dream without a plan.*

Where do you get a plan? You create one!

Out of that memorable session with a group of my heroes, a gathering of American veterans, a creative way to apply this lesson for anyone who wants and needs a plan for any pursuit was born. I dubbed this planning device the "C-5 complex"—so good for you it can be used as a change-your-life daily supplement.

The five Cs to supercharge your pursuit with a worthy plan are five words: *Clear, Concise, Compelling, Committed, Consistent.* The first example that came to mind in the middle of my remarks that day was from my family history, back in the 1940s, when many of my relatives, with no prior experience, planned to escape bigotry, poverty, and fear by traveling north to freedom and opportunity. My same three intrepid Gardner uncles who later served in the army were in that group. With a dream that clear and concise, they were motivated to pool their meager resources and mechanical know-how in locating a car to transport them from dirt-poor, rural Louisiana to "as far north as it will roll." As for compelling, in those days getting the hell out of the land of Jim Crow and lynch mobs was probably as compelling as you could get. Once they hit the road, with car breakdowns and misadventures, they could have stopped, given up, or even turned back, except for the *commitment* to the plan and one another. They had to remain committed, not just on safe, sunny days but on a *consistent* mile-by-mile basis, all the way to as far north as possible.

Actually, my uncles famously intended to go to Canada but broke down in Milwaukee and decided to put down roots and go to work there. Even so, their plan succeeded and their pursuit of a better life for themselves and their kids set the stage for everyone in the family who followed—including my mother, pregnant at the time with me.

Whether the endeavor is as direct a path as getting from point A to point B (or thereabouts) or as strategic as mounting a military offensive—as some of the veterans observed—or in planning an undertaking that is outlandish, massive, or over the top in scope, the C-5 complex is a tool that you can apply as you go, turning something fluid or complicated into something manageable.

Being *clear* first about what you want to do or where you want to go is mandatory. It's the most important "C" for me. This might be a conversation between you and you—to let yourself know where you're headed and make sure it's a priority. In our rush to go charging after dreams and desires, with all the static and distractions, sometimes we would do well to turn the volume on the hubbub down, find a place of stillness, and make sure we are *clear* about where we're charging off to.

Very often, in the course of making myself available to folks who have come to me for thoughts, advice, guidance, and/or inspiration, I find myself becoming frustrated by the lack of clarity as to what they're hoping to hear from me. In such a conversation or meeting, while sitting there and after honestly listening to people express their dreams and desires, without hearing them ask any questions at all, the first concern that comes to my mind is—"how can I help?" And many times, I've concluded that the best way I can be of help is to force the issue by simply asking, "How can I help?" Or "What is it that you want me to help you do?" Better yet: "What is it that you hope to accomplish?"

On the flip side, whenever anyone clearly presents their ideas or plans to me, my attention is drawn in immediately. The contrast was evident when I was approached by two young would-be community organizers in different ways. One was a former gang leader who came highly prepared with a small piece of paper on which he had written notes for himself. He was somewhat nervous and soft-spoken when he explained that most of his former colleagues were in jail or dead and that his dream was to motivate kids to avoid the pitfalls of gangs, drugs, and violence. He had already developed and tested a program for working with teens to create options that were legal, profitable, and educational. Sounded clear, somewhat promising. I assumed he was going to make a play for financial support. But instead, when I asked how he saw me helping him, his clear response was: "An introduction to a few community leaders who'll hear me out." I picked up the phone and made it happen.

Another would-be community organizer was much less clear about what he wanted from me, other than, as he said, "advice on how to help people less fortunate than me." Even though he was a college graduate and had an academic background, he was vague about what area of community organizing excited him, how to get started, what resources he might need, and what steps he should take to begin. It was beautiful that he wanted to help people, don't get me wrong. But he still needed to clarify what it was that he wanted to help people *do*.

Vagueness and ambivalence can be the kiss of defeat, if not death, in some pursuits, and are often why some folks get lost in their efforts whatever they are. Being clear allows you to see your plan unfolding in your own mind and then communicate it so that others can see it, too.

Being *Concise,* the second "C," is vital to your plan so that you focus your vision, not spin it out or re-create the universe in a day. Short and to the point. It's how best to communicate with yourself and with others. Like Shakespeare told us four hundred years ago, brevity is still the soul of wit. It doesn't have to be a clever bumper sticker slogan, unless that works for you. But if you can capture and distill what you want to do, concisely, to its essence, you will be practicing an art form that will serve you in other ways, too.

In my younger days, I can remember how challenging it was to explain my big dreams and visions without becoming too grandiose or going off on tangents. Whenever I was able to articulate an idea tightly—just as I learned to give short, snappy names to important life lessons—it gained major steam. In order to be concise, the operative takeaway is to keep it tight.

One of the veterans in the group that day talked about the red tape that he and his fellow vets had to endure in obtaining basic services, like medical care; he often had to go through a maze of paperwork and phone calls, while being shuffled here and there, having to tell his symptoms or concerns over and over. The ability to walk into an office and explain what he wanted, clearly and concisely, had made a huge difference in his pursuit of better all-around health.

As we speed through our days, faster than ever, it's all the more worth it to make an effort at being concise. In relationships, personal, professional, and familial, it's a form of respect, of letting the other person know you value their time as much as your own. In my desire to be the best parent that I can be, I want to be able to be clear and concise with my children, especially now that my son, Christopher, and my daughter, Jacintha, are young adults and have no time or tolerance for long fatherly speeches from me.

Being concise doesn't mean you have to talk in shorthand code that's so minimal nobody gets it but those who are trained in stenography. A concise plan might include a series of action steps to be taken, but they too should be concise and doable in such a fashion they can be checked off a list over time. If you want someone to sign on to your plan and support you, the ability to communicate your vision and action steps in five minutes or less is a good way to test how concise you are.

I'm the last person to go look at websites or review proposals or sit through multimedia presentations. Pretty much everyone these days has the attention span of a gnat, so to grab it requires an economy of language and motion. We may not like that reality, but it's a feature of modern living—another one of those "butt-naked, stomp-down" facts—as I recently told my creative son whom I was encouraging to be more concise.

When your plan of pursuit is clear and concise, you're then ready to make sure that it's *Compelling*. This third "C" is about engaging your own inner "wow factor." It means that you've identified something about what it is you want to do or the route you've chosen that excites you and others who can believe in your dream, too. Compelling means that you've sold yourself. After all, if you wouldn't buy it, why should I? If you are going to make it over the long haul, compelling means you gotta make it real as well. Is it a line of crap? Can't be. You must compel yourself onward. If this is the dawn of your time in the sun, find what it is that is the reason for the season. *Compelling* is your trump card.

What happens when, for instance, you don't know what your pursuit is and you decide that you're going to pursue finding out? Ain't no shame in that game. There were veterans in the group who dared to consider the possibilities of writing books, making movies, doing stand-up comedy. Why not? To do something that bold, you have to make it compelling for yourself and others. One gentleman among the veterans had served in Desert Storm in the early 1990s and had returned to Iraq as a contractor recently, coming home with observations that he wanted to write about; but he wasn't sure if he had it in him. As he told his story, everyone stopped and listened, wanting to know what happened next. That's compelling! That's grabbing others and having them want more.

Whenever I undertake something new, I will test-drive that baby to see if it holds up, offering the same intrigue for me as it does for others. If

I'm not getting a look of curiosity, or holding enough interest that when I pause, I hear, "Go on!" then I haven't found my flow yet. That's the motivation needed to galvanize action in order to follow the rest of the plan.

The "compelling" part of the C-5 complex can be your calling card, as it was for Shane Salerno, one of the hottest writer-producers in Hollywood, who arrived in town some years ago with a couple of scripts and a film he had produced on his own. Raised by a single mother, he was familiar with struggle and had no savings to support himself while he tried to learn the business. Salerno could have been overwhelmed by the competition from much more established screenwriters and how difficult it was to meet agents and producers who would actually look at his work, but, instead, he came up with a different approach. Rather than trying to get his scripts read or ask people to watch his movie, whenever Salerno met someone who might give him a break, he handed them a Xeroxed article about himself from a small out-of-town newspaper that showed him in a photograph working with inner-city youth on moviemaking. The photo alone spoke a thousand words about who he was and allowed him to stand out from other contenders. It worked as a powerful calling card that opened enough doors for Salerno to pitch ideas, find representation, and, as they say in show business, "take meetings." Before long he was chalking up such credits as the blockbuster movie hits *Armageddon* and a remake of *Shaft* with Samuel L. Jackson. That's the power of compelling.

Committed is about your level of passion. Can you be thrilled to get up every day and work at whatever it is to get you through to the next station? Are you committed to a path that is important to you? Good, because that kind of commitment is contagious! Commitment is my stock in trade, my old standby—whether it has been for breaking generational cycles or for breaking down barriers to opportunity.

Behind every successful pursuit of happyness that I've ever witnessed is a level of commitment that would have to be rated "above average," even borderline fanatical. When I asked one of my Wall Street mentors, Gary Shemano, what it was that made him decide to take a chance on me when I was still a very green stockbroker, he said that it was a tenacious commitment to learn—to attach myself like a pit bull to his thigh and not let go until I mastered everything that he knew.

For the veterans who inspired me to develop the C-5 complex, there was no mystery about the meaning of commitment to a plan. They had already shown that capacity in following protocol with the highest level of discipline and duty. They understood how to focus on a mission, how to break it down into the building blocks of action, and how to never give up. Now it was a matter of transferring that commitment to their own pursuits.

These vets also knew about the meaning of being *Consistent*. This fifth "C" is the proof of whether you can be committed not just on certain days but every day. It's the ultimate seal of the deal, the ingredient that determines whether you win or not. Consistency is about showing up in life and in your pursuit on a regular basis, in your relationships with others, in work, and in play. It propels you along on the arc of the journey, through the sum of the action steps you've set out in your plan. Consistency is your touchstone, the make-it-or-break-it part of pursuit that will take you anywhere and allow you to make possible the impossible, and then see your dream come to fruition.

The classic examples of consistency for me have always been those fanatically committed individuals, considered crazy by everyone else, who take up the cause of inventing something that's never been accomplished before—like Benjamin Franklin, Thomas Edison, Alexander Graham Bell, and Marie Curie. How many failures, disappointments, and duds must have occurred before electricity, the lightbulb, the telephone, and the lifesaving uses of radiation could be invented? For every inventor, no planned experiment could ever succeed without the consistency of trial and error that comes with no guarantees.

As most of us can agree, no pursuit comes with a guarantee—which is why this lesson comes with the advisory that plans may have to be retooled as circumstances on the ground change, rough patches are hit, and repairs are required. But don't let that keep you from asking yourself, right now, right here, what your dream is and how you plan to pursue it.

LESSON #2
We All Have the Power of Choice
KEYWORD: *Empowerment*

Every now and then, often in the least likely of settings, one of our most important life lessons comes sneaking up and hits us over the head like a ton of bricks to remind us of something we already know but have forgotten or have been ignoring. Whenever I'm fortunate enough to have that happen to me, the first thing I do is express gratitude to God for grabbing my attention. My next step, once the headache subsides, is to figure out what I'm supposed to do with the realization that follows.

That is exactly what occurred in the midst of a memorable occasion that became a turning point in my recent life. This was back in 2003 when I was honored to attend an event as the recipient of a fatherhood award being given to a handful of men who were selected for being positive role models. Typically, whenever offers for awards came in, I would decline—mainly because I'd always thought that getting to do what I love and being able to share success with others in a variety of ways was award enough. But when I heard the organization wanted to highlight the importance of men making the commitment to play active roles as fathers and mentors, I gladly accepted.

When I took my seat at this event, it was with pride to be in the company of fellow honorees—among them the great James Earl Jones (who, as Darth Vader, famously said, "Luke, I am your father"), security expert Frank Abagnale of *Catch Me If You Can* fame, and renowned jazz artist Dave Koz. Most of us were meeting each other for the first time and hit it off instantly. Of course, I had questions for all of them, and they were generous with answers not only that night but through friendships that began then and have lasted ever since. Meeting James Earl Jones, an icon, with his powerful voice and gaze, was enlightening.

He happens to be one of the most down-to-earth, kind, and generous people around. So is Dave Koz. Dave's power of presence and focus can be disarming. His many successes as a musician, radio host, entrepreneur, and philanthropist are not in the least surprising. Frank Abagnale, on the other hand, is full of surprises. Although I assumed correctly that there was more to him than the movie version of his story, I didn't expect to meet someone who had so clearly confronted the wrong choices he had made as a young con man and had chosen to repay his debt to society by helping businesses, law enforcement, and individuals to safeguard against all forms of security threats. As the father of three sons who are the light of his life, he is also a strong believer in the importance of mentoring—a value that I share deeply, as do Dave Koz and James Earl Jones.

So there I was, feeling fantastic when the award presentation began. Perhaps in an effort to move the program along or to create drama, the emcee read a startling introduction that suddenly changed the mood for me. Basically, it suggested that I was a *fluke*!

Not just me. Apparently, according to statistics, given the demographics of where and how some of us grew up, based on the households or neighborhoods where we were from, and our socioeconomic or racial backgrounds, it could be predicted that we would continue generational cycles, abandon our kids, and never amount to anything, much less become contributing members of society. As for happyness and a life that included its pursuit, that too was not supposed to happen to somebody like me who came from where I did or from a similar background. This logic suggested that success was for the gifted or talented few who manage to transcend their origins, those who are lucky, or basically flukes.

The longer I sat there listening, the more I thought the whole line of reasoning was a load of BS. I thought about my fellow honorees and the success as mentors, fathers, and human beings that they had attained, not because of silver spoons, but because they had chosen the paths that had brought them to this day. Not by luck or accident or because they were more talented than everyone else, but through the sum of their choices and actions.

As I listened to more depressing statistics, I actually started to mutter under my breath, saying "That's BS," but not so loud that anyone could hear me. I had to ask myself why this statistical slant bothered me so much, and I thought about the bigotry of low expectations for far too many of us that's been around for too long—even from well-meaning experts. As I recalled my childhood growing up in the 'hood in Milwaukee, which included stays in foster homes and with relatives, I remembered how my mother, Bettye Jean Gardner, my most important influence and mentor, had instilled the idea that it was up to me to choose who I was going to become in this world. She gave me that power. Not that all my choices were the right ones, but in the face of what could have been powerlessness, the decision to make them for myself helped keep me sane and gave me hope.

As I sat in my chair, not too comfortably, I saw my life pass me by as though in a highlight reel of important choices. For starters, I recalled my first major decision made at age six that when I grew up, I was going to be there for any children I might have one day. And it was because of that choice, when I became a single parent with a toddler son, we faced a period in the early 1980s of being among San Francisco's working homeless. The reason that I retained custody of Christopher Jr., rather than park him in foster care or send him to live with relatives until I had attained basic financial security, was the experience of being abandoned by my own father. It wasn't just that I didn't know him, I didn't even know his name, where he was, or why he wasn't in my life; it was also that I only met him once when I was in my late twenties. Yet the choice not to emulate his actions and the void his absence created in my life—what I've come to label as the "no daddy blues"—influenced many decisions that shaped me over the years.

Another pivotal decision that came to mind that night was the audacious choice, made at eight years old, to grow up to be Miles Davis. In my teens, of course, I had to make another choice when Momma set me straight that he already had the job of being Miles Davis. While I couldn't be Miles, I did resolve to be world class at something else one day—though it took more choices to find out what that was.

In this highlight reel were daily memories of Freddie, my stepfather, an illiterate, physically abusive alcoholic, who took pleasure in letting me know that he wasn't my daddy either—sometimes at the end of a shotgun barrel. It would have been so easy to become him. But my empowerment came from making the conscious choice to be everything that he was *not,* and to *not* be anything that he was, which I've indeed succeeded at.

Was I a fluke? Was I one of the lucky few to ever break out of the rut? Not by a long shot. There are folks everywhere in every walk of life who are defying statistics every single day. Far too few awards are being given to the millions across the country and around the world, and in every community, who are succeeding in parenthood and personhood. Not in spite of the odds, but sometimes because of them! Of everyone I've met who grew up in the bleakest of conditions to become the opposite of all our surroundings, challenges, and issues—all of us who could have easily become that which was right in our faces—I have never met anyone who was a fluke. The power of choice, not chance, was what made the difference.

But instead of saying that, when I went up to the podium, I couldn't help but say what I'd been muttering under my breath—that the statistics weren't the cause or the blame for successful or failed fathers. And as for the expert opinions? All I had to say was, "That's bullshit." For a second I thought—*oh, no, there goes my mouth, getting me in trouble again!* Fortunately, however, I was able to make my next point with a little less colorful language by saying that I didn't see myself as the exception to the rule; rather, I believed that I was a representative of everyone who came out of similar backgrounds but chose something different for ourselves.

That was the simple yet true life lesson drawn from that evening—that *we all have the power of choice* in determining who we ultimately become. This might not have made such a dramatic impact on me except for the tears in the eyes of a woman who came up to me after the speeches had wrapped up. "Thank you," she said, shaking my hand. "I came from one of those less fortunate backgrounds that they were talking about." She told me about being orphaned in her teens not long after her parents came to the United States. Every day, she walked through gang- and drug-infested streets to lead her younger siblings to school, supporting them with odd jobs that allowed her to graduate from high school in the top of her class. Though she didn't go on to college, she pursued her passion for dressmaking and was the proud co-owner with her husband of a prestigious D.C. boutique. All three of her children were college graduates. What was her secret? "I didn't want to be a statistic," she said with a shrug. "I decided to do something different!"

Right behind her was another person who offered words to that effect as well. Out of a ballroom of one thousand people, I heard countless stories from individuals who had overcome the odds, saying that they'd come from those neighborhoods and those homes, and didn't think of themselves as lucky, accidental, or exceptional. All of them could remember the moment of choice in their lives when they made up their minds and stated to the world, in essence—*I'm going to go another way; I'm going to be different when I grow up.*

And clearly, that empowerment had led to other choices to pursue possibilities that maybe hadn't presented themselves earlier. After all, the American dream and the ability to pull yourself up by your bootstraps is still alive and well.

The consensus of the evening was that limiting individual potential from studies of demographics was indeed BS. Even James Earl Jones, aka the voice of Darth Vader, tapped me on the shoulder to say that he was with me on that.

As I have said ever since that night—when Darth Vader says something is bullshit, it probably is bullshit!

The application of this lesson is that it gives us permission to call BS the next time we hear something that is not true to who we are or when anyone imposes limitations on us. And that includes calling bullshit on ourselves when we give too much credence to chance and not enough to choice. When circumstances outside of our control leave us feeling afraid, stressed out, and powerless, it is human to feel all those emotions. But we can't allow those forces to defeat us. It's up to me and to you to empower ourselves enough to find whatever it is within our current situation that we can control, no matter how small it may be—and start there.

If you haven't been flexing your choice-making muscles lately, you might want to begin by recalling memorable choices that you've made in your life so far. Have you ever looked at what was coming your way and said, "No, thank you, I'm going to find something better"? Have you ever ignored your wiser instincts and gone along with the program followed by everyone else, only to regret it later on? My opinion is that whenever you own your choices, whether they lead to better or to worse, you are empowering yourself. Now go flex those same muscles and take a look at the plan you're developing or contemplating for your dream.

Why not choose one small-sized actionable item that's in that plan and act on it today? With action comes traction and before you know it, you're empowered to take on the more daunting challenges. Just that one decision to do something, anything, can be your antidote to feeling outgunned, especially when the deck seems stacked against you, when you're feeling like bad luck and trouble are your only friends. You will probably feel empowered five minutes into the process. Then again, it's your choice.

LESSON #3
The Cavalry Ain't Coming
KEYWORD: *Attitude*

A journalist once asked me how I was able to hold my head up during the period when my son and I were homeless. He wanted to know how I was able to overcome the shame. My fast response was—"Wait a minute. We were homeless, not hopeless."

He seemed surprised and couldn't understand how that was possible, even when I pointed out that our state of homelessness never defined who we were. My attitude at the time was that it was only a temporary condition, one that I was being given the opportunity to change as I became skilled in the field of my choice. But I did have to admit that what was difficult was the awareness that my son and I had entered a class of people, invisible, even among homeless people—working families who are homeless, too. The reality is that invisibility does add to the weight of loneliness, of thinking that no one can understand your situation but you. That makes heavier the baggage that only you can carry to improve your situation.

One of the reasons, in fact, that I first decided to break my silence and talk about my story publicly was to increase the visibility of the rapidly growing numbers of people who are joining the ranks of those affected by what I've long referred to as "white-collar homelessness." Over the last couple of decades it has been estimated that 12 percent of the homeless in this country have jobs and go to work every day, and that in some communities the number is as high as 30 percent. These aren't the people you see panhandling or begging on the corners, but families who go to jobs and work as hard or harder to get ahead as those in better circumstances.

As of this writing, we don't yet have a full measure of the impact on individuals of the vastly fluctuating global financial markets in recent times. Whenever downturns have taken place, talking heads of television's business and news shows have been quick to point out how this corporate executive lost a billion dollars and how another unfortunate fellow lost

500 million. Well, what about the folks who lost it all? What about the employees who worked at those companies for twenty-five or more years, had all of their retirement dollars invested in the company stock, and believed they had responsibly planned for their future after retirement? Unlike younger workers, they're now fifty-five to sixty years old with a nest egg that is virtually worthless, and, oh, by the way, suddenly out of a job. They're not only jobless, but now they have to go out looking for work in an industry that is contracting—rather than expanding.

Although there's nothing new about working individuals and families suddenly thrust into homelessness, the landscape has been hit harder than ever by category 5 hurricane strength crosscurrents—exploded by the bursting of the housing bubble, combined with the toxicity of Wall Street's greed that fed the subprime mortgage foreclosure crisis, along with a credit and banking crunch. Add to those elements the stress of a recession, rising unemployment, dwindling wages, not to mention inflation for household staples. Growing hardships that we've been seeing include reports of college students unable to afford food and showing up at soup kitchens; elderly men and women forced to choose between paying for meals or prescriptions; families being split up because they can't find shelters that accommodate parents and children together; working folks opting to sleep in their cars, or even, yes, in public bathrooms.

Whether or not these trends have personally challenged you or someone you know, the lesson at hand that teaches us how to start where we are, even in crisis, should apply to you as well. After all, from my experience, we're all in this together. But just to be clear, let me define working folks in this first decade of the twenty-first century. If you do not command your own means for making a living—or have a stake in it—you are "working folk." Let me be a little more blunt. If you are not on the Forbes 400, you are working folk—because you aren't in charge and can be downsized, merged out, laid off, or outsourced at any time. You can improve your odds as a participant player—a shareholder or stakeholder. Or you can be a pawn. Whichever you will be is ultimately determined by your attitude.

So how was it that my son and I were able to weather homelessness without descending into helplessness or hopelessness? The answer to that was presented to me in one of the most important life lessons my mother ever tried to impress on me. It's one that I've sometimes forgotten, particularly when I become alarmed, for example, that more isn't being done by others to the remedy the suffering that I see and that could become epidemic. In those instances, I can almost hear Momma's voice asking me next, "Well, son, if you feel so strongly, why don't *you* do something about it?"

Whenever I recall that message of hers, it takes me back to my mother's even more pronounced mantra, which I first heard when I was in my teens—a foundation of the can-do, take-charge attitude she wanted to instill in me. Even though there would be a few close calls before I'd really grasp the point of this particular all-purpose, all-weather life lesson, it absolutely made an impression on me when Momma gave me the gift of her distinctive wisdom in the form of a passing comment.

It happened to be during one of the rare occasions when no one else was around, leaving my mother and me to share an experience that gave us both real joy—watching old classic movies on television. On this night, we were caught up in the story line of a vintage Western. At the climax of the action, just when all appears to be lost, and the bad guys with guns blazing are closing in on the lone hero—who must confront the reality that his horse has run off, his sidekick's been killed, and he's out of ammo—a look of worry finally crosses his tough guy face. As he gazes up at the western sky, with cactuses and armadillos in the background, he scans the horizon but sees no help in sight.

It was at that very moment that Momma turned to me and gave me a look that said—*pay attention, son, this is important*—as she pointed to the TV set and spoke words that would resonate forever: "See that? The cavalry ain't coming."

For a second, I refused to accept this edict, arguing that the sound of thundering horses and the cloud of dust kicking up in the distance was the sign of the cavalry on its way. The relieved expression on the hero's face matched my own assumption. Of course, that's until he looks again to see that it's the bad guys after all.

Needless to say, the lone hero in this Western prevailed in the end. And his victory against the odds had everything to do with ending his reliance on a cavalry to rescue him. Here's the hitch: before his own amazing ingenuity could make possible a reversal of his fortune, he had to reclaim the self-reliant attitude that made him a hero in the first place.

This lesson made sense from the get-go but was much tougher to apply in a concrete way to many situations that occurred in the years that followed—when I'd catch myself pinning my hopes on an elusive cavalry. But each time, whenever I'd look again at the horizon and see a cloud of dust, and hear the pounding approach of horses, it would turn out to be my own version of a bad guy posse—signifying that it was all about to get worse!

Eventually, the reality that no cavalries are being dispatched to any of us good guys, no matter how deserving of help we are, allowed me to be clear about the choices for all lone heroes. On the one hand, you can choose to blame the bad guys and feel as down and out as you please—even though that's not going to feed you or your loved ones. The other choice is to rise to the call and become your own cavalry.

How do we do that? The first step, I've learned, is to own up to where I am and how I got there. Nine times out of ten, extenuating circumstances aside, I have come to the conclusion that wherever I am, I've arrived there by choice. Yes, I can speak to factors outside of my control and blame them for the predicament or make excuses about why things didn't work out like they should have, especially if no one reached out to help me. Maybe it's all true. But that doesn't change where I am. Only by acknowledging, "Hey, here is where I am, and I'm here because I steered my horse here," can I make the next choice to ride on out to the sunset where I'd really like to be. Or, as I've updated this lesson to twenty-first-century terms, "I'm here because I drove here." Now it's going to be up to me, and no one else, to change direction and to drive to that better place.

You may find the easiest application of this lesson is to take inventory to see how well you own up to where you are and how you got there. You can start by asking yourself what I'll ask you—*where are you now?*

Are you on a path that allows you to feel hopeful? Are you at a place where you feel that you're being hit by the crosscurrents? Do you have a plan for moving forward? Where are you personally, professionally, emotionally, and physically?

Is it where you want to be, should be, or could be? More important, is it where you need to be? If you can answer yes to all those questions, count yourself blessed. If you're not so sure, break it down to how you feel about where you are. Are you raring to go but without means of transportation? Are you stalled out on the entry ramp, or stuck in a ditch, waiting for roadside assistance? Are you rollin' like a rock star but feeling like it's all moving too fast? Do you want to slam on the brakes and get off at the nearest exit ramp? Or are you open to the possibility that you may learn everything you need from being where you are? In any of those cases, you may be heartened to know that your feelings are shared by many others.

As you look at your current bearings and then ask yourself the critical question, "How did I get here?" even if you didn't set your GPS for this destination and would rather be anywhere else than here, you'll be moving into a higher gear with this lesson if you too can admit that, for the most part, "Well, okay, yes, I drove here."

And if you're not there yet, not ready to take ownership of your choices, you may benefit from some examples of folks who are still blaming the bad guy posse or waiting on the cavalry.

There's one cousin of mine who might remind you of someone you know. He is a walking soap opera, constantly caught up in drama that he apparently had no part in creating. Whenever he's had a shot at happyness, something disastrous and completely out of his control had to happen to thwart his dreams—something that you know, before he even says a word, he needs to borrow money to handle. Well, did aliens from another planet abduct him in their spaceship and force him to lose his car in a poker game? No, of course not. He drove there.

For drama junkies, as we all can be on occasion, it's never too late to change the dynamic by copping to the truth.

Maybe you also know someone who could be seen as my cousin's counterpart, overdriven individuals who keep taking on more and more responsibilities, yet who avoid acknowledging they haven't attained their goals because of their own choices. I'm thinking of so many people I meet and hear from—highly responsible men and women who run businesses and charities, raise families, juggle multiple duties and activities, yet feel that they've left their real dreams somewhere back in another life. They might begin statements by saying, "Oh, if only I had more time, what I'd really like to do is. . . ." Or "If I were younger, I'd be able to do. . . ." But when asked how they drifted away from what they felt so passionate about, they rarely own up to saying, "This isn't what I had planned, but, well, yes, I drove here." When asked if they've ever thought about reclaiming their dreams or reinventing their lives from scratch, there is usually an excuse why that won't work or what the downside would be. Still others are waiting for circumstances to come along to snap them out of where they are and transport them elsewhere. By any other name, that's still the cavalry.

A former Wall Street colleague who was running an office, raising her kids, supporting a spouse who had gone back to school, and taking care of ailing parents, once told me that she could see that she was neglecting herself and her dreams, but, after all, "I don't have any other choice."

In fact, nobody forced those commitments on her. Nobody prevented her from pursuing her highest aspirations. And if they had imposed that on her, she was allowing herself to be enslaved. As a first step toward liberation, my colleague finally made up her mind that she was going to take charge of her situation. She became her own cavalry when she discovered a very useful one-syllable, two-letter word in the English language that starts with "n" and ends with "o." Instead of upsetting everyone who'd been dumping more and more responsibility on her, when she started to say no to requests for all the extras and asked others to carry their own weight, they gained respect for her. Her boss hired her an assistant, her husband scaled back his classes so that he could play more of a role in handling household concerns, and her siblings agreed to pitch in more time and support with their parents.

"All these years, I've been everyone else's go-to gal," she told me. "Except for my own." Her can-do, take-charge attitude had been there all along, but she had been too busy being the cavalry for others. Now she was driving and could say yes to herself and her own pursuits—even an interest as minor as joining a book club, which she'd wanted to do for years.

Another kind of excuse comes from folks who can't admit they drove to where they are—based on claims that the system is stacked against them and they've been beaten down by "the man." We all know a few of these guys and gals. They see no reason to pursue happyness, they say, because with racism, sexism, and other oppressive isms, we're basically powerless. Not to defend any of the isms out there or any dehumanizing system, but isn't powerlessness what "the man" wants you to feel? The late South African human rights activist Steven Biko put it this way: "The most important weapon in the hands of the oppressor is the mind of the oppressed."

My mother and Steve Biko must have compared notes at some stage of the game! They certainly would have agreed that no matter where you are, only you have dominion over your mind, your beliefs, and your attitudes. So if you look at your situation and let go of excuses or blame, and you choose to believe that you can alter your position on your own, you'll deprive the system, the man, or the ism controlling you. First, you'll be taking your power back. And second, you won't be waiting for someone to ride in on a gleaming steed to make all your dreams come true or take away your pain. Instead, you'll get up again on the horse you rode in on, and do for yourself.

Whenever you want to energize your pursuit, the application of this lesson will not let you down. You can start by recalling those times in your life when your can-do attitude was front and center. Maybe you can remember as well when you didn't wait for someone to tell you what or what not to do, but you went ahead, rolled up your sleeves, and went to work. As you look at where you are now, you can also ask yourself if perhaps you have been waiting for the cavalry. However you answer, now that you know it ain't coming anyway, ask yourself what your next can-do step is.

Last, I should mention the advisory that habits of thinking often take longer to change than behavior. The key is to start and allow the initiation of action to create momentum. That's not an opinion, by the way. It's the law of physics.

LESSON #4
Start with What You've Got in Your Hand

KEYWORD: *Ingenuity*

You may have heard the old saying that "cleanliness is next to godliness." Now, although I value cleanliness quite a bit, another virtue has inspired me to revise that saying. As far as I'm concerned, resourcefulness is truly next to godliness.

The lesson that you can take what you've got—no matter how minuscule it may seem to be—and use your innate powers of ingenuity, together with hard work and focus, and make something meaningful of yourself and your life is fundamental to all pursuits. In my view, that premise speaks to the power of creating miracles that's given to each of us.

"Start with what you've got in your hand" is a lesson that originates in the Bible story from the Old Testament when God first appears in a burning bush to Moses and tells him to go down to Egypt and lead the Israelites out of slavery to freedom. You may know this passage and you may recall how at first Moses—who had once been an adopted prince of Egypt but is now a humble shepherd—insists he is the wrong person for the job and even argues with God, using the excuse that he doesn't have the means, the skills, or the power to make possible the impossible.

Moses asks, "Who am I that I should go to Pharaoh to lead the Israelites out of Egypt?" The Lord tells him not to worry, reminding him, "I will be with you," and then lays out his plan, which is for Moses to go and give Pharaoh an ultimatum to free the slaves or incur the wrath of God—who, by the way, the Egyptians have no knowledge of.

"But," Moses objects, "suppose they will not believe me, nor listen to my plea. For they may say, 'The Lord did not appear to you.'"

Then God asks Moses, "What is that in your hand?"

"A staff," says Moses, referring to his sheepherding stick.

"Throw it on the ground."

When Moses does as he has been asked, the stick hits the ground and turns into a serpent.

"Now, put out your hand," the Lord says to him, "and take hold of its tail."

This time when Moses does as asked, the snake turns back into a staff. Then Moses is shown how to use his hand to provide other signs to prove he has been sent by God—including the ability to make water from the Nile turn to blood.

All but convinced, Moses still argues that he can't do this task because he is "slow of speech and tongue," which eventually causes God to send Moses's brother Aaron along with him as a fellow spokesperson. But God's bottom line to Moses is that he must lead and he must go to Egypt with "your staff in your hand; with it you are to perform signs."

It wasn't until my adulthood that I came to appreciate how much this Bible passage has to teach us about not placing limitations on ourselves because of a perceived lack of skills or resources, or because we feel that we are not at a high enough station to dare to do great things. Moses had a lot more going for himself than he was able to admit. God didn't need to tell him exactly what to do, step by step. Instead, the point was that he should be resourceful and use his God-given gift of ingenuity to make the best of those resources—starting with what he had in his hand. Sure enough, as you may know from the rest of the story of Exodus, once Moses makes the choice to rise to the calling and accepts the guidance of God, he eventually goes on to attain the means, the skills, and the power to inspire others to follow his lead.

The reason that this passage has always resonated for me—and has become increasingly relevant as I've learned to apply it as an adult—is that it was taught to me on a practical basis from as far back as I can remember by my mother, the epitome of ingenuity. By direction and example, throughout many trials, Moms offered consistent proof that when any kind of resource appears to be lacking, you can still "start with what you've got." So many times I heard her say, "Boy, I've done so much, with so little for so long, that I can do anything with nothing." And as I saw her do it, the natural resource of ingenuity became not only my gold, but also part of who I am—how I made it this far while continuing to grow and flourish. In recent years, it has become even clearer that the choice to be resourceful like my mother was a way of embracing that aspect of her that was within me—within my "spiritual genetics" (as we'll explore in more depth in later lessons).

Growing up in dirt-poor, rural Louisiana, Bettye Jean Gardner and her brothers walked miles to school, suffering the indignities of being spat on and ridiculed by children whose parents handed that bigotry and ignorance to them. Part of my mother's determination to succeed in school and go on to become a teacher herself came from wanting to exceed the limitations put on her parents—especially her rock of support, my grandmother, who died without seeing her daughter graduate second in her high school class. But when my grandfather remarried, instead of being able to help her with the money to go to college, he allowed his new wife to decide how to allocate his resources. None of them were bestowed on my mother. Though she was devastated, Momma fell back on a multitude of skills with the plan of continuing her education and making the trek north to join her brothers.

By the time Moms got settled in Milwaukee, she had already earned the qualifications for attaining her teaching degree and license. The state of Wisconsin didn't agree. None of the training she had received back home was relevant. To complicate her options, she was now a single mother with two children—my sister Ophelia and myself. And then there was my stepfather, Freddie Triplett—abusive, controlling, and violent—who became her cross to bear. As is common in situations of extreme domestic violence, whenever she tried to leave him, he retaliated—twice with legal measures against her that put her in jail and us into foster care. I believe that at a certain point, my mother's mission changed. Instead of pursuing her teaching career, she chose to protect her children and survive Freddie, with her spirit intact, somehow, someway. And with every resource of her being, she was never going to let us forget that she had nothing but unconditional love for my older sister and me, and, later, for my two younger sisters.

How she did it, I continue to feel, was miraculous. Momma would have preferred to work with her mind, but instead she used her hands and was employed for years as a domestic. When she left the house each day and when she returned in the evening, it was with the same professional demeanor and dignity that she would have exhibited if she had been a tenured college professor. She drew from an unfathomable well to be able to do that, demonstrating ingenuity in its purest form—as only the greatest of teachers can do.

In the course of sharing with others how I saw her as living proof of the premise that you can start with nothing and do anything, I've discovered that many folks have someone they know who exemplifies ingenuity like my mom. For that reason, I would suggest that one of the best ways to apply this lesson is to consider borrowing from the example of the most resourceful person you know, and see how your own strengths rise to the surface of your awareness. It can be like flipping on a light switch in the dark—revealing assets to yourself that nobody, including you, has ever seen before. Then again, what seems like nothing in the eyes of the world, when properly valued and put to use, can be among the greatest riches.

Once you begin to recognize those underused strengths, your next step is to trust your own ingenuity to make use of them, to lead you out and lead you up. Yes, the staff you hold in your hand may not be anything out of the ordinary, but with it you can do miraculous things, as the Bible tells us.

Apply this lesson literally. Start with what you have in your hand. Maybe it's your determination or the determination of someone who has inspired you. It may be your parenting skills or your ability to learn. It may be your faith. It may be your story of overcoming challenges. It could be the pen you choose to put to paper. It may be your curiosity, your imagination, or your compassion. It may be your warmth, sense of humor, or unique style of fashion. It may be your quest to learn or your desire to impart wisdom to others. It may be your funky way with words or your ability to communicate with silence. It may be your hunger and need to put food on the table. Even if it seems to be nothing, this life lesson is that you can do anything you choose with it. Be ingenious. Be proud of your resourcefulness. Know that the tried-and-true adage "where there's a will there's a way" actually applies to you, too. Recall what it was that allowed you to attain earlier goals. Believe in yourself and in the infinite abundance of resources already at your disposal.

LESSON #5
Baby Steps Count, Too, as Long as You Go Forward

KEYWORD: *Purpose*

Many of the most profound, applicable life lessons seem so obvious or basic that we tend to skip over them. So it was with one of my favorite mantras—*baby steps count, too*—which is such a part of my pursuit of happyness that my team at the office got together a while back and printed that slogan on T-shirts.

Long before I ever could have appreciated this transformational life lesson or before those words had ever been spoken by me, its essence had first been demonstrated by one of the unsung mentors of my childhood—Uncle Joe Cook.

If it is true, as I have heard, that a mentor isn't so much someone who puts their hand on your shoulder and gives you direction, but rather someone whose job it is to help you identify your strengths and your weaknesses, then Uncle Joe would have definitely qualified as a mentor for me. Joe wasn't actually an uncle, but rather a cousin on my stepfather's side of the family, and he was possibly the only person I ever saw whose mere presence could diffuse the violence that threatened to explode from my stepfather, Freddie, at any given moment. Uncle Joe had an almost sedative effect on the old man. I never understood how he did it, but whenever Joe Cook was in our household, I felt that my mother, sisters, and I were protected.

At one time in his early days when he lived down south, Uncle Joe had been a wino and a derelict, but he had found religion, as folks used to say. It was his sense of purpose—the belief that he had something to contribute to the world—that inspired him to rise up out of the gutter to become a success in his own terms. What exactly brought about his transformation, he never told me, but what mattered was that he consciously chose to change, to live up to his potential to have a meaningful, purposeful life. For him, that had nothing to do with finding out what job he was best suited for, or going out to make a bunch of money. He never did any of that. He wanted to be a person of substance—someone who was respected for his point of view and who had the ability to bring out the best in others. His thing was not to *please* people but to *empower* them.

As to how it was he ended up with such a large extended group of folks who knew and loved him, Uncle Joe was fond of saying, "It's always best to make friends before you need friends." Nowadays we call that networking! He was also big on the need for individual ownership—especially of businesses—and, in turn, creating opportunities for others.

Uncle Joe walked with a kind of a limp, more of a hop really, such that he couldn't take a regular step at all. Even so, he had an aura of authority—a command that came from his knowledge of the different worlds through which he had traveled over the years. Whenever he said something, it had a punch, because it came from that authority and because of how he would say things, like a preacher, but never at length. Clear and to the point, his message stayed with you, even after you forgot his exact words.

The explanation for Uncle Joe's limp came from an astonishing story. Somewhere in the 1940s, when Joe decided that he needed an education in order to live up to his potential, he figured that the odds of attaining that goal would be much greater if he got as far away as possible from the racism and poverty of rural Mississippi; he thought if he headed north to Milwaukee where friends and family had settled, he would be able to find better access to night classes and employment. But how was Uncle Joe going to make that trip when he didn't have a dime? He was going to start with what he had—his own two feet. Putting one foot in front of the other, he walked all the way from Mississippi to Wisconsin.

What had he done to make that impossibility possible? First, he accepted the truth of the wisdom of the words used by Dr. Martin Luther King Jr.: "You may not see the entire staircase, but it is important that you take that first step." Next, he didn't give up, and he found ways to remind himself, no matter how slow going his progress was, to just keep at it. Baby steps got him there. They counted, too, because all that really mattered was that he was headed in the right direction.

His sense of purpose kept him going forward and helped guide him at different crossroads when choosing which step to take next. Whenever he was in doubt, somehow the right person would come along and steer him where he needed to go—or put him up for the night or cook him up a meal to tide him over. To me, that was miraculous! To Uncle Joe, again, it had to do with having made friends before he needed them. He could always find somebody who knew him from an earlier time, or knew a friend who could vouch for him. He never had to depend on the kindness of strangers because, as far as I knew, no fellow human being was a stranger to him. Or vice versa.

Of course, most of what he had to say was academic until my late twenties when I was able to put Uncle Joe's teachings to the test. That was when I became a father and my sense of purpose to be there for my son and to seek the reality of my dreams empowered me on the yearlong journey I took through the challenges of homelessness. At San Francisco's Glide Memorial Methodist Church, it was Reverend Cecil Williams who reminded all of us who sat in his pews, or who were fed downstairs at Mo's Kitchen, or who were given shelter at Glide's overnight hotel, that we were all individuals with something to contribute. Reverend Williams sent the simple but clear message of purpose to each of us—*go forward, take the journey, count the baby steps.*

Since those days this universal life lesson has never failed me. It's kept me on task when I've applied it to something as vast as learning how to be a successful parent, an ongoing quest, and in breaking generational cycles of abandonment, poverty, and substance abuse. It has been relevant for launching my own company and even now as I'm expanding my dream to bring private investment to emerging economies here and around the world. Purpose compels me forward. Commitment and consistency get the job done.

It's worth repeating to yourself whenever in doubt: As long as I go forward, baby steps count, too. You may be staggering across the finish line, but those stuttering, halting, inching baby steps count, any way you can make 'em.

Whenever you look at your own victories, I'm sure that you can remember the less glorified periods when your sense of purpose and willingness to keep on going, even when only inching along, allowed you to make it in the end. This lesson—that baby steps count, too—may have even seemed so commonplace that you didn't give it much attention.

Of course, the idea that we all need a sense of purpose to keep us headed in the right direction may be so obvious that we forget how applicable and useful Uncle Joe's example can be. That's why I should add the advisory that this happens to be one of those lessons that is like deodorant—it only works if you use it!

Most of us would much rather race ahead and take those quantum leaps toward attaining our most sought-after goals. If you've ever tried to go on a diet or embarked on a fitness program, you know as I do that any product or approach that promises speedier results raises our interest. And that's a multibillion-dollar industry that wants you to keep on buying their exclusive secrets, too. But do they work? Not in my experience. Nor do any of the get-rich-quick schemes guaranteed to banish your debt and make you a gazillionaire by the time you finish paying off what you're going to owe for learning the scheme!

Maybe one of the main reasons that I resist these magic wand approaches to happyness that advertise overnight success and easy money is that they undermine the importance of purpose, struggle, sacrifice, planning, and discipline required for succeeding in most meaningful undertakings.

This is why whenever I'm asked advice about getting out of debt or starting a company or finding purpose, success, or happyness, I have steadfastly pointed out that there is no secret to making a pursuit a priority through the power of choice, or to crafting a plan for yourself and then sticking to it. The "sticking-to-it" part comes from the basics of this lesson.

One comment Uncle Joe Cook would have added is that when it comes to persistence, remember the greatness of your purpose. Don't let the size of the smaller steps limit the possibilities for how great a distance you can travel or the possibilities for discoveries that can turn up at any point. They may be right around the corner. Or they might be way out in the galaxy, beyond the expanse of sky—an ocean of opportunity in which we all start pretty much the same as everyone else, nothing more than specks. But the dynamic changes the instant we become *purposeful* and *directed* specks.

I'm talking about the innate capacity to confront our doubts or flagging energies in those times when we think that we can't take even one more baby step. Long-distance marathon runners and other high-performance athletes speak to that moment when they think they've totally depleted their energies but somehow another gear kicks in that prevents them from quitting. My term for that higher gear we must activate to persevere is what I call *oceanic persistence*. This was an awareness that first struck me during some days of fierce struggle when I took a walk at the beach with Christopher Jr., and we watched the relentlessness of the tide inching forward with every wave, ebbing and flowing, but always moving with the purpose and power that nature had given it.

Think back, if you can, to a time when your sense of purpose allowed you to hang in, even at the roughest, most uncertain patches, and how that forward movement was possible. My bet is that you know how to tap your own reservoir of oceanic persistence when push comes to shove. If you're not sure what I mean, you may want to make the effort to step out of your regular routine and go visit the nearest body of water—the ocean, lake, river, or stream—or wherever you can feel inspired by the power of nature in motion. If you imagine yourself to be that tide pounding onto the shore, then receding, then returning again even stronger and more indomitable, or that river rushing forward, you may begin to experience how you can embrace that same energy and natural flow, even for your baby steps—for dodging rocks, taking dives going forward, like the forces of the universe that move the tides and turn the planets with purpose and persistence.

Uncle Joe might have put all of this in even simpler terms as he once did when explaining what it was that kept him going. Giving up was not an option, he said, especially because he was celebrating every step of the way.

LESSON #6
Stop Digging Your Potatoes

KEYWORD: *Instigation*

As any financial analyst will tell you, Wall Street generally prefers the status quo to the unpredictability of change. Frankly, I think many of us mere mortals feel the same way. It's often much easier to stay in our comfort zones, even when we've stopped being very comfortable, simply because it takes less effort to stay where we don't want to be than to summon the energy required to create the change to go where we'd rather be. Plus, the unknown can be downright scary.

At the same time, I have learned that change is necessary for growth, and that if we don't instigate the change that we desire for ourselves, the status quo will eventually change on its own—in ways that can make adapting even tougher. With all of that said, I'm the first person to resist rocking my own boat—especially in those instances when I'm convinced that I'm not ready.

How do you know if you're ready for change? That question is put to me so often, in so many variations, that I've had to review all the times when I couldn't wait to shake up the status quo and those times when I clung to it like a life raft, only to come up with the response that you rarely know if you're ready.

This is an issue that is relevant to many would-be entrepreneurs and community activists who submit proposals to me for my advice. Their ideas are sound; some of them are inspiring and distinctive. Many have the means to get their projects off the ground. They even have websites and business plans that they can use to incorporate the C-5 complex (Lesson #1). But before they instigate action, they are waiting for a green light, apparently, to tell them that, yes, they're on the right track and that they're going to be successful. They want someone else's validation that they're ready. In truth, no one else can provide that.

Back in the day after I'd gotten a foothold in the financial world and had started moving up in the ranks of working at a top Wall Street institution, I immediately began to flirt with the idea of having my own firm one day. But I waited. Besides the fact that I felt I had more to learn before striking out on my own, I was convinced that market-wise and family-wise the timing wasn't right at all. So I stayed the course. That was until I was fired, more or less, for being more entrepreneurial than my bosses wanted me to be. The blow of losing my job turned out to be a blessing that pushed me into action—ready or not. I had no idea what was about to hit the fan. Clueless, I didn't know you couldn't launch an institutional investment firm in Chicago, of all places, with a mere ten thousand dollars of capital, a telephone, and a stack of business cards, in a bubble economy that unbeknownst to me was about to burst.

Well, the moral of the story is that sometimes we're pushed by circumstances before we're ready. Other times, our own choices, conscious or not, are what move us into action. Again, not necessarily at the most opportune moments. Rarely are any of us given a green light to signal we've stumbled onto a surefire opportunity and we've got to grab it now or never. In other words—it's time to pop the clutch and roll!

One of the best stories that I often use to illustrate the point that there is never a better or a worse time to change your status quo is the all-time classic success saga of Ray Kroc. You may be familiar with the fact that before he ever dreamed that his future would have anything to do with a hamburger business venture he would turn into a household name—a multibillion-dollar global corporation with a worldwide charitable arm—Ray Kroc tried all sorts of endeavors as he bounced around between odd and assorted jobs, investing and losing life savings a few times over. What many people don't know is that in 1954 when he first came across the opportunity that allowed him to envision his ultimate pursuit, he was already fifty-two years old and one hundred thousand dollars in debt.

In the eyes of the world, he was the least likely person to be ready to take advantage of an investment opportunity. He had spent the previous seventeen years on the road, selling restaurant kitchen equipment, with no profit to show for it, and he had no capital to invest in any promising ventures—his own or anyone else's. What surprised me even more when I first heard his story was that in addition to his debt and a rocky personal life, he was also suffering from significant health problems, including diabetes and arthritis, on top of having lost his gallbladder and most of his thyroid. But as for suggestions from others that he was over the hill, he didn't let that enter his thinking. As he later explained, "I was convinced the best was still ahead of me."

Well, that kind of bold statement made sense to me. Clearly, the questions of whether or not he was ready to shake up his status quo or past his prime were never issues that Ray Kroc worried about.

But I also wanted to know what life lesson for success he was drawing from. On paper, up to this point, his fifty-two years of life included more struggle than anything else. He was basically an average working Joe, a midwesterner from Oak Park, Illinois. Maybe the boldest thing he had ever done was back during World War I, when at fifteen years old, he quit school and lied to the Red Cross about his age so that he could go to Europe as an ambulance driver. By the time he finished his training, however, the war came to an end, and he didn't make it overseas.

Kroc then took a more traditional route and went into sales for a company that sold paper cups to restaurants; he moonlighted at a radio station and, untraditionally, played jazz piano on air. His first major game-changing decision came when he met the inventor of an innovative five-spindled milk shake mixer. Certain that this was an opportunity not to be missed, he negotiated the exclusive marketing rights—in return for every penny he had to his name. And then some. Seventeen years later, carrying the baggage of debt, and health and marital problems, he didn't have much of a track record for having instincts about being ready to seize opportunities. But Kroc believed that if not for the initial investment in the milk shake mixers, he would never have had the chance to learn the restaurant business. Not to mention that he wouldn't have decided to visit two smart brothers out in San Bernardino, California, whose little hamburger stand was so hopping they were using as many as eight industrial milk shake mixers at the same time.

Ray Kroc was determined to find out what they were doing to generate that kind of excitement. As the story goes, the minute he arrived in San Bernardino and set eyes on the operation that the two brothers had created, he had a vision for turning what they were doing into something much bigger—something that would shake up not just his status quo but that of the entire food industry.

He didn't wait to mull this over but decided to pounce on his idea like never before. But without money for investment, what resources could he offer? According to lore, Ray Kroc went back to his motel, after promising that he'd return in the morning, and stayed awake all night coming up with his plan and his pitch—using his own version of the C-5 complex. When he returned to see the brothers the next day, he laid out his vision clearly and concisely about how they should use their model of simplicity and assembly-line efficiency to expand their franchise on a nationwide basis. When they asked him who had the know-how to build and run a company like that, he famously answered "Well, I do."

Then he made a compelling case for himself, describing his more than thirty years spent in sales, travel, and getting to know the competition. Had he ever run a franchise restaurant chain before? No, but he had a passionate belief in four keys to any successful business: *Quality Service, Cleanliness,* and *Value.*

There and then, in front of the octagonal-shaped hamburger drive-up stand, underneath a pair of golden arches, the McDonald brothers shook Ray Kroc's hand—agreeing that they had taken their vision as far as it would go and that it was time to change their status quo.

Far from an overnight success, Kroc went forward with committed and consistent baby steps that took him to a year later, when he opened up his own franchised McDonald's in Des Plaines, Illinois. In 1961 after selling almost two hundred more franchises, but still with little profit for himself to show for it, he sat down with the McDonald brothers and asked to buy them out. Again, he was altering the status quo at an even higher risk. He let them name their price. The two came back with the most extravagant amount they could imagine—2.6 million dollars. Kroc borrowed the money against his future profits, including those from the real estate venture that had been someone else's innovative idea. This was to be his real gold mine, built on the basic concept of purchasing the land where the franchisees were building their McDonald's franchises and then leasing the land to the owners, earning rent and a piece of their sales profits.

Almost sixty years old, Ray Kroc bet the bank again and went into hock as never before. Two years later, the McDonald's Corporation with five hundred franchised stores in operation, sold its billionth hamburger. That was the year Ray Kroc made his first million. By 1968, a the risks he had taken had paid off as his vision materialized into what was already the largest, most profitable restaurant company in the world. He was sixty-six years old and refused to retire or slow down an iota until the day he died, nearly twenty years later—with a personal financial worth of five hundred million dollars.

What stands out in the Ray Kroc success story isn't that he was motivated by money at all. What stands out is that he wasn't waiting for the right time for success or for evidence that he was ready or not. He wanted something more than the status quo, and he was willing to put himself on the line, win, lose, or draw, and make the most of it, whatever the outcome.

The Ray Kroc story and others like it have taught me that anyone who believes success comes to each of us with a start date or an expiration label has it wrong. It's been a reminder that no matter how young or old you are, your best days truly are in front of you. Once you've embraced that philosophy, you're primed to take your first step to changing the game and ultimately having the joy of playing it your way.

If there is a pursuit you have been postponing because you're not ready or because you're waiting for just the right timing, you may want to consider that there is never a better time than this very moment. If you have been hesitating, or needing permission, or a push, on the verge of whatever has been simmering up inside you for a while, you might want to ask yourself whether or not you've been digging your potatoes a little too long.

Now I don't know about where you grew up but in the 'hood in Milwaukee, Wisconsin, there was a popular term for those of us who hung out on the sidelines when a bunch of us were outside jumping rope. Picking that perfect entry point when you're jumping double dutch— with those two ropes swinging in opposite directions—is a practiced art form. For a lot of us rookies, the dance of hesitation we used to do, bouncing up onto the balls of our feet, and then balking before falling back onto our heels, was what we called "digging your potatoes." If someone stood there too long digging their potatoes, pretty soon somebody else would come along and just give that person a push. Once pushed, you might land on your feet just in time for the rope to miss you. Or you'd feel a smack of the rope that would knock you down and you'd mess up the game—for yourself and everybody else. High risk, yes, but much higher rewards.

This is one of those life lessons that may just have your name on it if you happen to be standing on the sidelines of your dreams. If you don't know whether you're ready or not, it might be helpful to think back to a previous situation when you instigated action by saying to yourself—"No more excuses, it's time to make a change." Tap that same resolve for this moment so you can stop digging your potatoes. And jump.

LESSON #7
What Would the Champ Do?

KEYWORD: *Inspiration*

Whenever I've been asked for the name of an uplifting book that has been memorably inspirational to me, I usually start with the Bible and then go on to add that much of what I've read for inspiration over the years has been stories of compelling individuals, mainly from biographies but also from fiction. As a kid, I fell in love with tales of heroic adventure—from the Arthurian legends to Greek and Roman mythology, to classic novels by a range of authors, along with an assortment of memoirs and nonfiction accounts of people who were remarkable in some way or another. I'm not saying that other kinds of books haven't been of interest, but what has most empowered me has been reading about the courage and stamina of those who were able to rise above all manner of obstacles and ultimately triumph.

I believe we all need the guidance and example of heroes. Perhaps this was especially true in my case because I was growing up without a father figure in my household who could champion and protect me. As a result, I felt a special kinship to the heroes that I met on the page, at the movies, and on television. They were more than role models. I considered them personal mentors—even though they weren't necessarily real and I had never met them in person.

One of the most transformational, inspirational moments of my life occurred when I finally had the chance to meet one of my most important heroes in person. It was back in the early 1990s, during a very challenging period, when I needed the life lesson that one of my former mentors helped me find that day. Now, I don't know if you've ever met someone you've admired from afar and been disappointed or shocked to discover that they're nothing like what you expected, but that's not what happened to me in this case—when the reality of meeting my hero exceeded every expectation.

This was during a time in my career after I set up shop in Chicago and had bet the bank on my belief that I could change the game. In the long run, my strategy was a winning one and would eventually become the industry standard. But in the short run, I was stretched thin with a growing company and overhead, in addition to having two young children who needed me there for them at the same time. Just as everything was starting to roll, I hit a major snag when I lost one of my key employees to a competitor. Adding insult to injury, this was a relationship that I had carefully nurtured. My disappointment over losing a valued employee was further compounded by my fear that 30 to 40 percent of my company's revenue could disappear. For reasons that may be obvious, the fear that I could lose a big chunk of business—when we were just taking off—rose to such a heightened level that I had to fight off visions of returning to homelessness.

In such a precarious state of mind, I headed off to New York to try to salvage the business relationships that appeared to be on the rocks. As much as I tried to tell myself not to let fear get the best of me, I couldn't shake the heaviness that seemed to hang in the air everywhere I looked. Well, that was until I arrived at the airport, made my way through security, and started off for my departure gate, when I recognized Lonnie Ali—the beautiful wife of Muhammad Ali—on a pay phone. We exchanged looks as if she knew just what I was thinking—that if she was here in the airport, *he* wasn't that far off.

Just thinking of Ali—THE GREATEST—was all it took for me to be ten years old again. In that instant I flashed on the time we brought home our first television, plugged it in, turned it on, and there on the screen the first person I ever saw was Cassius Clay, "I'm the greatest, I'm the prettiest!" It was as true then as it is now.

From that day forward, he had only risen in my estimation—when he became Muhammad Ali, when he fought discrimination, battled a war he believed was unjust, and sacrificed his career for what he believed in, and all the while he continued to be the Champ on every level. His greatness wasn't just about the boxing; it was his courage and the humanity it took for him to say of his own feats, "All I did was to stand up for what I believed."

Now he was standing in the airport, in the early 1990s, with a cart holding his baggage, and, apparently, no one but me had recognized him.

Beside myself, I ran over and started blurting out greetings like a ten-year-old, "Hey, Champ, wow, how ya doing, what are you doing?"

My questions poured out of me as I watched him try to calm his tremors. I was familiar with the symptoms of Parkinson's from my time as a navy medic and from my five years working in a hospital setting as a director of medical research—my field of pursuit before I went to work on Wall Street. As I knew, Parkinson's affects the motor skills, though not necessarily the mind. Finally, I was able to ask a single, coherent question, "Where are you going, Champ?"

In his low, raspy but audible voice, he answered, "I'm going to L.A."

"Whatcha doing in L.A.?"

Not missing a beat, he declared in his familiar breathy voice, "I'm announcing my comeback!"

Unbelievable! I wanted to laugh, but his humor was so poignant it was all I could do to keep from crying. What do you say to that? The two of us sat down for a minute and got a chance to talk. Before it was time to say good-bye, I could feel my earlier worries creeping back in and had to ask him for some wisdom. "Champ," I began, "have you ever been scared?"

Ali said, "Yeah." He paused, then admitted, "I'm scared now. I've got a disease and there is no cure. But I'm still fightin'." That was that.

For a minute there, I was too humbled to imagine that I, too, could access some of the same resources for overcoming fear that the Champ was using. But then it occurred to me that this was a life lesson that I could grab on to and put to use immediately. After all, isn't one of the main benefits of being inspired by our heroes the reality that they show us possibilities we're having trouble seeing for ourselves?

The takeaway for me from this encounter was the question posed by this lesson that has been enormously steadying in times of challenge—*What would the Champ do?* It has been an indispensable tool for finding a source of inspiration needed to confront fears—real or imagined. Of course, we all have our own champions who inspire us in different ways. Yet we all have equal access to the exemplary ways they overcome obstacles.

In my estimation, fear is the most common obstacle that stands in our way or holds us back from our highest aspirations. We all know deep down that nothing and no one else can make the source of the fear go away for us. We can, however, choose to combat whatever has caused the fear with whatever means are at our disposal.

On the day of that unforgettable encounter, the Champ himself answered the question for me as to what he would do—keep on fightin'!

With that, I flicked the gnat causing my panic off my shoulder and gave myself a tough lecture, that went something like—*Hey, you know that thing you're scared about in New York City? Get over it. It's not threatening your life, not threatening your health, and if the Champ says, 'I'm fighting something right now with no cure,' you, Chris, can handle this crisis.*

And I shook his hand, thanked him, got on the airplane, smiling all the way to New York and I lit that city up, retaining all my business and then some.

Whenever I've seen the needle on my fear monitor start to wave or when doubts have set in, I have applied this simple lesson right at the outset by allowing myself to be inspired by the Champ. Sometimes I even imagine having Muhammad Ali standing there in my corner, telling me that he can do it, and so can I.

If you don't have an example in your life right now of your own champ, this lesson may come as an encouragement to ask yourself who inspires you. None of us are too old to have heroes. None of us are too old that we don't need a boost of inspiration now and then—whether it comes from a parent, a friend, a role model, a famous person long departed, or even a fictional character. If you're still stumped, I'm more than happy to share my hero with you. His example may not dispel all your worries, but if you can face your fear when you're down for the count, admitting that you're still scared but you're still fighting, you might find the inspiration you most need—whether it's to get back up on your feet or to announce your comeback.

LESSON #8
Say "Peace Be Still"

KEYWORD: *Perspective*

Though there is nothing new about crisis, judging by the number of letters that refer to feeling higher-than-ever levels of anxiety, it's likely that many of us will continue to be in for some turbulence for a while in many areas of our lives.

Maybe you've been feeling overly anxious yourself or know others who seem to be having more than their share of a tough time. Or, like me, you may be picking up on a generalized atmosphere of uncertainty—perhaps from the extremes in the economy, a downturn in a particular industry, the upheaval of politics and war, or agitation about the weather and natural disasters. But it's not only the stress-induced factors that seem to have ramped up the nervous energy a lot of us are feeling. New technologies, innovations, opportunities, and potential pursuits are cropping up on the horizon as lots of folks race to be part of the excitement. Many feel optimistic about the dawn of a new era of progress and possibilities, but others panic that they're going to be left behind.

With worry and hope battling it out for our focus, the media deluge and information bombardment have added to the static and distractions, causing almost everyone I know to have some form of ADD (attention deficit disorder). It has been said in many quarters that it's a shame that the actual news has been canceled, and I agree. What passes for news instead is packaged to get our hearts pumping, to keep us hooked on sensation-stirring stories, if we'll just wait until after the commercial— with televisions everywhere we go, on our computer screens and hand-held devices, even on our cell phones. By the time we start to process one story, another exposé arrives, and we have to scramble to take it in.

With the rush to stay tuned, as our minds and bodies speed up to remain "in the know," health studies have suggested that as we try to keep awake longer and sleep less to get the information to do the tasks required of us, the twenty-four-hour day is shrinking by as much as six hours. You can imagine what this does to our natural biological time clock and rhythms that help us keep in tune with the movement of the planet. No wonder the pharmaceutical companies are doing so well!

In this jump-and-jive environment, I try to fend off feelings of anxiety that tend to go viral very quickly even when there isn't a true crisis. For that reason, when I received a phone call from a longtime friend in the brokerage business who had gone from making half a million dollars a year working for one of the top investment banks to now being out of work—and willing to start for a fraction of that—I felt terrible for my friend, yet assumed this was an isolated case. But after many more calls exactly like that one, I knew that many of my former colleagues were unmistakably in a world of hurt.

My first advice to anyone who has played at the top of their game—in the employment of others—is to consider starting with the experience that you have in your hand and open up your own shop. In this economic climate, you'll be at a profound advantage over the *Titanic*s that are constantly sinking.

My second piece of advice to anyone in real crisis—job related or otherwise—is to find a place of calmness and stillness in the storm where you can gain some perspective. Only with a reasoned outlook can you find the solutions and empowerment that are already there for you but have been obscured by the crisis.

This lesson was first presented in entertaining terms, straight out of the classic film *The Wizard of Oz*. I have fond memories of watching this movie in our household, especially because I knew that my mother loved Judy Garland, or felt a kinship to her, perhaps for the sadness she masked behind her distinctive voice and beauty. As I recall, the movie came on television once a year, and whenever it was scheduled, my mom, sisters, and I would look forward to watching it together as a special occasion. Of course, I knew many of the lines, could hum along with the songs, and had learned to anticipate some of the terrifying scenes that scared me every time. The music that played whenever the Wicked Witch showed up got my heart pounding, and managed to capture everything that I felt whenever my stepfather, Freddie, went on an abusive tear. And those flying monkeys still scare me!

Looking back, I can see that the story was just what I needed when danger, real and perceived, required me to fend off the feelings of powerlessness. Maybe I didn't see it at the time, but on a deeper level the idea registered that sometimes the only way we can discover our true power is by living through the crisis we feared. As it was portrayed in the movie, it takes those life-and-death challenges for each of the main characters to realize that the very thing they want the Wizard to give them is already within their capacities. The Scarecrow doesn't think he's smart enough to endure difficulties, and yet all along he's the guy with the logic and reasoning that guides the group to make the right choices. The Tin Man thinks that he's worthless because he was made without a heart, except that his compassion for others and his passion for not giving up are what keep everyone going. The Cowardly Lion, of course, is ashamed that he lacks the courage that should accompany being the "King of the Beasts," but when put to the test, he acts with courage in the face of fear.

As a kid and even later on, I dug the Lion. My favorite scene in the movie is when the Great Wizard of Oz tries to send Dorothy and her friends away, even after they've accomplished their mission. It turns out that it's the Lion who steps forward with the real cojones to confront and expose the man behind the curtain who has assumed a role of power he doesn't deserve. The other standout in the story was the lesson of the ruby red slippers. The whole time Dorothy had struggled to get home, thinking only the Wizard could help her, she had the power to do so all along. Her ability to understand the power of what she already possessed was obscured by her fear.

I forgot much of that movie until my own children were growing up and I had a chance to discover it again with them. Now I could watch it from a different perspective after various tornadoes had ripped through our lives. The adult lesson was to not lose sight of the fact that whenever panic sets in, logic, reason, and the power to find solutions fly right out the window on a broomstick as well.

You may have experienced this in some form or another, too. Whenever I talk to folks who've grown up in unstable households like mine and who had the need to stay on high alert, I hear stories about the importance of clearheadedness amid crisis. I've heard the same from professionals who work in such arenas as law enforcement, firefighting, and the medical field, in which they're required to keep an even keel, at the same time that they make sure all their senses are sharp. Similarly, when people face loss or must cope with illness of their own or in the family, instead of being swallowed up by despair, they speak of maintaining perspective, and making their way to solid ground as a result.

Our natural survival skills give us the capacity to find our own state of calm in the midst of crisis, our own shelter in the storm. This was taught to me by watching my mother react to the possibility or threat of violence that could explode at any time from my stepfather. Instead of engaging, reacting, or exploding in return, Moms had the ability to become absolutely motionless, quieting her breath, her heartbeat, even involuntary movements it seemed; she attained a state of stillness on a physical, cellular level that I've never seen in any other human being. The ability to become that still saved her life and mine on more than a few occasions.

Although I had the close and in-person example of how to achieve that kind of stillness—and have learned to create a similar Zen state when necessary—I have also developed other responses to off-the-chain anxiety levels. There are times when becoming immobile in the face of an onslaught is not enough to quiet the crisis. Sometimes we are talking about employing our fight-or-flight mechanisms. More often, I employ the get-up-and-go option, which is to consciously change the mental channel either by shifting my focus or by getting up out of my office chair and going for a brisk walk. By stepping outside of the crisis, even for ten minutes, perspective can usually be found.

You may have your own version of standing your ground or of getting up and changing the channel to create some distance between you and the offending concern. You might also choose to speak directly to the crisis with firm authority as is taught in the biblical passage from the New Testament—through the parable told in the books of Mark and Matthew—which recounts how Jesus and his disciples traveled in a small boat across the Sea of Galilee. While Jesus slept, a ferocious storm came up at night and his followers frantically went to wake him, certain that they were all about to die. When he was awakened, he rebuked the roaring winds and shouted to the waves, "Peace! Be still." As it is written, suddenly the storm ceased, and the wind and the sea stopped their rage, all followed by a dead calm.

The disciples were in awe while Jesus reminded them not to allow their fears to overwhelm them. By demonstrating that Jesus was able to confront the storm by speaking directly to it and saying, "Peace! Be still," the parable teaches us that we, too, have the option to respond similarly when storms of different kinds beset us.

As you may have also learned from watching or reading *The Wizard of Oz*, there is something to be said for riding out the twister to wherever it takes you—even if it's to teach you that there's no place like home. Maybe you can recall those times when the crisis you survived gave you a different, empowering perspective about yourself and your situation. Perhaps you've also had the opportunity to use your own strategies for changing the channel and moving away from a source of anxiety, or for speaking directly to the storm and telling it to cease and desist immediately. If you haven't, by decree of me—not a wizard but someone who's done it for himself—you now have permission to say "Peace! Be still," anytime you choose. You can use those words or your own to calm wound-up co-workers, rock babies to sleep, manage personal relationships that may be fraying, take the edge off when outcomes are uncertain, or when you or those around you are headed into a tailspin.

As a dear colleague reminded me recently, the wonderful children's book *Where the Wild Things Are* by Maurice Sendak teaches this lesson for the entire family. In that story, as you may know, a young boy named Max is behaving like a beast and is sent to his room—and soon is transported to a place where wild, beastlike creatures live. When they show Max their teeth and claws, he shouts right back at them, "Be still!"; he infuriates the beasts, his hitherto friends, thereby taming the Wild Things. In a grown-up·sense, Max not only gains perspective on whatever crisis set him off but also on his own capacity for detaching from his anger and finding calm.

And, one more thing—there is nothing passive about seeking peace. Nor is there anything negative about being prepared for different forms of crisis. Maybe you've heard the saying that it wasn't raining when Noah built the ark. That's yet another reminder that at whatever point we choose to solve the problems of the day, seek perspective first, and start there.

LESSON #9
Even Lewis and Clark Had a Map
KEYWORDS: *Research and Development*

Got a question for you—Are you crazy?

To be more specific—Has anyone ever said you were crazy for want-ing to pursue a particularly ambitious idea? Let me rephrase that again—Has anyone ever told you that your idea for your very ambitious pursuit is crazy?

Well, if you've ever had your aspirations dismissed out of hand in such a manner, I've got a few choice words (not suitable for publication) that you may opt to use the next time somebody makes a comment to that effect. But even better than wasting your energy being upset or offended, you can skip the drama and employ what I believe is one of the most practical life lessons that I can offer you—and one that has been used by humankind since the invention of that crazy thing called "the wheel."

The essence of this lesson is that for every pursuit you can dream up, there is a very high probability that somewhere in the world or in history, someone has been there and done that, or at least has tried—and can provide you with a very helpful overview of their struggles and discoveries, as well as their downfalls and triumphs. Contrary to those who believe that you must ignore all predecessors and forge your own path into the woods where no one has ever gone before, my experience has been that, when starting out, it's smart to ask for directions before heading off into the wilderness. After all, the pioneers who traveled west to new frontiers did so only after explorers like Lewis and Clark had charted the "there" there. Not only that, but as this lesson reminds you—*even Lewis and Clark had a map.*

Ain't no shame in starting with someone else's map, blueprint, or guidelines. If you ask me, it's crazy not to! In any case, I've learned that whenever I have chosen to trek out on my own, using the maps to suc-cess that others have created, by adapting those maps along the way, eventually I've learned enough to come up with my own methods to share with those who'll soon be coming up behind me. I've always referred to this approach as asking questions and then testing out the answers for practical usage now and later. Others call this process R&D—research and development—a term that I'm also happy to borrow.

My mother never used that term, nor did she tell me that I was crazy for wanting to be my idol Miles Davis. Instead, she encouraged me to do the legwork to learn everything that Miles had to do to become the world-class jazz icon that he was. At great sacrifice, she bought me a trumpet, arranged for lessons, and, over a period of nine years, encouraged me to study, perform, even to play professionally during my high school years. That period of R&D was an intensive program of discovery that let me see it wasn't his genius that gave him the power of mastery, but his own years of study combined with his boldness to push musical boundaries. When the day came for her revelation that I couldn't be Miles Davis, because "Baby, there ain't but one and he already got that job," it wasn't a shock at all. From my research I knew that at my age Miles was in New York playing with Quincy Jones and John Coltrane. I was still living at home, playing with some cats named Pookie and Ray Ray! The conclusion was that I was going to have to do the legwork of more R&D to find out what it meant to be Chris Gardner. But what I took from the model provided by Miles Davis was the burning passion to become world class at something one day—and the desire to develop the mastery to claim that title.

Moms also gave me a crash course of R&D when I ran another aspiration by her at one point, that I was considering the possibility of becoming a famous actor. She didn't tell me that I was crazy. She did nod in the direction of the newspaper to check out how many "help wanted" listings I could find for actors. A short while later when I was on my way out the door to go to the movies, still insisting that I had the brilliance to be a star one day on the big screen, I set myself up when I asked her for five dollars. Momma tested me again by saying, "Well, why don't you *act* like you got five dollars?" If that wasn't enough to dissuade me, the more that I learned about the odds of making it, my research revealed that I didn't have enough of the burning desire to be an actor that I'd need to make it.

Later, after my service in the navy led to specialization as a medic, I was fortunate to attain a working understanding of R&D in cutting-edge medical research when I was mentored by one of the world's leading experts in heart surgery, Dr. Robert Ellis. In the realm of science and technology, research typically refers to several phases—studying precedents, creating controlled tests, performing analyses, and drawing conclusions from all the data; development usually refers to the process of applying those findings toward creating new procedures, treatments, and technologies. In my Wall Street career, I've come to highly value the business version of R&D—where research is seen as a commitment of resources toward increasing knowledge about what's happening in the marketplace, and development is about turning that knowledge into products or activities for the company. Governments and organizations devote resources to R&D as well, as do global alliances and whole economies.

Think, if you will, of the times in your life when you naturally employed the resource of first doing research before you developed your game plan. Most of us do this all the time, with everything from asking around for the name of a reputable doctor or medical specialist that we might need, to locating an ace accountant around tax time. Think of how many times we do research using MapQuest for something as basic as driving directions. Most of us like to comparison shop before making significant purchases—another form of R&D. We also tend to weigh decisions that will require a commitment of time by finding out in advance what's going to be involved.

Yet for all the things that we would never think of putting our energies toward without first doing the legwork of research, it's surprising how many people I've encountered who aren't sure how they ended up in their particular line of work or in a pursuit that occupies their time. Sometimes they say their profession was a given because their parents expected it. Sometimes it was just what came along. If you can relate, now is the best time to retool your plan with forethought.

That's exactly what a woman named Meg decided when she came to a turning point in her life. We met at a publishing industry trade show that I attended a few years ago when I spotted an energetic, smiling petite lady in her early sixties walking the convention floor with several copies of her unpublished manuscript in her hands. After I asked her when her book was due to hit the stores, Meg explained that she didn't have an agent or a publisher yet.

"Any takers?" I asked.

None, she admitted. But that wasn't the point. Her goal for this venture was to ask questions, get advice, and make contacts. Yep, she was conducting her own R&D. When I asked what it was that put such a happy smile on her face, Meg told me about how she had spent much of her adult life as an office manager in the medical field. Even though she had enjoyed her work and it had helped her and her husband put three kids through college—one through med school and another through law school—her true dream had always been to write science fiction. As every year passed by, she saw her possibilities for doing that fading from her grasp. Then, not long before it was time to retire, she decided, finally, "that it was time to put up or shut up."

Meg's family and co-workers were horrified. They called her crazy and begged her to reconsider. Financially, the time was all wrong, they reminded her, not to mention that her husband's health had recently taken a bad turn. Meanwhile, Meg had begun to think that if she didn't try her hand at writing the science fiction stories that had been cooped up in her imagination for all this time, she really would go crazy. So what tipped the scales in making her decision? Meg shrugged and answered concisely, "J. K. Rowling."

Meg had started with her own R&D by following the map of one of the most successful publishing examples in history. In fact, when I was writing *The Pursuit of Happyness* and was doing research of my own about the marketing process, every time that I went into bookstores, no matter what city I happened to be in, the first sight that welcomed me was dramatic displays of a book with a mysterious blue cover and the face of an English schoolboy with glasses on it—it was *Harry Potter and the Order of the Phoenix,* which was the fifth title in Rowling's series.

Though I knew the books had been incredibly popular—later making them the top book series of all time, selling 400 million copies between 1997 and 2007—up until then, I had no idea what a phenomenon this truly was. When I started to pay attention, I realized that it was another British invasion! Everywhere I went, children, teens, even young and older adults, were scooping up copies of the new book like hotcakes. That in itself was astonishing. To see young readers so excited about reading was beautiful, not to mention that the book was nearly nine hundred pages.

Of course, the part of this triumph that makes it so compelling is the personal story of how J. K. Rowling pursued happyness on her own terms—by starting where she was. That was in 1995 when this British single mom, living abroad in Edinburgh, Scotland, chose to pursue her dream of writing at a time when doing that and supporting her baby girl meant opting to take public assistance.

Although I knew the broad strokes of her classic success story, like much of the public, I had been fascinated to learn more of the specifics of what Rowling had accomplished and how she had done it. Not surprisingly, there was a crazy idea that set all the wheels into motion. It seems that five years earlier, while on a lengthy train ride, Jo (short for Joanne) Rowling had struck upon a vivid story line for a book. As she began to visualize her main character, a boy who attended a boarding school for wizards, she was flooded with all kinds of details, as if the story was telling itself to her. But as she later described to reporters, she had no functioning pen with which to start writing down all of this magical stuff that her imagination was cooking up. As to why she didn't borrow one from another passenger, Rowling admitted that she was too embarrassed. But that turned out to be a blessing because not having a pen forced her to refine the details in her mind over the course of the four-hour train ride.

As I learned, Jo Rowling had been writing continuously from the time she was six years old, was a university-educated scholar of French, and had worked, among many pursuits, as a researcher for Amnesty International. When she began writing what became the first Harry Potter book, not only did she have natural gifts and transferable skills from other areas, but there were many classic examples that could help give her a structure or map to follow for getting started. Besides such obvious influences as J. R. R. Tolkien's *Lord of the Rings* trilogy and T. H. White's *The Once and Future King* (both of which include wizards), there were other sources of inspiration. These famously include Shakespeare's *Macbeth* and many popular books for younger audiences that were set in English boarding schools.

Those literary predecessors gave her structures to follow. But after coming up with her plotline, it was not as simple as sitting down, using those maps, and churning out her masterpiece. There was a move to Portugal, marriage, a child, then divorce, single parenthood, and a serious bout of depression. During all of that, Jo wrote when and where she could, but it was in Edinburgh that she decided to commit to her pursuit as she never had before—"in a frenzy," as she put it, pushing her baby in a stroller to a nearby café, where Jo wrote in every spare moment. Certainly, as a single father who had journeyed through homelessness with a toddler son, pushing his stroller up and down the hills of San Francisco to drop him off at day care so that I could go to work and pursue my dream of making it in the financial world, I could relate.

It was also meaningful to find out that Rowling wasn't overly focused on writing something that the publishing industry was dying to have. Her priority was to follow the inspiration of her literary heroes and tell an unforgettable tale. So instead of writing a commercial young adult novel that could have been merely entertaining, Rowling was bold enough to write about the estrangement, darkness, and fear also experienced in childhood, as well as the enchantment and the light. All of those feelings went onto the page.

As an aspiring writer, my acquaintance Meg was wise to do her

R&D by taking a page out of J. K. Rowling's playbook. No doubt what she learned from her research was that if any one of us ever thinks we can't make time to do what we most want to do, the years between 1994 and 1997 for J. K. Rowling prove otherwise.

Consumed by her project, it was the doing of it that empowered Jo and made her happy, long before she saw a penny for her efforts. Her motivation had nothing to do with becoming a billionaire, even though that was what would happen. How was that possible? Again, research and development. Not magic. Like every other would-be author, she did the legwork, following an age-old model by sending out query letters to agents and suffering the standard rejections. Eventually, however, she landed with an agent who submitted her manuscript to several publishers, receiving nothing but no's for a year—until an editor at an English publishing house, Bloomsbury, decided to have his eight-year-old daughter read a chapter. The response? The editor's daughter was hooked and wanted more!

That was in August 1996. Rowling's first advance wasn't enough for her to afford to write full-time but, again, R&D led her to a grant that helped tide her over until 1997 when the rights to publish *Harry Potter and the Sorcerer's Stone* were purchased, earning her an advance of $105,000. When asked how that felt upon hearing, she famously said she "nearly died."

At that point, I suspect, Jo Rowling threw away the maps and used her own vision as she went on to conquer the book and film marketplace in a franchise that is today worth 15 billion dollars and counting. Her philanthropy includes support for organizations like "One Parent Families," and she plays an activist role on many global issues, particularly those affecting women and children. The road there was her own. As for where she started, it began with a crazy idea—and her passion to tell a story that could matter. And then she followed maps left by others, never gave up, and never gave in.

As a result of applying her version of the lesson that *even Lewis and Clark had a map,* Meg had said that she was not too far off J. K. Rowling's pace for finding an agent. She'd been at it for nearly a year.

But she wasn't discouraged in the least. First, she explained, "I've completed two books on my own that I absolutely love. How many people can say that?" And, second, even though she was willing to consider self-publishing as a last resort, she was mindful of how many of the most famous authors in the world were rejected countless times before they finally were accepted. Before we said good-bye, Meg summed up her takeaway from all of her R&D with a smile and an always useful reminder that "it only takes one person to say yes."

Let me repeat, again, just for the record: maps are useful. If God didn't want us to use them, he wouldn't have put them in our glove compartments!

LESSON #10
Find Your Button

KEYWORD: *Passion*

Until I had the privilege and challenge of telling the grittier, often more painful parts of my story, I thought that many of the aspects of what I'd gone through and how I had reacted were unique to me. Nobody, as far as I was concerned, could have ever dreamed the same thing, feared the same thing, felt the same thing—whatever it was. For example, I thought it was just me who dreamed of being world class in some capacity one day. True, it took me a while to find the right venue in which I could attain mastery and find real passion. Before I found my niche on Wall Street, there had been stints in the field of music and then medical research after that. Did everyone take such a circuitous route in finding their way? Apparently not, if comments that I've heard from so many are any indication. Indeed, it has been validating to hear time and again that lots of folks have had the same experience, and many of them have confided, "I used to think it was just me."

Those were the words sent to me by Susan, a talented graphic designer and artist, who had never shared with anyone her desire to become world class at something. Her great dream, she went on to say, was to have her own serialized comic strip—hip, smart, and edgy. Of course, so far there was no money in it to be made, as far as she had learned. For the time being, she was resorting to the backup Plan B, putting her energies into doing the office work that paid the bills. If she could earn enough money, Plan A was to eventually freelance as an artist. At the same time, she had to admit that she fantasized all the time about quitting her day job to do her comic full-time—even if it meant doing it for free and being homeless. Then she wanted my advice. What should she do?

This life lesson, which first clicked for me at age twenty-eight and has continued to show up at various crossroads since that time, is that *there is no Plan B for passion.* Do what you love and love what you do. Plan A has to come first. Besides, Plan B sucks!

Yes, it is true that many individuals are grappling with unprecedented financial challenges in their lives. I've been asked frequently if it isn't foolish or irresponsible to put passion before practicality. My contention is that it's erroneous to think that we have to stop dreaming because of an economic or other crisis. My belief is that you can be responsible to loved ones and yourself without betraying your dreams. Let me take that a step further by arguing that there is nothing more practical than harnessing the power of passion.

So let's get to the billion-dollar question—definitely the number one most frequently asked of me and that I asked for many years above all others. It's not the what, when, why, or how that may assist you in finding valuable answers. It's the question of "where." *Where* do you find that "something" you can strive to be world class at? *Where* do you locate the venue in which you can attain mastery? *Where* can you ignite that part of yourself that makes you feel that you love what you're doing so much, you'd do it for free? *Where* will you discover affirmation that you're where you're supposed to be and that fires you up to be not just good but great?

By the time I left home in my late teens, I had eliminated what were then considered to be the few proven options for attaining greatness for someone from my background. The only ways to make it big in our 'hood, as far as most of us were led to believe, was if you could sing, dance, or dunk balls. Since I was convinced that out of every young black male in America, I was the only one who couldn't sing, dance, or shoot hoops well, that didn't seem very promising to me. Playing the trumpet and composing groundbreaking jazz was off the table, since Miles Davis had that market cornered. Football had actually allowed me to develop valuable leadership skills, although I had quit the team when the coaches put me on the line instead of at QB. Ironically, there were later opportunities in the navy for me, thanks to football. On the whole, however, I had come to the early conclusion that the ability to run, jump, and catch balls was, frankly, overrated. On the other hand, on one memorable occasion when I was watching the NCAA basketball championship playoffs on TV, I couldn't help but observe out loud that a couple of the star players were certain to make a million dollars one day. Momma set me straight on the spot, walking in from another room where she had overheard me. She laid down the law, letting it be known that I, too, could attain that level of success—in whatever financial or other terms I so specified. That was, of course, as long as I heeded her one caveat: "If you want to."

She was egging me on, opening the door to the rest of the world—the big, wide *where* out there for discovering what I most wanted to do.

The first major discovery as to where I might begin to look was to do everything within my power to search out individuals who were at the top of their game, no matter what it was, who could show me where they found what they were meant to do. In answer to my quest, I was blessed with an abundance of opportunities to learn from some of the best and brightest in their respective industries. Early on, starting in the navy, while serving as a medic in the armed services hospital at Camp Lejeune, North Carolina, I was fortunate to have Lieutenant Commander Charlotte Gannon take me under her wing. Bold, forceful, enthusiastic, and no-nonsense all at the same time, her leadership style was one that I continue to borrow from today. In that same time period, I met and went to work for Dr. Robert Ellis—who took me on

his journey to understand and improve conditions in which heart surgery and transplantation occur. He brought to his work a level of brilliance, precision, curiosity, imagination, and fanatical focus that was
akin to Miles Davis on the trumpet and that I was determined to incorporate in whatever I did. Meanwhile, Rip Jackson, the man who trained
me to set up and run the research lab, was an unlikely mentor. A good
old boy from down south, he didn't bother hiding some pretty racist
views that could have made it difficult for me to learn from him. But I
couldn't help acknowledging his considerable abilities, especially his
scrupulous attention to detail and to planning—leaving no stone
unturned and nothing to error.

Each of these three was unique unto themselves, but they had one
quality alike that was my biggest clue to finding my venue for mastery.
Gannon, Ellis, and Jackson all had found and turned on their button
for passion. Was this because they were born with special gifts and had
found their callings? I didn't think so. It seemed to me that they would
have been able to use their button for whatever they chose. For lack of
a better description, they were simply *turned on*—firing on all cylinders, operating at peak levels, revved up to the point that sleep, food,
and other human needs seemed to barely concern them.

The more I thought about this idea of a button that's in all of us, the
more I started to pay attention to how certain people had that energy
and presence about them. When I left my job in medical research and
found employment as a sales rep for a medical supply company, I found
more examples of people in that field who appeared to have found their
button. This was true not only of individuals who were in sales but also
of those on the buying side of the equation. Sometimes the most
turned-on folks were not even at the top. They were secretaries, interns,
custodians, security guards—but they were striving for mastery nonetheless. It wasn't that they had found their calling so much as they were
able to bring passion into where they were.

Does this sound like something you've witnessed or experienced? If
you have found the button that engages your wow factor, but aren't sure

if it's turned on all the way or whether or not you're in the right venue, my next question is, "What are you waiting for?"

I hear many reasons about why some say it's impractical to think about changing their "whereabouts." And I also hear folks rationalizing about how they're satisfied *enough* to stick it out and hang on to the dependable salary. Sounds like dreams deferred to me. My honest to God feelings are that if your button isn't engaged on the job, a paycheck isn't enough. It may not be enough that you're good at something or you make a terrific living at it, or that it validates you in someone else's eyes. The only eyes that matter are the ones you see in the mirror. You can and you deserve to love what you're doing so much that you'd do it for free, that you lose sleep because the sun can't come up early enough in the morning for you to do your whatever it is.

Why not follow your bliss? After all, if you don't feel it, you can't fake the funk. Go look for it.

That was the message sent to me when I met my paternal grandmother for the first time. As a new father in my late twenties, I had made the trip to Louisiana with my baby boy to finally meet my biological father and the rest of the Turner family. It was emotional, challenging, and wonderful—most of all because of what I learned about myself from my eighty-two-year-old grandmother, Ora Turner. After taking her time to study me and make an assessment, she said knowingly, "Boy, your way is always going to be different from other folk; and every opportunity you get, you've got to run your race with a passion."

That sounded weighty and meaningful, but I didn't fully grasp the implications until that next Sunday when I saw her wearing her high-top Converse sneakers to church so she could help "old people" to sit down! That's passion. Pure and powerful. She accepted herself fully and completely as she was, wherever she was, and lived her passion to the hilt. She had found her button.

By no coincidence, a short time later in San Francisco I sat down for the first of a few cups of coffee with stockbroker Bob Bridges—who gave me my first introduction to the basics of Wall Street. The more I learned after that, the more interested and passionate I felt to learn more. Then came the moment of truth when I visited the stock exchange in San Francisco for the first time. The energy was spectacular. I'm standing there and the ticker tape is going, bodies are flying all over the place, tickets are getting stamped, traders are shouting out orders, furiously scribbling their trades down, with bells and whistles ringing madly. I had died and gone to heaven. Though I'd never seen anything like it and had no previous glimpse of a trading floor, I was at home. That's when something inside of me clicked into place, and I recognized the flow, structure, and movement of Wall Street—just like music. This was where I was supposed to be. It wasn't—*Oh, yeah, I can do this*. But—*This is where I'm supposed to be*. I had found my button.

I hope you know what I'm talking about either because you've found it or you recognize that you have not—which is just as essential. Once you've found your button, what comes next is the passion that fuels your drive. You are in pursuit. You should feel a blast of simplified, uncomplicated happyness. Yep, it's a little like falling in love. It will be up to you to be bold enough to commit to more passion to come.

I have applied the button test when observing world-class rock stars of the financial world—starting in San Francisco with Gary Shemano and Marshall Geller, later with Bob Muh and then Ace Greenberg—all different, all completely plugged into passion. The same has been true of folks whom I've met in the entertainment business and in the non-profit, civil rights, and educational sectors, and those whom I've rubbed shoulders with who have helped shape my global consciousness. All turned on. I still think of my grandmother in her high-top sneakers on Sunday morning. That's called being happy!

There is one side note that I've had to confess lately. I do have trouble sleeping because I can't wipe the smile off my face! The choice, however, is not a tough one. Sleep or happyness? Your call.

Two / The Thorny and Golden Past

History is a guide to navigation in perilous times. History is who we are and why we are the way we are.

—David C. McCullough
Historian and author

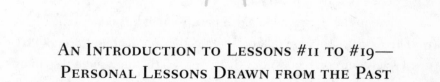

An Introduction to Lessons #11 to #19— Personal Lessons Drawn from the Past

Most of us have read or heard some version of the saying "If we ignore the lessons of history, we are doomed to repeat them." As many times as I'd heard that point made, for years my reaction was to use Tonto's line when the Lone Ranger says, "We're in trouble," and Tonto responds, "Who the hell is *we*?" If I had any clue that there was something useful to be found in studying the lessons of my own history, I wasn't about to fess up.

Over time, however, I came across the context for the original statement written a hundred years ago by George Santayana—a Spanish-born American philosopher and author of *Life of Reason*. He never said "we." What he actually said was, "Those who cannot remember the past are condemned to repeat it."

Ouch. He was talking about me after all. Even though I could accept the premise that it was important for all of us to study our personal histories, it still took me years to summon the fortitude to revisit and recall the chapters of my own past. Well, I'm here to report that even though the journey was painful, the knowledge that I unearthed in the process has turned out to be my own buried treasure—which was waiting for me all along, right in my own backyard. I'm also here to say that if you're anything like the way that I used to be—either avoiding the chapters of your own history or giving it too much power to hurt you now—you, too, are missing out on the buried gold that can be found in your past.

Now I know a lot of us would rather skip over whatever happened back in the day, because it's painful or obsolete (as some would say), because there's nothing to do to change it, other than to let it go or get over it. But if we do that, we risk losing our knowledge of what really makes us happy: the pure essence of joy that we knew as children. And if we don't take the time to reclaim the dreams that we may have left back there in the thorny and golden past, we will be poorer for it.

The treasure that I'm talking about comes up in almost every Q&A that I've ever given, in questions that I hear all the time about resources that many consider to be rare: "Where did you find the hope that you wouldn't always be homeless?" "How were you able to see your dreams coming true, when nobody else could?" "Where did you learn to believe in yourself?"

The answers consistently take me back to the past, to the soil of childhood, adolescence, and my early adult years—even to events and people whose lives came before me. That's where we all can hit the mother lode. And yet, the irony for many of us is how much we resist going to dig in the first place. That's why I call it "thorny" as well as golden. For much of my adulthood, my feeling was that I was glad to have gotten out of there alive. What could possibly compel me to go take a tour of my personal hell? Well, for starters, listening to others tell their stories allowed me to come to the conclusion that we've all got our own versions of hellish moments and memories. Much to my surprise, it turns out that nobody grows up with the picture-perfect, fairy-tale life. A big awakening! No matter what 'hood or easy street you come from, there were painful passages for all of us. Such is life; such is the past. On the flip side, even in the thorniest, most difficult pasts that I've heard others recall, there were also pockets of light, humor, pleasure, discovery, accomplishment, and triumphant decisions.

The recognition that it wasn't just me was one incentive to brave the journey back. But the main reason I had to choose to do the work was that until I dealt with residual issues—fear, disappointment, shame, loss, abandonment, powerlessness—the memories were going to haunt me anyway. Amazingly, when I finally decided to stop being haunted and to turn around and say "Boo!" right back, I found a freedom that I'd never known. Painful? No question. But it's the most important decision I ever made that has freed me to pursue and claim the happyness that has blessed me beyond measure. Who would have known?

At almost every book signing, I will spot someone at the end of the line waiting to share something with me that they may have never told anyone else. This was the case on one memorable occasion when a gentleman who had waited for some time approached me, shook my hand, and went on to say that hearing about my past had reminded him of something in his. For years, every time he removed his belt and heard the sound of it slipping out of his belt loops, he was overwhelmed by fear. It was the same sound he had heard as a child when his father took off his belt before beating him and members of his family.

"But you know," he said, "I never gave myself credit. I'm fifty-three years old and I've never whipped my son. He's sixteen." That was a conscious decision that he had now remembered—an important discovery about himself that he'd overlooked all this time. That conscious choice was part of who he was and had guided him to find other ways of being a strong parent. You can give a child positive direction and discipline without hitting, he insisted, through other means of leading by example and with thoughtful communication. The feeling of pride in his parenting skills that he had only just come to fully appreciate turned out to be a golden discovery about himself.

We both felt validated to be standing where we were. Without making the connection to the past, we wouldn't have had that freedom.

I have also discovered that when making decisions about the present or the future, there's no better place to look for guidance than the past with its storehouse of personal experience and education—a virtual "Library of Resources," as I call it. And that's not just me. We each have such a place in our memory vaults where wisdom waits. We can figure out where we became stuck with faulty beliefs that still stand in our way, how to free ourselves from our fears, or how we can reconnect to empowering beliefs. Best of all, we can come away with evidence of our strengths and our potential, which we may have forgotten or left behind.

Remember that when looking into the past, just one of many areas where we can find useful resources, it's not necessary to relive every moment. The purpose of taking an inventory of your earlier personal lessons is to reexamine and learn from those that left their mark. You'll then be able to look at where you are now or where you're headed and say to yourself—*Oh, yeah, I've seen this movie before!* That information is golden because at a certain level nobody else was there but you. How did you handle it before? What mistakes did you make? What did you do wrong? What did you do right? You have this wonderful opportunity to make use of what didn't work before by admitting—*oh, yeah, here's where I screwed up earlier*—and then perhaps seeing that you're headed for a repeat of the same mistake. You can spot patterns that haven't been working for you and choose to change the things you've been doing to perpetuate them or find alternate ways for reacting to situations that keep cropping up. If you've been pushing a boulder up the hill only to have it roll back down on you every time you get to the top, your past may hold a needed lesson that you haven't yet learned or been able to apply in order to alter the dynamic once and for all.

Yes, getting to the knowledge can be like climbing through thorny vines that obscure the path. It's not an overnight process either. Anyone who has been in therapy or has dealt with issues from the past through writing or other outlets can attest to its difficulty and its value. This isn't to discourage anyone from the hard work of unearthing the gold of who you are—nobody can do that for you but you. On the contrary, if you are too cool for school when it comes to your past—as I once was— you're missing out on a lifetime of dividends you could be earning from the stock you own that you don't even know about!

That's how a dear friend of mine put it to me some years ago when I told her that the past was of no interest to me and was more or less off-limits. An artist and children's author, my friend then told me a fable about a beggar who was missing out on his true potential. Was she talking about me? I was not into this story but I listened anyway. This beggar—poor, homeless, in rags, with nothing to eat, out in the cold—always sleeps in the same spot, unaware there is a pot of gold buried just below the patch of dirt where he's been camping the whole time. Until he awakens his awareness, with the conscious choice to do so, he is cursed every day to search elsewhere for handouts, or look for other people to tell him where the gold is buried, to live the pain, humiliation, misery, and confusion of his circumstances.

"What exactly does that mean?" I asked her.

"Whatever it means to you." That's why it's a fable, she explained.

Different interpretations have occurred to me over the years. The gold could symbolize the hidden truth of who we are and what our potential is. Some have suggested that it could represent the "collective unconscious," or the "master mind" that contains all thought and knowl-edge, past, present, and future. Others have shared their interpretation that the gold symbolizes enlightenment and the pure joy of being, while the misery comes from seeking it outside of ourselves, rather than within, right where we are.

The point of the fable that reverberated for me is that it put another twist on "rags to riches." It's a reminder that until you are at home in yourself, familiar with the knowledge of the gold of who you are, where you come from, where you've been, and who you were meant to be, you'll be basically "homeless." In other words, until you can come to value all experience, and find some happyness in everything you've lived and will live, you will be without your ultimate riches.

As an overview to the lessons that we're getting ready to cover, an e-mail from Scott in Michigan can give us a jumping-off place. Scott began by noting, "While we are different in many ways (I am white and grew up in a different generation), there are some similarities." Though he considered his childhood to be nowhere near as challenging as mine, he said there were enough similarities that he felt compelled to recall forgotten events from his past that were enlightening for him. A very successful banker and active volunteer for several meaningful causes, Scott realized that his leftover worry from his younger years kept him from savoring his success:

> My parents divorced when I was an adolescent. Both remarried within ten months and since that time I felt a substantial amount of instability, until the last few years. . . . During the more intense times of fear I always worried about being home-less someday even though it was probably not realistic. Because of this, I even took in a homeless man one winter when he was begging. . . . In addition to a daughter from earlier in my life, I recently married a widow, and now I have two more children. I am truly blessed to have what I have now, but hope that some-day I can help those in need in much greater ways.

Scott's story gives us a terrific example of someone who is con-tinuing to learn more about himself from his thorny and golden past and leads us into the resources we'll be exploring next in Lessons #11 to #19:

> #11 Instead of avoiding the gold of where he came from, Scott
>   already had chosen the **freedom** that comes from recalling
>   his past.

#12 Like Scott, we all can gain a greater sense of **self-aware-ness** whenever we're willing to go looking for it and put it to use in new ways.

#13 As his e-mail indicates, instead of being overwhelmed by the past, we each have an opportunity to choose a path of **discovery** about where we come from and where we're headed.

#14 Scott's example shows us the importance of knowing who we are and what we have to offer without allowing others or our circumstances to determine our **identity.**

#15 For him and for everyone, the past can empower and guide us in an ongoing lesson of **forgiveness.**

#16 As a key to understanding relationships past, present, and future, Scott and many of us can attain vital insights about how we were taught to **trust** ourselves and others.

#17 The effort that any of us takes to reclaim dreams left behind will reward us with knowledge about the power of **motivation** in all of our pursuits (a great lesson!).

#18 Just as Scott looked at how early events caused him to worry, we can use this lesson as a tool for gaining our **independence** from thoughts or beliefs that do not serve us.

#19 Perhaps most valuable of all, the past holds a reminder lesson for Scott and the rest of us about the **courage** we earned in the face of our toughest tests.

Some of these personal lessons to be drawn from the past may be familiar to you already. Perhaps you've been doing some digging of your own for a while and this will all be just a stroll in the park. And if it isn't, be resolved that you're not going to be one of those people doomed to repeat the past. You're here to set yourself free.

LESSON #11
Who's Afraid of the Big, Bad Yesterday?

KEYWORD: *Freedom*

There's a guy I know very well who got to a place in his life, somewhere during his early forties, when he finally acknowledged that there could be something of value in his past and dared to go dig under his feet. In the eyes of others he already had his riches, having attained many important objectives that he had set out for himself. Very few people knew the extent of what he had overcome, and the generational cycles he had chosen to break, although it was apparent to them that he was a self-made man. In fact, he was a very happy person, and he had much to celebrate—success as an entrepreneur, fulfillment as a parent, meaningful personal and business relationships, and rewarding outlets for empowering others. For all intents and purposes, life was great, and he had no complaints.

But until he made a decision to deal with darker stretches of his life, he wasn't sure what to do with lingering memories from the past— mainly the painful years of his childhood and youth, experiences that he rarely if ever shared with anyone else. Abandoned by his biological father, whom he never knew, he had spent time in foster care when his mother served jail sentences for her attempts to free herself from his stepfather's violence. This guy had worked hard to compartmentalize those memories and the powerless feelings of being a child and not being able to protect his loved ones. He had kept the most painful events, like the time in his teens when he was a victim of sexual assault, as firmly locked-up secrets. After all, he came from a long line of people who practiced their version of "Don't Ask, Don't Tell," of not discussing painful or unpleasant matters. He saw no incentive to change the tradition.

If this story sounds familiar, you've probably figured out that the guy is me. Today, my life is literally an open book. But there was once a time when I was the Undisputed Heavyweight Champion when it came to avoiding the past! If you have never had a similar aversion and already have the freedom to access the meaningful memory files of your life, count yourself blessed. If, on the other hand, you've stamped some passages "secret and confidential"—never to be exposed to the light of day, even to you—it's probably time to gently ask yourself, *Who's afraid of the big, bad yesterday?*

By the time I was in my early twenties, it might have taken some interrogation, but in answer to the preceding question, I would have eventually forced myself to raise my hand and admit—*I am!* Instead of doing anything about it, however, I had other priorities—or so I told myself. It was much more important, or so I felt, to contend with questions about the present and the future. For instance—had I rushed into marriage without taking the time to find out if I was emotionally ready or not? And then there was the issue of that prestigious but low-paying job in medical research. Was I actually living up to my younger dreams of being world class at something one day? Or was I lowering my expectations because I'd never gone to college and didn't want anyone to know where I came from?

Ironically, many of my answers could have come from doing some R&D into my own past. But that area of investigation was off-limits, and I wasn't going there. After all, I'd already locked the door and gotten rid of the key!

The first chink in the armor happened one night when I went out with friends to one of the hot and happening comedy clubs that were booming in San Francisco in the early 1980s. The act we'd gone to see was Richard Pryor, the headliner, already the reigning King of Comedy, and the recent survivor of a freebasing accident in which he had allegedly been picked up by the police for running down the street on fire. Early into his set, Pryor started joking about what many rumored hadn't been an accident but a suicide attempt by explaining that it was set off by an explosion when he tried to dunk an Oreo cookie into a glass of pasteurized milk. His deadpan expression at proposing such an innocent far-fetched story brought down the house. Then he talked about waking up in an ambulance surrounded by white people and thinking, "Ain't this a bitch? I done died and they sent me to the wrong @#*$$! heaven!"

If that wasn't irreverent enough, he topped it all off by making the same cheap joke that lesser comics were trying as he waved a lit match onstage and laughingly said, "What's this? Man, it's Richard Pryor running down the street!"

I was amazed that he could take the most painful experiences from his life and turn them into material. And that's what he did with everything, digging down into the depths of his most private pain, holding it up to the light, and squeezing every last laugh out of it. He talked about his weaknesses, shortcomings, and things that were embarrassing, about sex, dysfunctional families, racism, politics, and everyday spirituality. Pryor talked about his ne'er-do-well daddy—a boxer, pimp, and the meanest so-and-so he ever knew—who made the Mafia seem like teddy bears. And he brought to life a crazy cast of characters that he must have observed in the insanity of growing up in a brothel run by his grandmother, where his mother worked until she split when he was around the age of ten. It was there that he had learned to fend for himself; I had read elsewhere that when he was young, he had been molested by someone who lived in the neighborhood and by a local priest. But somehow instead of blaming and being victimized, he was able to stand up and transform all of that pain into storytelling that was hilarious and spellbinding at the same time.

At first, I thought it was just me who was laughing so hard that I was crying and doubling over in my chair, until I looked around and saw that everybody in the room had been seized by the healing spirit of humor. It was like being in church, and Richard Pryor was telling truths like a preacher, freeing us from some of those same dark places where he'd been before.

How did he do it? He turned over every stone that had something interesting to reveal from his past—his rocky relationships, all the odd jobs he'd worked after he was expelled from school at the age of fourteen, his ill-fated stint in the army. Nothing that he had lived through was off-limits.

The thing about Pryor that made him perhaps the most influential comedian of all time was that as much as he made you laugh, he also made you think. He certainly made me think about the possibility of being able to examine the darker memories of my own past. Was the prospect of doing that scary? Of course it was. But the thought also occurred to me that by avoiding the terrible stuff from the past, I was missing out on all the good stuff, too. Not only that, but for the first time, Richard Pryor's act had convinced me that I probably had some pretty funny and dramatic material stored back there! Let me quickly add that I had no desire to do stand-up comedy with it or tell my story someday to the world at large. And I'm not saying that Richard Pryor was a model of mental health, although he was finding his own form of therapy through humor. What compelled me was the vision of having the same freedom that I had witnessed that night to make something useful out of everything or anything that I had experienced.

Almost another twenty years went by before that vision came to pass. If not for the nudging that came from loved ones, and my choice to make sure that my children didn't inherit the "Don't Ask, Don't Tell" policy, it might have taken longer for me to break the cycle of silence. The few times that I had ever brought up questions to my mother about vital information that I needed to know—like who my father was, why I didn't know him, or why she couldn't leave my stepfather for good— Momma changed the subject. There was no point in talking about something painful; it was water under the bridge. The few times that I found myself shutting down when my son or daughter asked me a question about our family history, I caught myself. Not that my answers were in-depth, but it was a start at breaking the generational cycle of silence that persists in many families.

The real impetus for finding the key and unlocking the cage where the big, bad yesterday was fattening itself up, at my expense, was a speaking opportunity in front of a group of urban middle-school kids.

From the comments and questions that were being voiced by many of the teenagers, I understood that they'd been hearing the same negative messages about their futures that had been sent to me. When one of the boys announced that he might like to have his own financial planning firm one day and the rest of the group started to snicker, I said something that later was included in the film version of my story— something that was said as much to those kids as it was to the boy that I had once been. "Don't listen to them," I said. "In fact, don't ever let anybody tell you that you can't do something. Not your parents, your teachers. Nobody."

Then I found myself talking about events and circumstances of where I'd grown up that I hadn't shared with anyone for years. Suddenly, they all leaned forward in their seats, and the light of possibilities came into their eyes. The incredible freedom that I had just found to finally talk about where I'd come from was better than anything I could have imagined. What was more, it was contagious. The one boy who had been willing to share his aspirations started a trend. Other hands shot into the air as advice was sought. One of the girls asked, "Mr. Gardner, why people gotta keep you down when you have your dream?"

Again, I was having a long overdue conversation with myself. "Well," I said, "people who can't do something themselves, they're jealous, so they wanna tell you that you can't do it. But you know what? You got a dream, it's yours and you gotta protect it. So, don't let anyone tell you that you can't. If you want something, go get it. Period."

When I left that day and hailed a taxi to go back to my office, I started to tell the cabdriver some other memories that I was now free to remember and to talk about—from homelessness to being a single parent of two teenagers, and every topic under the sun. And I kept on talking. Cabdrivers became my therapists. Why not? I was paying.

From then on, I continued to strive to be as free as Richard Pryor to drag out whatever part of my past that could be turned into something useful for myself or for others. Though it was going to be some time before most of the thorns had been cleared, the most freeing discovery that I made, right off the bat, was that even though it was very painful to remember and reopen past wounds, *I no longer was powerless.*

The crazy part was that all this time, the past had held on to its power over me. Now, by facing and remembering everything, the bad, the ugly, as well as the good and the great, I was taking my power back.

A few empowering steps for applying this lesson can be taken by anyone who is ready to admit to the fear of yesterday. The first step is to remind yourself of what you're missing by disowning so much of who you are. That was what Sonya, a painter, did when she was in her sixties. I was amazed by a series of paintings she did of herself as a child in the strange, colorful household where she grew up. Sonya said that for many years, she had avoided recalling the events that took place there. She had also swept aside memories of her unconventional family. Besides the painful parts of the past, she said that much of it was cloudy and confusing to try to remember. That was until an image popped into her head of the beautiful carpets and antiques that she had spent hours admiring as a little girl. It then dawned on her that what she was missing was the part of herself who used ordinary surroundings and the quirky characters in her family to inspire her art. With that realization, Sonya began a series of personal memory paintings that have turned out to be the most successful of her career! The freedom to dip from the well of the past had changed her life, she told me.

The second step to freeing yourself from the power that the big, bad yesterday may have over you is to come meet it armed with questions. You're not intending to live in the past or allow yourself to get swept up in old stories. Rather, you're on an important fact-finding mission. If you've ever seen interviews of stand-up comics like Richard Pryor, you've probably heard many of the top comedy stars talk about how they'll write down a topic they want to rant about or expound upon and then go hunt for material directly from their pasts. You, too, are entitled to the same freedom. Jot down a topic of interest or a vivid experience and see what wisdom and life lessons you can retrieve from yesterday.

You really do have the option to embrace your inner Pryor and find a new take for how you dealt with setbacks, challenges, failures, adversity, and mistakes. Perhaps you're tougher than you've let on and owe yourself some overdue credit. Or is there a way to apply what you learned from those situations now? Whatever you decide, don't forget to enjoy the freedom of no longer being afraid of the big, bad yesterday.

LESSON #12
In Your Library of Resources, Value All Experience

KEYWORD: *Self-awareness*

Not long ago, I had lunch with a Wall Street colleague who had recently retired and had planned on spending more time with family while catching up on his reading, hobbies, and philanthropic efforts. "Chris," he said, "retirement is the worst thing that ever happened to me!" Like many highly driven individuals, he had never known what it was like not to have every single minute of his day plotted out for him. The luxury of free time, he swore, was going to kill him. If it didn't, apparently his wife was going to do the job instead. No matter what she suggested—everything from launching a new business from home, to traveling around the world on a sailboat, to teaching a class at a local community college, to studying far-out subject matter like astrophysics—it all seemed pointless.

He had even tried therapy—which for him was true desperation. "C'mon, man," he added, "that's for crazy people." My friend said that the therapist assured him that he wasn't crazy but then fired him on the grounds that he was unwilling to open up about his past. The diagnosis was that he was suffering from a radical loss of identity that had been completely tied to his professional life. All of a sudden, here he was, home alone, a stranger to himself. His job had become who he was. Without it, he had ceased to exist.

Countless individuals today may be finding themselves suddenly disconnected from who they thought they were—due to the loss of a job, not necessarily from voluntary retirement. When who you are is based on what you do, the shock of no longer doing it can be devastating. We're seeing this in the tens of thousands in the financial field as folks have to ask themselves, not just "what do I do now?" but "who am I?" This doesn't have to be the end of the world. Rather, it can be an opportunity to seek the true balance of what matters in life, as well as a chance to focus less on what has been lost and more on the value of acquired experience.

Along these lines, I reassured my friend that he wasn't alone in feeling estranged from himself and that there were plenty of others who could relate. I'd been in similar shoes before. Now, to be fair to myself, maybe I wasn't as stubborn or as set in my ways as this guy. But I promised him that if I could overcome my own unwillingness to deal with the past, so could he. The first step was to go on a quest for self-awareness—a major reward that awaits any of us who are willing to get past the thorns.

How? Well, I suggested, like starting out in any other pursuit, by educating yourself. Only this was an education as to your own history. That was, after all, one of the logical arguments that I'd made to myself. But where should one go to get that education and earn new self-awareness? What came to mind next was an image of a kind of library— much like the beautiful old branch of the New York Public Library with the grand entrance guarded by a pair of marble lions. My idea was that each one of us has such a place, our very own Library of Resources, where we can visit and check out any book or article about any aspect of our lives and experiences that we need to access.

This concept appealed to my friend. But wouldn't going in there be overwhelming? It would almost be like putting in any word on an Internet search engine. How would you know which of the millions of results was relevant?

"Great question," I admitted. Then the essence of this very personal life lesson became clear to me—that everything we've experienced is relevant and part of who we are, whether we like it or not. As Einstein wrote about what constitutes an education, "All true learning is experience. Everything else is just information."

Hence—*In your Library of Resources, value all experience.*

My friend decided that it was worth the effort to peruse his past to see if there was something of value he could find that might help him understand why retirement bothered him so much. The self-awareness that he gained from the process allowed him to acknowledge that way back in his early days there was a lonely child. What he thought had been a privileged life, on second glance, involved spending more time with a nanny than with his parents or older siblings who were gone by the time he was in school. It was painful to learn that he never knew much about the people who mattered most to him. But then his practical side, one of his strengths, came up with a solution to learn more about all of his relatives. The next thing I knew, he was busy doing extensive genealogy charts for both sides of his family. No, he couldn't give himself another childhood in place of the one he'd missed. But he could have fun getting to know himself, starting where he was. His next plan was to travel to some of the places where his ancestors had come from.

In the meantime, I've been able to do some further recollecting of my own as to why the idea of a Library of Resources is compelling for me. Not surprisingly, the answer has taken me back to my growing-up years and to the memory of what a marketing genius my mother was when it came to promoting the wonders of Milwaukee's public library system.

There was nothing out of the ordinary about her encouraging us to spend time at the library. Moms was like most parents who value literacy and education as building blocks for success. In the 'hood, if you wanted to move up in the world—I'm talking literally—your goal would be to go north, less than a mile up the road, where a migration was well under way for educated people of color. If you lived above a certain street, that meant you had studied how to get ahead, had built your own business, or had pursued college degrees and professional jobs—teachers, civil servants, lawyers, bankers, doctors, and so forth. Below that boundary, it was assumed that you were uneducated or lacking in the means to make something of yourself and your family.

Of course, for my mother, education was more than a requirement for upward mobility. It was what she had journeyed so far to attain, what she sacrificed everything for us to have. It was the only thing that made sense out of chaos. In her book, education was as necessary as breathing, eating, sleeping, and praying. Like Einstein, she valued all learning and all experience, and she conveyed her point of view like no one else.

Momma's ad campaign for why the library was where we should go hang out was unique. Rather than suggest it would be nice for me to spend an afternoon in a safe environment that would help me cultivate my mind, what she said was, "The public library is the most dangerous place in the world."

The most dangerous place in the world? Why was that? "Because," she explained to me, "you can go in there and learn how to do anything."

Years later I was surprised to hear a similar idea expressed by my ultimate hero, Nelson Mandela, who said, "Education is the most powerful weapon which you can use to change the world."

Moms had never heard that quote, but she was clearly tapping the same universal wisdom. And she knew exactly what she was doing. She was giving me a mighty sword to help me fight my own battles up ahead. If it's the case, as I've also heard, that a mentor can see the potential that you can't see for yourself, but can't tell you what it is or lead you all the way there, and must prepare you to face unforeseen obstacles, then Bettye Jean Gardner Triplett was playing the role of Obi-Wan Kenobi in my life. She didn't paint the vision for me. But whenever I found myself lost in thought, imagining possibilities for the future, I felt that she was encouraging me, saying, "Son, are you seeing ghosts again? And if you are, it's okay as long as you're seeing them with the eyes of your soul, 'cause if that's how you're seeing them, ain't nobody got to see them but you."

This was her way of saying that if I didn't pursue my dreams, they would remain nothing more than ghosts—misty possibilities that would haunt my days. To avoid that fate, well, there was the dangerous public library—chock-full of free resources, where I could learn to do anything. In the process, I could gain self-awareness to make wise use of the resources I learned.

Without question, Momma's strategy worked. To this day, I must go into a bookstore or up to a newsstand daily. I can't pass either up. Back home as a kid, whenever I entered our local library, I had a feeling of adventure and excitement. With its high ceilings, polished floors, and musty, mysterious odor, the atmosphere made me feel like I was in a spy movie every time I headed to the card catalog, like a detective, where I could use a code—the Dewey decimal system—to hunt down books, articles, reference guides, even old stuff stored on microfilm, on all manner of subjects.

Among the many perks that went along with a visit to the library was the fact that I was free to wander in the stacks and make up my own mind as to what might be interesting or relevant to my life. There was also that very stern person, sometimes a woman and sometimes a man, who sat at the reference desk and answered questions when I wasn't sure where to find material about a certain subject. Not overly friendly at first, the typical reference librarian would suddenly turn into Sherlock Holmes when asked to join me on my mission to locate hard-to-find material.

My concept for a virtual visit to your Library of Resources can be applied with the power of your imagination whenever you feel compelled to find valuable experience from your own archives. You might be surprised to learn that you probably are already doing this on your own whenever you choose to learn something new. It's a natural reflex when you're transitioning to an unfamiliar stage of your life to refer to the past as a ready-made guidebook. The challenge, I've learned, is to remember to not just skim the surface, but to crack open those files and get to the self-awareness stored within them.

As a recent example of the value of all experience, I will share a portion of the beautiful, handwritten letter that I received from Pat, a married mother and grandmother in her early seventies, retired and living in Omaha, Nebraska. Pat had responded to hearing my "story of us" by making the decision to look more closely at her own story and where she came from. In spite of the fact that we had almost nothing in common in terms of gender, age, race, or cultural background, Pat recognized that some of the more difficult parts of our journeys had been similar.

She recalled what it was like growing up in an orphanage in St. Louis, where she and her three siblings were sent to live when her single mother couldn't support the four of them. Even so, her mom managed to visit them every other day, taking three streetcars each way to make the trip.

Pat could recall going to school in the dead of winter with only a light sweater to wear. When people asked if she was cold, she would say, "Oh, no." When her younger sister became ill and needed medicine, Pat refused to accept that they couldn't afford it. Her ingenious solution, which nobody else was doing at the time, was to go through the alleys and find milk bottles that she could turn in for five cents apiece—eventually raising the money required for the medicine that helped her sister survive her illness. Instead of seeing her life as full of hardship, Pat described herself as enormously blessed. She was thankful for her marriage of many years, for her wonderful daughters and grandchildren, and for the opportunity to work in various jobs starting in her early teens. It was very moving to see how the past had helped reconnect her to strengths that were part of who she was, and to how she used them to deal with a struggle that had occupied her for years:

I made it thru 8th grade, how on earth I do not know. I could not read or do math. . . . Then 15 years ago I did go back and went thru math and reading for my G.E.D. I went every night and on weekends. . . . It took forever, I had to do five tests, but I made it! I still have to work when I read books—but now I can. And now I can write letters like this one to you.

The process of recalling her past had done so much to energize her self-awareness that at the end of the letter, she acknowledged how a new mission had become her pursuit of happyness. Her dream was to work with older people like herself who had never learned to read or write. Pat observed, "We hear so much about 'no child left behind,' but I would like to have a 'no age left behind.'"

Pat was not a woman of significant means in terms of money or formal education, which she stated plainly, but it was evident from her letter that she had come to believe that she had much to offer. "My special gift," she confided, "is that I am able to feel the pain inside of others, because I have felt it too, and I know how to make them feel good about themselves." To demonstrate the potential for gaining literacy later in life, she was thinking about writing her life story—something she once could have never dared to consider. Pat was confident that she had the tenacity to do it. That level of self-awareness probably wouldn't have been possible without a visit to her Library of Resources.

For anyone who has ever considered putting pen to paper and telling all, let me echo what I wrote to Pat—*Do it!* You don't have to wait until you retire to begin your remembrance and use of times past. Don't worry about whether or not what you have to say is salesworthy or if anyone else will appreciate what you've written. The operative action is simply to tell your story. If it's meant to be shared with others, be assured that it will find its legs.

LESSON #13
Draw the Line of Your Life

KEYWORD: *Discovery*

Imagine for a moment that you're standing at the reference desk in your very own virtual Library of Resources—where vital experiences and lessons from your past are stored—and would like to be directed to this legendary treasure that supposedly can be found by digging in your past. Instead of giving this job to the know-it-all who sits at that desk, you have the opportunity with this life lesson to create a sense of order out of all the material by drawing the line of your life. That's your treasure map.

If your first reaction to that is "what?" then join the club. I, too, had that reaction during a nonprofit organization's strategic planning meeting in 2003. The professional strategic planner suggested that before we talk about issues confronting the organization, we should each identify what role we could better play in the collective pursuit we had undertaken. And in order to share the special strengths and skills each of us had to contribute, our strategic planner asked each of us to write our life story down on one piece of paper. She then took out Magic Markers and passed them around to the group. Everyone assembled, eight or nine of us, exchanged confused expressions. "Oh, it's easy," she said, "just draw the line of your life."

The grumbling began. I was the loudest. We were all pressed for time, many of us busy executives, with other agendas. The strategic planner explained that we all have our stories of how we arrived at where we are—in life, in our jobs, in our relationships—wherever we are. Telling our individual stories, she insisted, was important in personal and professional contexts, whether we were doing an organizational history or mission statement, or putting together a professional curriculum vitae. By drawing the line of our life, apparently, we could tell our own story in shorthand—and by doing so create this treasure map to the major events, turning points, and stepping-stones that had brought each of us to the strategic planning session.

It all sounded out of my league. But her recommendation was not to think about it, just do it, as there were no rights or wrongs. The point was to be as visual as possible, to start as far back as an earliest memory and then draw the line without words, but with all the twists, turns, ups and downs, bumps and grinds, highs and lows. Though I needed more than one piece of paper, when I was finished, I looked and saw the line of my life that I had just drawn. It reminded me of the Bay Area Rapid Transit maps, and the many times that my son and I had slept on the train—riding it out as far as it would go and then returning again. Stark as the memory was, I could see how all the stops along the way had been necessary for my growth and movement forward.

Many different emotions swirled inside of me as I appreciated all the ground that had been covered. Instead of my early days looking as dark and dreary as I'd remembered, I could see the pockets of light that had been there and which I'd forgotten. Then she suggested that we give our drawing a title. There was only one word that came to mind for me: "Pursuit."

My fellow participants were excited about the discoveries they had made by drawing their life stories on paper, even though each of our lines was different. Some were reminiscent of waves on the ocean; others looked like jagged cliffs. Some of our lines incorporated sharp edges and rolling curves. Interestingly enough, when the strategic planner brought the meeting back to the particulars of short- and long-range goals for our organization, we were a much more cohesive group than we had been before the exercise. We had gotten to know one another's stories through our lines—and we could better respect the past experience that others brought to the table. With the discoveries we made about ourselves and one another, it seemed that our discussion about where we wanted to go as an organization was more directed and results oriented than it would have been without doing the exercise. No doubt about it, I was schooled!

The strategic planner later explained to me that she had developed this tool in settings when she worked as a therapist helping individuals who were suffering from posttraumatic stress. The idea was that by standing outside of your experiences—by drawing them, rather than talking about them—it becomes easier to get some distance from the painful part of an experience while still being able to look at it and discover the truth of how it may have impacted you. She had then applied this technique in working with businesses, organizations, and groups of people that need to come together quickly on the same page with agreement about their organizational history. The examples she gave me were of companies and other bodies needing to reinvent themselves, adapt their strategies for new growth, recover from losses, or start fresh.

This approach struck a familiar chord with me. After all, if you as a business entity don't know how you arrived at where you are, how can you chart the course for where you hope to go? How can you know what you've been doing that's working and what you've done that hasn't been working? By looking at the big picture—after you've drawn the line of the company's growth, much like a stock graph—successful versus unsuccessful strategies can be all the more apparent.

The point of this lesson, as I've learned increasingly the more that I've recommended this practical tool to others, is that it gives you a fresh perspective on the past. One of the discoveries that I've made in looking at my personal line of pursuit was where it showed an avoidance of remembering certain events and where I was holding on unnecessarily to memories.

At that time, the year of homelessness was something that had lived inside of me for too long, even while I'd avoided talking about it. It occurred to me that for years, whenever I went back to San Francisco on business, I'd chosen to stay at the same hotel in a room with a view overlooking Union Square Park, where my son and I had to sleep too many nights. It had been important to remember where I had come from and that I was never going back there again, ever. Meanwhile, I was living with the fear that everything good, joyful, safe, and secure in the life that I'd created for myself and my kids would somehow be snatched away. Somehow, my defense mechanism told me that if I stayed at the hotel and looked down to where I used to be, that would keep me on high alert to prevent such a disaster from happening again. By drawing the line of my life, I finally was able to see that my fear had gotten the better of me.

That discovery was as profound as an exorcism. The next time that I headed for San Francisco, I booked a room at a hotel on a different side of town—and loved it! Will it be my new Bay Area digs? Maybe or maybe not. The gift is that I'm free to choose.

Not long after that revelation, I had the opportunity to speak at a juvenile detention program and decided to try out the power of discovery with this lesson. I suggested that the youth in the program could tell their stories of how they got to where they were in that setting by drawing their lines. One of the teens who was set to be released soon—vowing that he never wanted to repeat his earlier mistakes—allowed me to keep his drawing and share it as an example:

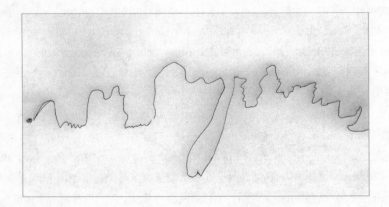

He narrated his drawing with captions, calling his high points "excellent" and his lowest point "lost" and then described other ups as "OK" and downs as "shaky." It was clear that he wanted his future to be brighter. But as his drawing depicted, he wasn't sure that he could make it. My suggestion for him and the others in the room who really liked this exercise was to look again at their pasts and put an "X" at every point on their drawing where they had made a choice that influenced the direction and shape of the line—the good, the bad, and the ugly. Very few of the teens had trouble acknowledging that their choices had been driving their line—not the other way around. The next step was to recognize that their choices could determine the shape of the line that had yet to be drawn. As for the young man who was getting ready to go out into the world and wasn't sure how he would fare, his discovery was that he could take the same pencil and a fresh piece of paper in order to draw the line of his life that was still to come—while making the same positive choices that had led to the "excellent" outcomes earlier.

To apply this lesson, I recommend that you take the leap and dare to explore your line. You'll discover that from a bird's-eye view, the major turning points and particular chapters will draw your attention to them first and foremost—like a topographical map. You can note your important choices, where you struggled, when you fell down, and the places where you got up again as well as the places where you stayed too long. The discovery available to any of us when we draw the line is that in the midst of what seemed like chaos, instability, or boredom we were able to find our own coherent order, shape, and direction. And we can also see the connection between the lessons that we learned and built upon—or that we failed to learn at our own peril.

You may want to think this one through in your imagination, or do the exercise as we did with the strategic planner. You merely need to trust your treasure mapping skills. It's a simple exercise. This is your story and you get to tell it. You can choose whether you use pen, pencil, paper, crayons, Magic Markers, or paints and poster board. You can use an Etch A Sketch or graph paper with your compass and protractor.

The reason that I view this line as a map to your treasure is that it lets you see that there is a shape, direction, and purpose in the flow of your life—your story. Each moment in the line of your life is a lesson. Every loop, backslide, dip, elevation, peak, and plateau is reflected there in an event or a memory. Put them all in. And don't forget to draw the curves!

Maybe you know someone who has ridden that smooth, straight line that points to the stars and never falters, veers, crashes, or dives. But for those of us who can proudly say that we're here, thanks to every pitfall and bump in the road, would we really want that? Without the gyrations and fluctuations, you're just flatlining—and that ain't living!

However you draw your map, the treasure of discovery that awaits you is nothing less than the rhyme and reason to your existence. The through line of your life gives meaning to everything that you've experienced, suffered, and enjoyed. It lets you look back and see the design— how the seemingly disconnected pieces actually fit together like a jigsaw puzzle, and how changing just one piece of the journey would reconfigure everything else. It's the discovery of self and the confirmation of three very personal, golden truths: (1) you were meant to be here in this life, to learn, love, and be loved; (2) you are the hero of a meaningful story that is yours alone—a trajectory that has a shape, direction, and purpose; and (3) everything and everyone are in your life for a reason.

My advisory is not to accept these truths on face value. Discover them yourself.

LESSON #14
Whose Child Are You?

KEYWORD: *Identity*

While speaking at a fund-raising gala in Florida some time ago, I had a chance to talk with a woman involved in putting on the conference, and she recounted a story that many of us may find familiar. There was a lesson for both of us that came from her account about how we choose to see ourselves and how our pasts hold the key for us to claim our rightful identity.

For many years, she confessed, she had been aware that she was compensating for a feeling deep down that she was never going to be good enough to achieve her true aspirations. In her late fifties, she was attractive, charming, an accomplished event planner, community volunteer, wife, mother, and grandmother, with multiple interests that she was passionate about. But as for her dream to take her creative ideas to the next level as an entrepreneur, whenever it came time to take that first meaningful step in her pursuit, something stopped her cold every time.

When I asked, "Where's that insecurity coming from?" she shrugged uncertainly and started to laugh. But then she stopped herself and admitted something that had bothered her for a long time. She told me, "When I was little, my mother used to tell me that I was a mistake." As the youngest of several children, she came along at a time when her parents had lost passion for each other. Moreover, they weren't interested in growing their family. So she was conceived on a rare night of intimacy. The woman said, "Isn't that horrible, to be told you're a mistake? That you were unwanted?"

I agreed that it was horrible and unacceptable, even when said in jest. Then I shared with her how I'd felt the same painful feelings when my stepfather used to berate me, rubbing it in my face that my biological father had abandoned me. Talking to her as I once had to learn to speak to myself, I said, "Well, you're not a mistake to me." Then I gave her a hug—intended for both of us, and for every kid ever sent a message that he or she doesn't count.

"I'm so glad you said that," she said. "Because I'm not a mistake to me either!"

We talked about how stupid remarks like the one her mother made can leave a cloud over our identities that have nothing to do with who we are. As children, very few of us have the capacity to fend off demeaning, negating comments, even the ones that are made without malice. Our work as adults is to make the choice to not pass those words on to our kids and to reject cruel or unthinking remarks about ourselves—to flick 'em off our shoulders like dandruff!

Of course, as this lesson made clear to both of us, it's not always easy to reject the identity that was handed to us based on where we

come from. It's especially challenging to reject the identity that is connected to who our parents were.

The challenge made me think of a passage from a book by poet
Nikki Giovanni that had been given to me around that time. During
my high school years, at a stage of life when the world was sending
negative messages about my identity, a particular line of her poetry had
allowed me to boost my self-esteem by reciting it whenever in need: "I
am so perfect so divine so ethereal so surreal / I cannot be compre-
hended except by my permission."

The more recent book of Giovanni's, though not a collection of
poetry, deals with the issue of identity as well—but from a very different perspective. Entitled *On My Journey Now: Looking at African-
American History Through the Spirituals,* it also emphasizes the need to
study the past—even when it involves confronting the darker days of
slavery and powerlessness. Nikki starts out by asking how Africans who
were first brought to this country and enslaved here not only managed
to survive but ultimately, through their descendants, to thrive. How
was it possible, she asks, that people whose existence was totally controlled by insanity were able to stay sane? It had to do with holding on
to their power over the only thing they could: their identity. To stay
sane, they had to keep that identity separate from their condition of
enslavement. How did they know who they were? How could they
declare to others and to themselves, "This is who I am"? They did so,
she writes, by teaching their children through the spiritual grapevine of
songs that "if anybody asks you who you are, tell them you are a child
of God."

That message translated in such a way that you would never call
yourself a slave or tell anyone that you were a child of slaves or that you
belonged to a slave owner. As a child of God, you were not a mistake,
or a product of lust or rape, but you were meant to be here, to learn,
love, and be loved.

I referred my new friend in Florida to Giovanni's book and also to the uses of the question that is the essence of this lesson—*Whose child are you?*

She smiled and got it right away, answering, "I'm a child of God." And then she added that she wasn't religious at all. But allowing herself to embrace that answer gave her an identity that made her proud, and that gave her a sense of belonging in this world.

The lesson that comes from asking "Whose child are you?" is therefore a reminder that regardless of the station in life into which you were born and wherever you live in this world, you're free to choose your place of belonging and to identify your parents in your own terms. Perhaps you think of yourself as a child of God. Or maybe you're a child of the Universe or of Nature, the Ultimate Divine Mother. The point is that you are here—just as you were meant to be as an essential part of the total design. You absolutely matter to the whole of life.

Taking this one step further, I will add that Giovanni's book also reminds us that the spirituals were lifesaving because they helped ground those who sang them in the promise of survival. The belief that they would eventually be free became an integral part of their identities, too. The spirituals they sang told them that they were God's children and were being guided with love so that one day they could look back and see that all the parts of the journey, even the worst hardships, had happened for a reason. That's why those of us who have been in the storm can look back and quote, "On my journey now, Mount Zion / Well, I wouldn't take nothing, Mount Zion / For my journey now, Mount Zion"—a sentiment echoed in the previous lesson as well.

If your identity has been marred by a false message sent to you in the past, you can reject it as untrue anytime you so choose. You always have the option of asking yourself whose child you are, and answering in a way that validates you. However you do answer, know that in this journey of your life—the only one you've got—your identity is as the star who shines above all the rest, as long as you dare to claim that billing.

LESSON #15
Check Out Your Own Version of Genesis

KEYWORD: *Forgiveness*

Many years ago, before I pursued a career on Wall Street, when I was employed in the field of medical and scientific research, I read a report that said over 50 percent of visits to the doctor are caused by symptoms that seem to have no physical cause. All of the symptoms are real, the medical experts said, but they couldn't reach a diagnosis. Their thesis was that stress was the real cause—anger, worry, fear, and other emotions that had often been eating away at their patients since early childhood.

It was only recently that I heard about Dr. Dave Clarke's book, entitled *They Can't Find Anything Wrong!* From his studies of stress illness, his position is that the first step to healing undiagnosed symptoms is to return to the past and seek out those early stressors—through the act of remembering. In a majority of cases, his patients experience full recoveries because they are able to understand how their pain started emotionally before it became physical. With understanding, Dr. Clarke observes, some patients are even able to forgive those individuals and experiences that may have been responsible for factors that first triggered the pain.

This is where we can see the obvious thorns and the potential gold in lessons from the past that help pave the way to forgiveness—including forgiveness of ourselves. Granted, not all of us have physical manifestations of stored stress from the past. But it's also true that until we do something about the baggage of old hurts, resentments, and different forms of anger or guilt that we carry around with us, we're limiting our experience of happyness in the present.

Then again, when we feel strongly that we've been wronged, forgiveness can be a tough hill to climb. How can we begin? In answering that question for myself, I have done much soul-searching, questioning, and reading. On the subject of who was the most hurtful, stressful presence in my childhood, I can easily state that had to be my abusive stepfather, Freddie. Even at a young age, I can remember wondering how he had been allowed to trample on so many of the positive aspects of my early years. And as time went on, I began to ask the question, If everyone is in our lives to teach us something, how could such a negative force as Freddie be there, too? The answer led me to the Bible, to our human origins in the Garden of Eden story.

It was eye-opening to revisit this story that many of us know from various interpretations—from Sunday school, literature, and art—and look at it for the first time as a story that might be personally relevant not just to me but to others. What could it teach us about our human condition and our ability to forgive others and ourselves?

As you may recall, we enter the scriptural Garden of Eden, a paradise, as we meet up with Adam and Eve—who have an abundance of everything they need to be happy. They are loved, protected, and guided by God, who gives them their purpose—to appreciate, cultivate, and care for the Garden. As long as they don't break the one rule—never eat from the Tree of Knowledge of Good and Evil, which will result in death—Adam and Eve can stay in the Garden forever, never to grow old, never to die. But there is a negative force in paradise with them, a being who goads and tempts Eve to break the rule and take a bite of the forbidden fruit. He tells her that she won't die at all; in fact, if she eats the fruit, it will give her the power of seeing with the eyes of God, to know good and evil. After she goes for it, and Adam follows suit, the consequences for disobedience are certain to be grave.

God bestows his forgiveness on Adam and Eve, but he doesn't let them off without punishment. He is especially unhappy with Adam, who first tried to cover up what they'd done and then tried to blame it on Eve. When the role of the negative force is revealed, God curses that force to live as a snake and to forever slither on his belly as the lowest of the low; he further curses the snake's descendants, leaving not even the slightest potential for growth. But God doesn't curse or disinherit Adam and Eve. For their disobedience and for falling to temptation, their punishment is that instead of staying in the Garden and continuing to eat from the Tree of Life, which makes them immortal, they must leave. They are banished to somewhere "east of Eden"—the world that some of us know as our first neighborhood—where they have to learn to grow their own food from tough, thorny soil, and where they will eventually die. In spite of their mortality and the hardships they will endure, they will retain the God-like resource of knowing good from evil, right from wrong. As to what to do with that knowledge, they are given the power of choice, or free will. That is our human gift.

Their Father/Creator doesn't split. He's still there to provide guidance, love, and other miraculous resources when needed. But as to determining their path, their purpose, and how they will pursue their potential—that's now all on them.

The role of the snake in this story and in ours is really interesting. The lesson for forgiveness, as I see it, is that we can't blame the negative forces—because that would mean we are stooping to their level. Perhaps you can see in the environment where you were raised how there were influences that could have taken you down—through temptations to respond from your baser instincts—that were at play in your life. Maybe they weren't embodied in a human being but rather in the circumstances of where and how you grew up.

Again, it wasn't a stretch for me to identify the snake in my version of Genesis as my stepfather. On the evolutionary scale of things, this guy was definitely subhuman—illiterate, alcoholic, violent, lacking in any moral awareness. In my own anger and fear over a sense of powerlessness, the temptation to respond to his rage with my own—and to become him—was always there. The gift of free will, however, allowed me to choose not to do that. In time, I came to terms with the possibility that he was in my life to teach me exactly what *not* to be. Was choosing not to be Freddie to prove that I was better than he was? That I could "show him" or "get back" at him for telling me that I was worthless all those years? No. That would have been a judgment rather than a decision to empower myself.

Along those lines, I have been helped in making sense of my own father's absence in my version of Genesis. My choice was not to go his way, to break the generational cycle. That didn't make me forget the void and the hurt, but it did allow me to eventually forgive.

Because I can choose to forgive but not to forget, I don't have to carry around the baggage of hurt and anger anymore. I'm also very grateful that the symptoms of stress illness that could have manifested in adulthood were vanquished long ago.

If you've ever wondered where the stress comes from that might be triggered in the present but is connected to something bigger that happened long ago, checking out your own version of Genesis can yield many insights. If you see the influence of a form of darkness that has limited you, the understanding of its influence on you can pave the way for letting that baggage go. When facing our own shortcomings and mistakes, when we have been tempted, if we have been self-limiting and allowed our baser selves to take over, the message of the fall from grace of Adam and Eve is that we are human, not immortal. Yet since we also retain the spark of the Divine, just as we can forgive, we can be forgiven.

Let me add the advisory that goes with the act of forgiveness—it takes practice and focus. Again, the operative phrase is that we can forgive even when we don't forget. Both are separate experiences.

John F. Kennedy said it well when he advised, "Forgive your enemies, but never forget their names." To which, I might add, "Or their addresses."

LESSON #16
Who's Who in Your 'Hood?

KEYWORD: *Trust*

Most of us are familiar with one of the all-time classic statements about the pursuit of happyness, coined by Henry Ford, "Whether you believe you can do a thing or not, you are right."

I'll sign on to that statement without hesitation. There is no doubt that belief in yourself is a key ingredient to any pursuit you can tackle. In fact, in most Q&A sessions that I've been a part of, several questions arise about where that belief comes from, how to cultivate a sense of certitude about your possibilities, and how to reconnect to those feelings when they seem to have fled.

From my own experience, I count myself infinitely blessed that my mother's most important message to me was that "you can." This was also echoed by other individuals and teachers whose opinions I sought out and believed. Because I knew they loved me and wanted the best for me, I trusted them and their belief in me. The critical part of the equation that I've come to understand, however, is the issue of trust.

The lesson taught by *Who's who in your 'hood?* is here to shed light on a variety of trust issues that show up in relationships, on the job, and in our daily existence as we strive to get through tough times and thrive in better ones. It's meant to alert us to the power of past relationships to influence our lives for years to come.

This was a topic that arose in a memorable conversation that took place in Oregon after a book signing one night when two gentlemen, Dan and Jim, stayed behind to ask for advice. Both were high-level managers in the same national retail business, and both had recently been given notice because of store closures. As for future prospects, when it came to looking for new work, each had different trust issues.

Dan had all the belief in the world in his own abilities to adapt to a new career in another setting. At the same time, he was pessimistic about his chances because he didn't know anyone he could trust to open doors and guide him to opportunities that were becoming fewer and further in between—in his opinion. Jim, on the other hand, had friends, contacts, and strings to pull that he trusted to have him reemployed in no time. But he wasn't sure he would be able to deliver on their belief in him because deep down, he admitted, he didn't trust himself to be able to adapt to a different job.

My curiosity was definitely raised. How did the two of them happen to have such different trust issues? In each case, the past and details of the "Who's who?" in their respective 'hoods held the clues.

Dan recalled that his most important life mentor—his father—had died on the night that he graduated from high school. Up until then he considered himself a happy-go-lucky person who generally liked everyone else. But without another mentor or supporter to fill the void, he chose to learn to depend on himself. Although he had cultivated wonderful personal relationships, was happily married, and was a very proud father, Dan had always seen himself as the guy who was supposed to make things happen—rather than looking to others to give him a sense of security. Actually, his father had been that way, too. In telling me his story, he was able to laugh, as he observed, "My challenge is the willingness to ask people I admire for help and direction, even though I'm the one usually offering it to others." As he stated that, I actually saw his whole mood lighten.

Jim described his upbringing as being as close to an ideal childhood as possible. He had been a star on his basketball team, president of his class, and the "big man on campus" ever since he was in kindergarten. Looking back at his "Who's who?" he noted several individuals from the past—his parents, teachers, buddies, and girlfriends—who had sent him the message that he was going to be a superstar and most likely to succeed at whatever he did. Doors had always opened easily for him, he recalled. Whenever he needed a favor or to depend on someone to help him pull a string or two, he never had to want. But deep down, Jim admitted, he wasn't so sure that he deserved all the praise he was given. "You know what," he remarked, "high expectations can be a lot of pressure." He went on to say that many of his adult relationships—on the job or with women—had ended with him thinking or saying, "You just expect too much of me." His challenge, unlike his friend's, was to be there as much for himself as his "Who's who?" was able to do.

As you can see, there are a few different ways to apply the lesson that our earliest relationships are instrumental in how we each deal with trust issues. The most basic application, of course, is the act of looking back and recalling who the messengers were that shaped your belief in yourself and in others—messages that you carry around with you today.

When you do this, you may discover initially—as I did—that some of your first "Who's who?" might be individuals you haven't thought about for years, and when you try to bring them to mind, they appear as dim faded photographs. But as you ask yourself certain questions about the messages they sent you, often you'll capture a memory that brings them into close focus. One of my colleagues in the publishing world offered an interesting example of this phenomenon recently. My colleague frequently talks about the challenges of weight loss. "I fail at every diet that I start," she'll say. Other times she says, "Well, I come from a long line of short, chubby people so why should I be any different?" Finally, one day, I replied, "Says who?"

She stuttered for a moment and then went silent, falling into deep thought. Something in her past that had been buried much earlier came to her. She recalled that as a teenager, everyone complimented her petite figure and attractive appearance. That was until the head of a modeling agency, and a friend of her parents, tried to discourage her from pursuing an acting or modeling career by saying, "You're not thin or tall enough." As if that wasn't bad enough, the woman shrugged and predicted, "You're always going to have a weight problem."

When my colleague shared this memory with me, it was a reminder of the powerful influences that others have on our belief systems—including individuals who might not have played major roles in our upbringing, who don't really know what they're talking about, and who we should perhaps not trust. There is nothing wrong with being in the present and asking, "Who was she to tell me that?" and then deciding, "Well, maybe I'm not going to have a weight problem after all." It's never too late to make the choice to trust your own judgment.

I love this straightforward application of asking *Who's who in your 'hood?* because of the simple joy it brings me to remember the richness

of the characters who were part of my past. In exploring those relationships of the past and remembering folks whom I loved, resented, missed,
or wondered what had become of them, with hindsight I'm able to let go
of judgment and just appreciate how they enriched my experience.

If you have trust issues, don't skip the effort it may require to reflect
on your past and the early relationships you developed at home, in
school, and wherever you hung out. By consciously choosing to see
whose words and actions influenced you—and may still—you may be
surprised at how vividly the cast of characters from your movie of the
past will step forward with review lessons that you might just need. At
a restaurant in Miami some time ago, I was talking to a gentleman at
the next table who had chosen to pursue a teaching career, rather than
following the guys from his neighborhood into risky entrepreneurial
endeavors. He was grateful that he had seen them as examples of what
not to do and that he had found the good sense not to trust their promise of overnight riches. He was sure that if he hadn't trusted his own
better judgment, he would be dead or in jail today.

The issue of trust is the focus point and keyword for this lesson, but
it is also about love. So as you allow yourself to recall your "Who's who?"
do take advantage of the opportunity to better appreciate the love you
were given, even when it wasn't expressed the way that you might have
preferred. You can then look back to feel love in return and value everyone who has made your life richer and your journey more interesting.
You will also have a chance to gain new appreciation for the lessons
that those different people were in your life to teach you—even when
you didn't particularly like them at all, whether they were a role model
of what *to do* or what *not to do,* or they were a royal pain in your butt.

A good friend of mine used her "Who's Who?" in deciding to open
up her own business. She had realized that every toxic boss she ever
had was an updated version of her father. She recalled that he had
never respected women in the workplace and had encouraged his sons
to excel but not his daughters. No matter what business success she
achieved, her father could never give her the praise she needed and

wanted. After giving up on ever changing him, she went to work for high-powered men, reminiscent of her father, hoping to earn their approval—but to no avail. When my friend realized how she was perpetuating the message that she was never going to be good enough, instead of blaming the different authority figures, all updated versions of her dad, she decided to become unstuck from the pattern. She chose to become her own authority figure. The minute she stopped caring about the approval of others—but, rather, trusted her own approval of herself—and established her own company, on her own terms, her relationship with her father improved.

My advisory that goes along with this lesson is that the more you appreciate everyone who has played even a modest role in your past—whether to reinforce, challenge, entertain, or inspire you—the more you can trust that perhaps you touched their lives just as much. That may be your cue to write a letter to someone in your past, whether you need to send an overdue thanks, deliver an apology, say hello, or just because. Whether you believe that you can value your original "Who's who?" as a meaningful resource in your life now, or not, you are right.

LESSON #17
The Red or the Yellow Bike?

KEYWORD: *Motivation*

"What is your why?"

That was a question I first heard a fellow speaker ask when I attended a conference for Northwestern Mutual Life Insurance. Since all that time I'd been asking *what* and *how* others pursued their dreams, I now could appreciate this most revealing added question of *why*. In fact, only a short time later I asked it of an impressive young man introduced to me by a colleague at a nonprofit fund-raiser that we both attended. As he and I got to talking, I learned that he had recently taken over the reins at a private charitable foundation—what he described as his "dream profession."

When I asked, "What is your why?" he wasn't sure what I meant.

Well, I said, when people say that they've attained a dream, I'm curious to know what motivated them to pursue their goal in the first place. For example, I asked, "Why philanthropy? Was that something you always knew you wanted to pursue? As a kid, did you see yourself making a difference in the world one day?"

He laughed and admitted none of that had crossed his mind. What he always wanted to do, he explained, was to be the first in his family to go to college. From the time he was young, he had a sense of himself as being different, and the most daring ambition he could set for himself was to one day seek higher education. As for discovering his dream profession, he said that had to do with the question "The red or the yellow bike?"

Then he told me his story. He was from a blue-collar background and had grown up in the rural Midwest where the majority of graduating high school students, like his siblings, didn't go on to college. As a senior in high school, he caught his guidance counselor off guard when he expressed interest in applying to a nearby state university. The guidance counselor discouraged him from doing so, telling him that he should learn a trade instead because he "wasn't college material."

Now deep down that didn't sit right with this guy. But it did fire up his motivation to prove otherwise, so that from then on, every choice he made was as if to say, "Says who?" But starting where he was, he decided that if he loved learning, he might as well enroll at the technical trade school to become an electrician. After two years he was happy with the skills he had acquired, enough to wonder, "If I could master a trade so easily, how tough could a bachelor's degree be?"

With part-time work as an electrician, he was able to pay for tuition at the local state university, although he couldn't afford to buy a car. For transportation, he decided to buy a dependable used bicycle. He shopped around with listings from the want ads and narrowed his choices down to two: a red bike that was nothing special but well made and sturdy; or a yellow bike, which didn't look as sturdy or well made but was a wonderful yellow color that was eye-catching, not run-of-the-mill or commonplace but exciting in its own way. What made more sense to him, the red or the yellow?

As I listened to the description of the two bikes, I knew right away, he had to go with the yellow. That was the daring, different choice—something to smile about, to make him feel happy riding along in all kinds of weather.

For some people, that might have been a bad decision. If he had chosen the red bike, it wouldn't have broken down and he would have stuck to the plan of living off campus. Of course, as expected, the yellow bike broke down within a short time of owning it, which forced him to move closer to campus. Finding affordable housing nearby was impossible at that time, so because of the broken-down bike, he had to take the only thing he could find, which turned out to be a room in the housing units for foreign students. If that had never happened, he wouldn't have eventually discovered his interest in becoming a linguist. The daring, different challenge of pursuing his course work in linguistics was so motivational, he managed to attain a master's degree, and he then applied and was accepted to a linguistics doctoral program on the West Coast. The selection of the yellow bike had emboldened him forever.

Since his choices were working for him, he figured that he might as well knock off a master's degree in social anthropology while completing his doctorate in linguistics.

Finding a job proved to be daunting. "To my knowledge," he said, "there was no position out there that would use both those degrees." Then, just when he was going to give up and consider a more practical field of study, another chain of events helped him land an opening at a foundation that needed someone who understood how best to provide funding to global programs that were aimed at cultural growth, health, and peace around the world. His degrees were tailor-made for doing that. And none of that would have happened, he says, if he hadn't chosen the yellow bike.

One of the things that I found most impressive in his story was that

he managed to stay connected to the motivating power of his dreams—
his why—throughout his teens and early adulthood, a time when all
kinds of outside pressure can make many of us second-guess ourselves,
our whys, and our choices.

The takeaway from the lesson posed by the question "The red or
the yellow bike?" is that if we look back at that time in our own lives
between childhood and adulthood, we can often identify what our whys
were back then. We can see how they did or didn't affect the choices
we made in terms of career, relationships, education, lifestyle, and
other kinds of pursuit.

In my case, this process enabled me to recall making the decision
to search for the right venue in which I could one day become world
class. Looking back at this time period in my past also revealed something that I'd never thought much about—what was behind my desire
to reach that high? Since I didn't know what my dream profession was
going to be, or who I was meant to become, my primary motivation
came from knowing deep down that I didn't want an ordinary life. I
wanted to travel, internally and externally, as far as it was within my
capacity to go, do, know, see, and experience.

Again, part of what shaped my why was following the real-life
adventures of heroes who had rejected the ordinary for the extraordinary. Even though I didn't know them personally, I was inspired by
those examples and possibilities—from the way heroes like Miles Davis
pushed musical boundaries, to how Muhammad Ali defied the boxing
world to take a stand for what he believed in, to how others committed
to causes larger than themselves.

The memories raised by the question "The red or the yellow bike?"
bring to mind as well the reality that there are complicated consequences
to face as the result of choosing bold pursuits over options that are safer,
more predictable, and less exciting. Even so, if we disregard our true
motivation—often more evident in our younger years when we may have
been less concerned about security issues—we may miss finding what
gives us our own definition of happyness. And when we identify our why,

if we honor it, even when we make choices that result in complications, we find the path that we were meant to follow all along.

As I've learned when struggling over decisions or offering advice to others who are trying to make a choice that may have significant ramifications, when there are no clear-cut pros and cons—go with what you feel, not necessarily with what you know. Usually that's what's going to motivate you over the long haul. If the yellow bike is different, more daring, more exciting, and less practical, so be it. If it's a lemon, I don't have to tell you what you can make out of it, do I?

If you have been choosing to stick with the safe routes laid out for you by misguided guidance counselors, it's never too late to try a different approach. And while you're at it, relive the best of your younger years and recall what motivated you back then. What gave you the most joy? What's your version of the red or the yellow bike?

LESSON #18
Sometimes You Gotta Give Up Christmas
KEYWORD: *Independence*

While leaving my Chicago office on a cold December day in late 2006, I was approached by a stylish, professionally attired woman who recognized me from a recent media appearance. She introduced herself as a professor who taught at one of the universities, and she went on to say that though she came from a different background—white, affluent, suburban—we had a lot in common. One part of my story in particular had helped her see something she had never known.

"What's that?" I asked.

"I always thought that I was the only one who got robbed of Christmas."

She explained how the holidays had always brought out the worst in her household. In her imagination, every other family in the world had the picture-perfect Christmas—stuffed goose with the trimmings, sugarplums and all. Even now, happily married with children of her own, she planned well in advance to avoid having to make a pretense of joy when her memories told her something else. In fact, whenever winter holidays approached, she would plan a family vacation out of the country—simply in order to graciously turn down invitations to parties.

We were alike in that we had found ways to observe the spirit of the season, attending church or contributing to community services that bring the holidays to those who would go without otherwise. But as for trying to ritualize the Hallmark version that had actually been a horror film in our pasts, we had both come to the conclusion that *Sometimes you gotta give up Christmas.*

"Anyway, I just wanted to thank you," she concluded with a laugh, and she used a phrase that I hear often, as she remarked, "I used to think it was just me."

After I thanked her for the acknowledgment, we went our separate ways, and I started to reflect on the disastrous Christmas Day memory in my own past, wondering if perhaps it was time to just get over it. After all, as awful as that day in my late teens had been, it did give me the impetus to leave home and go out to seek my independence. So some good had come of it.

Then again, I didn't know if I really wanted to be so philosophical when it came to a rotten, hurtful experience that had ruined Christmas for me from then on.

What was ironic to me, all these years later, was that on the day in question I had congratulated myself for opting out of going to the annual holiday family gathering that I knew would end up with drinking, demeaning language, yelling, and then knock-down, drag-out fighting. Instead, I was going to take advantage of our empty house, enjoy a long hot Christmas Day bath, and then take my girlfriend out on a date. Too lucky to be that lucky, I should have known that my stepfather would not have allowed me to celebrate on my own terms. Not that I could have anticipated Freddie's sudden return home or the sight of him bursting into the bathroom, with murder in his eyes, or that he would put me out of the house at the end of a shotgun barrel. Standing there stark naked on the freezing porch in broad daylight as a kid passed by and stared—obviously not knowing what to say except "Merry Christmas, mister"—I came to a crossroads. Time to give it up and say to myself, "Never again."

Most likely, you, too, can recall those times in your past when you faced a crossroads and made a decision to change the circumstances of your life—much to the contrary of what others expected of you. Whatever it was that prompted your decision may not be as important as the fact that you came to it on your own. If this is the case for you, it may be worth your while to look back and remember those choices made at crossroads that perhaps you could put to use in the present—especially if changing your life for the better is on your current wish list.

For me, this life lesson resulted in my independence, which came as the result of making up my mind as to when too much is too much.

The road to independence isn't just about giving up illusions about the way that we think the charmed life is supposed to be—although it's a start. Along the way it also means owning our reactions to the events of our lives as opposed to blaming them on others. If we want to be free of controlling or abusive authority figures who lord it over us, we have to choose to own the actions we take next. This includes not only the joys and victories to come, but the mistakes, failures, disappointment, hurt, and insult that we'll encounter as well. The price of independence may be that you have to give up blame altogether.

As you look back at the time in your life when you were first setting out for adulthood, it's valuable to remember the independent decisions you made, right or wrong, and how they taught you lessons in terms of what I call the three As. Those are the three additional keywords that go along with independence—*authority, authenticity,* and *autonomy.* These three capacities are some of the most empowering resources you can seek: (1) to *know yourself* (authority), (2) to *be yourself* (authenticity), and (3) to *choose for yourself* (autonomy).

The three As are there to validate you, for example, in those cases where you need to say enough is enough. As was the case with the professor I met, you are entitled to independently cancel the holiday or celebrate your own way.

In the weeks that followed our encounter in Chicago, I received countless pieces of correspondence from others who felt similarly vindicated to learn that they didn't have to suffer by themselves as the holidays approached. Many others have told me that they can relate because of memories of events that are traditionally seen as happy ones by the rest of the world but were not happy to them. Then again, some folks couldn't relate and suggested that I was being overly dramatic.

The eye-opener of this lesson for me was that sometimes giving up Christmas—or its equivalent in your life—isn't going to please, impress, or educate others who just don't get it. Not everyone is going to feel your pain, even though it may turn out that lots of other people know exactly what you mean. It's all part of the process. The truth is that everyone in the flock of humanity has their own version of a rotten Christmas, holiday, birthday, Valentine's, or Groundhog Day somewhere in their past. The gift of independence is that we can cut that cord anytime. We don't have to reinvent it or dress up the memory or make it more appealing for other people's needs. Instead, we can call it rotten, accept it for what it was, give it up, and be grateful that we can.

We can also wake up one December morning and decide we're ready to rekindle the lights of the season and institute our own holiday celebration anew. A fellow I met at the airport while waiting for a flight gave me food for thought about how to do that. At fifteen, he had run away from a violent, dysfunctional home and was taken in by distant relatives who slowly but surely introduced him to love, stability, and normalcy. Even then, he said, he would wake up on Christmas morning and break into hives, unable to accept the gifts they'd placed under the tree for him. It wasn't until he moved across the country to pursue a career and was living on his own as a young adult that he and some friends living in his apartment complex got together and organized an "Orphans' Christmas." Some of his group had families elsewhere but no relatives to invite them over for a feast. Others had also broken ties with their pasts and had experiences that weren't too different from his. Everyone pitched in and brought something to their potluck celebration. He was amazed that even though the meal was not lavish in the least and that the small inexpensive gifts were not items of value, it was one of the happyest experiences of his life. Now the head of his household and well off, he told me that thirty years later that same group of friends, many with spouses and children, have managed to get together for their "Orphans' Christmas" every single year since.

Using his example, the advisory that comes with this lesson is that independence allows you to change your mind over time. You can reject a lousy childhood or a painful memory and choose not to allow it to be part of your ongoing journey. You can also reclaim your right to joy, camaraderie, and community by creating the celebrations and the life you truly desire. Simply stated: independence gives you those options.

LESSON #19
No Test, No Testimony

KEYWORD: *Courage*

Whenever I'm asked how it was that my son and I became homeless, I opt for the short version. I start to explain the particulars of the breakup of my relationship with my son's mother, how I was sent to the state penitentiary for ten days on parking tickets (yep, parking tickets!), and how I was then released to find my family and our belongings gone without a trace. It was in the midst of desperately trying to locate my son that I moved into a low-rent boardinghouse, which was all that I could afford on my entry-level stockbroker trainee position, before finally my ex showed up with my son one night and said, "Here he is." Because the boardinghouse strictly forbade children, we were immediately, effectively homeless. From there, as the situation grew more complicated, to make the story shorter, I usually just summarize the rest by saying, "Life happens."

The majority of the correspondence that I receive comes from people of all ages who've had their own experience of "Life happens." All of our circumstances vary dramatically, but what we have in common in our ordeals is suddenly having to pass the hardest test of all—one that brings us face-to-face with our fears, lets us know who we are, and reveals whether we have the courage to stand on faith at the most uncertain points.

We can refer to those chapters of our lives as rites of passage that take us from shaky, uncertain ground to finding our firmament. This was the experience of a woman I met at a book signing in Albuquerque, New Mexico, who described her situation as hopeful but also one that was testing her on every level. A single working mother with two children, she had undertaken a dream to go to her "Promised Land" as an entrepreneur. Her current pursuit was to attain the means to open up a restaurant in Santa Fe. Coincidentally, she pointed out, a couple of characters from the musical *Rent* come up with the same dream and sing about it. The bonus for her was that she had a theme song to sing!

The irony that I shared with her was that during my journey through homelessness while seeking my Promised Land I kept humming the tune to "California Dreamin'."

Her observation was that you never know what you can accomplish until you're challenged to find out. "I never planned on a career," she noted. "I wanted to be home with my children, that was my dream." When things didn't work out in her marriage, the rug was pulled out from under her. "Twenty-nine years old and I didn't know how to do anything on my own. I was lost in the wilderness." Her version of "Life happens" had taught her what she was made of, had helped her find her faith, and gave her courage that she didn't know she had. Now she was on her way to opening up a restaurant in Santa Fe.

Her story stayed with me and got me to thinking about how a lot of us come, for different reasons, to turning points in our lives where we can stay stuck in the same place or we can seek deliverance, a departure, or an exodus from where we are to the destination we determine. Given the hardships many folks are encountering, including the exploding crisis of white-collar homelessness that I knew all too well, it seems that we're all being tested, and we could all use an added boost of courage, maybe now more than ever.

Then again, as Momma used to say whenever courage was needed and faith was being tested, "No test, no testimony." This was biblically inspired, no doubt, but drawn from the many trials she herself had faced. And she always framed it for me in secular language that I could understand and apply; that is, if you ain't been tested, you got nothing to say, nothing to add of value to the conversation.

So I understood how the journey to start a new life in Santa Fe that the woman described was a test of faith and courage. Her comments also motivated me to take a closer look at the actual book of Exodus.

There are many ways to interpret the metaphor of the exile into slavery, God's deliverance of his people out of bondage, and then the journey of having to travel on foot for the next forty years before being able to cross the river Jordan into Canaan, the Promised Land. For African Americans, that is the story of deliverance out of four hundred years of slavery. The parallels include our escape not from Pharaoh but from the slave master, a journey on foot for runaways who followed the northern stars and traveled the Underground Railroad to freedom. It took almost another century for a modern Moses named Dr. Martin Luther King Jr. to appear in our midst and lead us farther along the way toward economic and political equality.

Dr. King talked of the mountaintop where he could see the other side, and he told us about his dream—so that we could all see it and be moved to attain it—in a speech that he gave in support of striking sanitation workers on April 3, 1968, in Memphis, Tennessee. Many of us know a small part of the mountaintop speech, but not everyone knows the circumstances surrounding his remarks. That morning Dr. King had flown in from Atlanta, Georgia, after a flight delay caused by a bomb threat that required all bags to be searched—even though the small plane had been under guard the previous night. In addition, Dr. King was concerned by outbursts of violence that had occurred at a recent march in Memphis. He was also tired. For those reasons, he had decided it would be best not to go to Mason Temple to deliver his speech. But when other leaders arrived and saw the multitude of citizens who had turned out to hear him—the overflow waiting outside on the streets in the midst of a terrible storm—they were able to convince Dr. King that his presence was needed to help quell the chaos.

From the start, the focus of his speech was on the plight of the sanitation workers who were being treated no better than garbage, who were losing hope in their fight for dignity and a living wage. Dr. King asked them not just to have faith but to act on it—to march for their rights and not be afraid, even though they'd been attacked by dogs, hoses, Mace, and worse. He acknowledged the fearful times afflicting everyone:

> . . . the world is messed up. The nation is sick. Trouble is in the land. Confusion all around. . . . But I know, somehow, that only when it is dark enough, can you see the stars. And I see God working in this period . . . in a way that men, in some strange way, are responding—something is happening in our world. The masses of people are rising up.

He went on, borrowing biblical passages, rallying spirits in the collective march for justice and human respect, reminding everyone how far God had already brought them, and infusing all those present with the certainty that the Lord would not have brought them this far to abandon them. And only at the end of Dr. King's speech did he talk about himself, how grateful he was to have survived a near-fatal stabbing some years earlier, how in spite of other attempts on his life and increased warnings, he had decided to reject fear. The speech concluded:

> Well, I don't know what will happen now; we've got some difficult days ahead. But it really doesn't matter with me now, because I've been to the mountaintop. And I don't mind. Like

anybody, I would like to live a long life—longevity has its place. But I'm not concerned about that now. I just want to do God's will. And He's allowed me to go up to the mountain. And I've looked over, and I've seen the Promised Land. I may not get there with you. But I want you to know tonight, that we, as a people, will get to the Promised Land. And so I'm happy to-night; I'm not worried about anything; I'm not fearing any man. Mine eyes have seen the glory of the coming of the Lord.

That next day, as though he had been speaking prophetically, Dr. King was shot and killed in Memphis, Tennessee. But he had told us what Moses said to his followers, in essence—*I can't cross over to the land of milk and honey with you, but you will get there, because I've seen it, and you will be delivered there if you go forward on faith, not fear.*

Over the years, I have thought about why Dr. King compared him-self so closely to Moses, who in the book of Deuteronomy went up to the mountaintop to die. But I've also wondered why Moses wasn't allowed to cross the river Jordan with his followers. After looking into it, I found the explanation had to do with a time early in the Exodus when Moses lost his faith. The people were grumbling, starving and thirsty, and in frustration, Moses regretted trusting in the Lord to pro-vide for their needs along the way. When God told him that he would bring water from a desert rock, Moses defied God's instructions to touch his staff to the rock and speak to it. Moses decided that was crazy, and justified his anger, telling himself that he had done every-thing that had been asked of him, and more; and now that he saw that this journey was going to take much longer than he had ever antici-pated, he gave in to his fear and resentment by striking the rock. Well, the water poured forth for the people anyway.

But because of that incident, Moses had to face the consequences— that God would continue to be with him throughout the journey ahead, but he would not be allowed to cross into the Promised Land. And Moses wasn't happy about it, but he traveled on.

By the time he arrived at the mountaintop before making it to the river Jordan, few of his original traveling companions had made it. Most of his followers were from younger generations who had been born along the way, no longer slaves but homeless wanderers. When Moses told them he couldn't go on and they understood he was going up the mountain to make his peace and to die, they were full of sorrow and fear. But he reminded everyone of the tests they had already passed, what they had been taught and how God had never left them, as he roused their resources of wisdom and strength to build the lives they had been dreaming about during all their hardships. He filled them with courage to go on.

Similarly, Dr. King understood the arc of his own journey and the role that he had played, and as his last act admonished everyone in the struggle with him, black and white, people of all religious backgrounds, that we had to go on ahead, courageously, and finish the journey on faith. That was forty years ago, and though we've made enormous strides, there is more work to do for everyone for Dr. King's dream to be realized here in America and around the world.

But we can still stand on the shoulders of the faith that brought us this far and know that if God didn't give up on us, how can we give up on ourselves? That's the other lesson of Exodus that I have tried to incorporate into my search for light, even in darkness, the essential pursuit of happyness.

Yes, a year of homelessness with a baby on my back lets me testify to that. Goodness and God showed up in bold and subtle ways. We were blessed by everyone from Glide Memorial Church with spiritual nourishment and actual soul food when we were hungry, given without judgment. There was the opportunity of this career that I was pursuing and belief that I was making headway. There were people who quietly supported us without looking for their payback, Underground Railroad style. And there was even a bathroom at a transit station where we could sleep and be safe.

Toward the end, when it started to become dark inside of me, when the faith that had led me and fueled me was being the most severely tested, I found resources that I didn't know I had, ones that I still draw from every day.

In this period, running from pillar to post, even as I came closer to the destination of being settled in our own place, I found courage in the examples of others. At the grocery stores or on the street, I'd be overwhelmed by having to struggle with a growing two-year-old, my briefcase, laundry, a bag of groceries, and wondering how I was going to make it. Then I'd see a woman with a briefcase-sized purse, laundry, a bag of groceries, and *two* babies! That's courage. All I could say to myself was—if she can do it, so can I.

Struggle is in our genes. We are here on this earth to choose to journey from one place to a better one. The Bible doesn't tell us that, but it shows us that it's all been done before, by others we can follow, and will be done again by those to follow us. Struggle was not invented just for me or you or any of us. We either go forward in the struggle, or we give in to our fear.

With courage we can pass the test of our Exodus and find our faith that overcomes fear and empowers us to offer testimony. By the way, there is no religious requirement for what or who inspires your faith, even according to Scripture that says, "Now faith is the substance of things hoped for, the evidence of things not seen" (Hebrews 11:1). You don't have to believe in anybody else's version of God but yours.

Like the song says—"whatever gets you through the night is all right"—as you overcome fear and find what you need to keep forging on. On a primal level, maybe it's possible that your faith comes from nothing more miraculous than the power of your own two feet to take you to your Promised Land.

As you recall what may be your Exodus, look at how far you've come and take courage. Now allow yourself to be your own Moses, and lead on.

Three / Hitting the Anvil

I learned the value of hard work by working hard.

—Margaret Mead
Anthropologist, writer, speaker

An Introduction to Lessons #20 to #29—
Marketplace Lessons for Success

Long before anyone thought to ask me for my "secrets for success," I had come to the fairly straightforward conclusion that there was no such thing. First of all, if the knowledge, tools, and techniques for assuring success were so secret, wouldn't that mean that only the most elite among us would ever succeed, while the rest of us would be doomed to failure? And that's not the case. Or, by contrast, given how much folks like to tell secrets, wouldn't everyone be in possession of the secret by now?

Well, all this is to say that when we go in search of the means for attaining success, we've got ourselves an embarrassment of riches. Where do we start? We can borrow what's already known from other people's success—which is available for free everywhere we look. And we can also use what we already know from our own experiences and life lessons learned while hitting the anvil of any past and current pursuits.

Here's what I believe—that everything we'll ever need to know for our greatest successes can be learned by the sweat of our own brow and through vital knowledge taught by the marketplace. This is from common sense, more than anything, since most of us first interacted with the laws of supply and demand, buying and selling, and various forms of marketing long before we left home. More than that, most of us began to pursue different forms of employment in our teens and will eventually go on to spend the majority of our waking hours for much of our lives at our jobs. Of course, part of that is to earn our wages and produce whatever we're being paid (or paying ourselves) to do. But in the wide, wonderful working world, we're also continuing our education—through OTJ, or on-the-job, training—and lessons that keep evolving with new relevance as we grow.

My belief in the value of OTJ training was first inspired years ago by an image that's stayed with me since childhood, that of an old-fashioned, wise blacksmith, a tradesman in pursuit of excellence, working away in his shop, always learning, adapting, and mastering his craft, pounding his anvil for all of his worth. Ironically, for most of my life I never knew of anyone who still did that for a living. That was until I heard of Ralph Figlow from Pennsylvania, who raises and trains Standardbred champions and has a bustling shop that shoes horses and makes other equestrian supplies. As a blacksmith, Ralph has taken his skills to the next level by creating statues of metal men as art pieces (that first brought him to my attention)—along with lines of philosophy and poetry that he composes to accompany his works. For all the years that I had admired the image of the noble, hardworking blacksmith, it turns out that Ralph Figlow happens to be the real deal—and a rock star of a human being to boot.

The image of the classic blacksmith also helped to inspire the concept of the five Cs—Clear, Concise, Compelling, Committed, and Consistent—which reminds us that only with commitment and consistency can success be reached. Again, it's no mystery that success comes from hitting that anvil, pounding not until you're done, but until you've done your best. You'll find in the process, as I have, that happyness doesn't arrive just from the admiration of others or by taking it to market for all the rewards, but also in the act of doing. The high of knowing that you're giving your all, that you're leaving everything you've got at the anvil, pounding with all your might and then some, can be the purest, most unadulterated feeling of joy.

Now, you may be puzzled by this nonsecret. If we can locate all the knowledge we need to be successful by grabbing it from our own experience and the thousands of years of marketplace lessons for success, why, then, do a high percentage of us believe it can't be that simple? One answer, I suspect, is that some masterful marketing and PR over the past millennia has fed that mentality. As long as we buy into the pitch that we can't possibly already know how to better ourselves, then those claiming to have privileged knowledge will keep it that way.

My other theory for why we have trouble believing that we each have the knowledge we need to pursue happyness and attain success is that we haven't done the work of defining those terms for ourselves. And that part isn't easy. Look at history. Almost 235 years ago Thomas Jefferson and his collaborators wrote in the preamble to the Declaration of Independence that they held certain truths to be self-evident: that we are all created equal and endowed by our Creator "with certain unalienable Rights, that among these are Life, Liberty and . . ." of course, the pursuit of happyness. Right off the bat, life and liberty didn't need defining. But that third concept, of what was being pursued exactly, has been an ongoing subject of serious, even legal debate.

Is pursuit of happyness defined as the quest to attain property, status, and wealth, as some would say? Or is it the protection of the rights of all citizens to work as hard or as inventively as they choose in order to attain whatever fruits of their labor they so determine—in emotional, intellectual, and/or economic terms?

In my reading of it, and my understanding of the American dream (which really has been embraced all over the world and is now the global dream), the unalienable right to the pursuit of happyness gives us the choice to make of ourselves and our lives what we can, will, and do. It also gives us the right to choose what we won't do. In 1776, it was outrageous and radical to propose that just anyone born to any particular background whatsoever could be deemed a success. Today, the very word *success* seems almost quaint.

Maybe the reason people don't want to embrace the word or what it represents is because they don't want others to feel jealous or insecure. Or maybe some of the flash and bling associated with the trappings of success have been a turnoff. It's possible, too, that we've grown cynical with the materialistic emphasis, rather than the emotional centerpiece, of why we strive in the first place. Perhaps that tells us that any definition of success should no longer include any monetary reference. What if, instead, we defined success in terms of the amount of peace we brought to a transaction or situation? We could measure success in units of goodwill or in commodities that enrich ourselves and others in nonmaterial ways.

Although I'm going to leave it up to you to define success and its true measurements for yourself, I'll tell you right now that in my experience the trappings—the stuff—ain't it. Instead, you might want to consider the working definition that's helped me. Simply put, success is the result you get when you apply what you've learned in productive, practical ways. More potently put, I believe that success is the result of tactical and strategic applications of learned knowledge toward objectives pursued with passion. That to me is nowhere more true than in the marketplace—one of the more important classrooms where we're taught the life lessons that significantly shape our lives. You might also find some interesting definitions by asking questions of those you know who appear to be successful. You could even ask them "what do you do?" and "how do you do it?"—two questions that both started me on my journey and are frequently asked of me.

Whenever I've gone in search of how others embrace success on their own terms, the diversity of answers has been amazing. Take this e-mail that I received from Alex, a gentleman who had come here as an immigrant looking for a better way of life for himself and his family:

When I was fortunate to come to this country from Eastern Europe, I worked twenty hours a day as a janitor, a cabdriver, and a dishwasher. I never starved but if it meant food for my daughters, I could go without. After a while, I noticed that many of the businesses where I worked had poor bookkeeping standards and I offered to help. Before long, I was so busy with bookkeeping I hired an assistant. My company grew from there. I then partnered with a technology firm to develop software for various business needs.

His secret? "Hard work." He also defined success as having the ability to open doors for others who were starting at the bottom.

Then there was a letter that came from Madison, a twenty-four-year-old law school graduate from rural Arkansas. The first to go to university in her family, she had always considered herself to be ambitious and tenacious. But she had come to believe that only from facing challenges had she discovered her own mettle, and the depth of her desire to be a "world-class lawyer" and not settle for just any job:

> I know that I probably don't need to write you about how difficult it can be to find jobs in this economy. But what I've learned about my "Pursuit of Happyness" is that if I define my goals and remain true to self-belief, that keeps me going. After two years of job hunting, I landed a part-time temporary position that I decided to embrace as if it was my dream job. Not surprisingly, I was given more hours and greater opportunity. Now it looks as if I may be given full-time, semi-permanent status. The terms aren't the best, but honestly I've never been so proud of myself! From here on out, I feel that there is no limit.

For Madison, the secret so far had been staying at her anvil. She was also motivated by the opportunity to inspire other young women in her extended family to raise their sights. Her obvious enthusiasm was going to be a plus for her in the marketplace no matter what.

An inspiring definition of success was given to me by Darrell—a

thirty-four-year-old father of two working for his city's board of education in the areas of truancy and gang prevention. He went on to describe
his pursuits outside of his job description:

> You could say that I'm a rule breaker because I will break a rule
> for the betterment of a child. Up until last year I didn't fully
> know what I needed to do. Now I do, working with kids from
> juvenile corrections to foster care, to children who have been
> sexually molested, beaten and verbally abused, scared to go
> home, homeless, hungry and worse. . . . Working with two part-
> ners, we came up with the idea to create a clothing line that
> would fund itself so we could give away most of the gear to the
> kids. We developed a following of youth that we started uncon-
> sciously mentoring and helping, just out of instinct and good
> nature. It's given us a direction and purpose. We're not in it to
> make money but we are looking to save lives, and if we can do
> both at the same time that's what we'll do too!

Darrell and his partners might not have put their enterprise on the
map, *yet,* but they were already at the highest level of contributing to
their community—and ours. That's success.

Alex, Madison, and Darrell may not share the same goals or come
from the same backgrounds, but each has found his or her own way to
make the most of a combination of the marketplace Lessons #20
through #29 as you can see in this preview:

#20 Each well understands the rule of hard work and values the
     leverage of **initiative.**
#21 Like these three, we all can access the power of **confidence**
     when we appreciate core strengths that are learned or part
     of who we are.
#22 For anyone who dares to raise the bar for themselves, as

Alex, Madison, and Darrell are doing, the successful use of **transferable skills** can be transformational.

#23 As we all learn from the ups and downs of the marketplace, a do-or-die ingredient is **resilience.** This lesson about how we connect to that resource and put it to use is required reading.

#24 Continuing education about how to access the power of **marketing** benefits everyone, no matter what the pursuit or how far along we are.

#25 The often overlooked resource of **authenticity** comes in this lesson for these three and for all of us who are looking for a competitive edge.

#26 Alex, Madison, and Darrell provide excellent examples of the **discipline and character** that hard work teaches—a lesson always worth revisiting.

#27 Just as these three are expanding the uses of **networking,** we all can be reminded of why this is an evergreen marketplace resource.

#28 We can always use a refresher as to the importance of **focus,** as this lesson is poised to give us.

#29 Like many of us, Alex, Madison, and Darrell each speak to the desire to use success to contribute to the greater good of the **community.**

As the lessons ahead will emphasize, the only success that matters is that which you claim for yourself. You may already know what I mean, and you may have done your large share of hitting the anvil. In that case, the lessons coming up may be ABCs you've known for a while. Even so, it's never too late to go back to basics. In fact, it's never too soon.

LESSON #20
The Law of Hard Work Is No Secret

KEYWORD: *Initiative*

There was a time in the early 1980s when I was convinced that somewhere out there someone had a lock on privileged information that would give me the key to success on Wall Street. By any other name, I was looking for the secret.

Two years later, I held the key in my hand—literally. The process of getting to that pinnacle involved working two jobs simultaneously—one as a medical supplies salesman, which paid the bills, and one in pursuit of an opportunity to work as a stockbroker, which gave me a crash course in cold calling, getting past gatekeepers, and making sense of the numbers game as I knocked on doors of every branch office of every brokerage in the Bay Area; I heard more than a year's worth of noes before catching my first real break. Once I did get my foot in the door as a trainee at Dean Witter & Company, after my trainee workday was done, I studied ferociously in order to pass the exam for my brokerage license—a feat that coincided with becoming a single parent and subsequently homeless. Without any margin for failure, I set myself a quota of making no fewer than two hundred sales calls a days. Meanwhile, my other OTJ training was figuring out the logistics of where to sleep, how to pay for quality day care, and how to feed and clothe my toddler son and myself, with enough left over to put a roof over our heads.

Many or even all of these efforts may resemble those that you have undertaken in your life, or those that you may undertake in the future. In such cases, we all know that we're not alone in having to juggle efforts—whether they include an entry-level position on the job or seeking new work, finding places to stay, as well as needing to make choices for transportation, and budgeting the living needs for ourselves and our loved ones. It doesn't alter your circumstances to remember that others have gone through similar straits, though sometimes that message can help you keep going. And if you've forgotten about the most essential resource of initiative, let me remind you that it has to be one of the first tools out of the toolbox. Because if it's not, the toolbox may never be opened.

Initiative is available to everyone, regardless of where we went to school or what connections we do or don't have when starting out in any endeavor.

Though it took a year to land a job and another year of hitting the anvil, with initiative and persistence I was able to survive a beginner's mistakes and conquer the basics. It was then that I finally looked up and saw that I'd built my "book" of clients. That was not only a success that validated my efforts, but in cold, hard cash terms, I could finally afford a place of our own to stay. Our first place of residence, after a year without, was a basement unit of a house in Oakland that I'd found when we passed by and I spotted the roses that were growing out front. Roses in the ghetto! We were home.

It wasn't the end of the journey, only the beginning. But I must say that after our first night sleeping there, when Christopher Jr. and I left that next morning, the single little metal key given to me by the land-lord made me feel as if I were the richest person on the planet and that I had completed the hardest assignment ever. Nothing has compared since. For the first time in a year, we could leave our belongings at home, secure in the knowledge they would be there after I finished up work and picked up Chris Jr. from day care.

Just the feeling of the weight of the key in my hand is something that I will never forget. It defined for me the proving grounds of a life lesson that I'd known all along—the first and last rule of the market-place—that *the law of hard work is no secret.*

You can write it on your arm in permanent ink and on the inside of your skull. It will not fail you. No matter what your current or future field of endeavor, whenever you take the initiative to make of yourself and your life what you will, and back it up, you're in possession of spe-cial knowledge about how to succeed in the marketplace.

There are other rules and requirements to learn about how to corner and command your market, to be sure. But this life lesson has been the most crucial for me at every stage of the game, confirming that Thomas Edison had it right—there *is* no substitute for hard work.

If it seems that I'm overstating what should be obvious about the importance of this first rule of the marketplace, it's because of the many questions I hear from people looking for an angle, any angle, to skip the heavy lifting of laying a foundation—and get to the big time right away. Again, that can sometimes take us back to the land of magical thinking or to the belief that somebody else has a special formula that we're lacking. Of course, it's empowering to consider strategies that have worked for others—as long as they don't become distractions to us doing our own work.

The best angle for optimizing opportunity for each of us, in my opinion, isn't in someone else's repertoire but inside of ourselves. And sometimes it requires rote repetition, trial and error, and slogging it out in the trenches, before we find out that, hey, whatever works is specific to each one of us.

Again, I'd love to be a genie, snap my fingers, and give everyone their angle. I wanted it for myself! It turned out to be the application of this lesson. Hard work was required for starting out, just as it was when it came time to push myself to the next level. It was similarly applicable later when it was necessary to start over and reinvent myself, and likewise meaningful further on for pushing me to expand my frontiers. At no stage of my professional development has hard work not been essential.

During a Q&A session at an annual conference for a real estate company back when the subprime mortgage debacle was beginning, a good-looking, well-dressed man in his fifties stood up and asked, "If you were thinking about changing careers in this tough economy, how would you recommend attracting the right opportunities for that?" Frankly, I had to smile. The reality is that while pounding the pavement sounds like a cliché—it still works! Not that I disagree with the positive uses of the power of attraction. But without the active pursuit of possibilities, that approach could well be slow going. The best advice I could offer was something he'd already learned early in his real estate career—do the work, go the extra step, and stay on it. Rather than attracting opportunity, he would then be in the driver's seat and initiating it. Initiative!

Take it up a notch and put it on top of the menu. Initiative is a first cousin of pursuit. It's what's for dinner, lunch, and breakfast, too. Initiative puts you in the kitchen and at the table. So if you don't have some in stock, go get it, now! Because ain't nothing coming but the bills, taxes, death, and trouble. Then you can decide how you want to serve your initiative.

When you recall your efforts in the workplace as well as in other areas of your life, you might be surprised at the role that initiative has played in some of your accomplishments that you never thought of as such. What about that school fund-raiser you good-naturedly organized that was such a hit? Did you ever run an idea up a flagpole at the office that you were given the job of overseeing that turned out amazingly, but you just took it in stride? Or how about the success of the arts and crafts items that you create as gifts to others? The funny thing that happens when we're engaged in something that we've decided to do on our own is that it doesn't even seem like hard work. Wouldn't it be great if we could tap that same natural ease and capacity for initiating action when facing the daunting prospects of entering or reentering the working world? Well, I think we can. And the most successful do. Yet we still sometimes hesitate in taking initiative.

Part of the problem is fear. Who relishes calling up potentially cranky people? Who looks forward to hearing that there are no openings at this time? And then there's the resistance we all can feel about being a commodity out there for sale, or the anxiety many have about the marketplace in general. I have heard it said that job hunting is among the top causes of stress—right up there with having a child, losing a loved one, marriage, divorce, illness, and moving. It may be even more stressful for individuals who, for various reasons, are returning to work after time spent in other areas, or who are changing careers in midlife (however we choose to define that these days). Understandably, they're worried about not being able to maintain the lifestyle they used to be able to afford. Plus they're competing for fewer jobs with younger candidates—who may be willing to work for less or who may have had more recent training.

Fear of the unknown is common to all of us when we put ourselves out there in the real world, out of our comfort zones, in situations where we feel that we may be judged, criticized, possibly rejected, and where we can't control many variables that will affect the ultimate outcome. Knowing that has helped me to better understand why one of the most severe panic disorders, agoraphobia, literally translates as "fear of the marketplace." Fear of not having control, not being able to escape or survive mishaps and unforeseen events, can be tough to overcome for some folks—who avoid leaving their houses or steer away from public gathering places.

Even for those who don't suffer from such an extreme aversion to the public arena, it can be nerve-racking to put yourself out there, hat in hand—asking for something. It can be less intimidating if you know that you've done your preparation, making sure your tools of the trade are in order—that is, your résumé is updated and easily accessible, your websites and marketing materials are current—and you've made sure that at absolutely all times you've got a business card and an ink pen on your person, at the ready. You can find me butt naked on a desert island, and I will have a business card and an ink pen on me somewhere! Be prepared.

All those tools of the trade are for you to keep in working order. How you respect your instruments of industry can be a clue as to how you respect yourself. The working world responds well when you keep your materials sharp and your methods tight.

The stone-cold truth is that the marketplace is not your friend. It's not designed to be a loving, welcoming entity. It doesn't care about you. You can mark that down as another rule. Whenever you take the bold step to put yourself on the line—with your creations, ideas, wares, dreams, and desires—rarely will a welcome wagon come out to greet you with flowers and chocolate. You may be the most sensational undiscovered star, but you're not a shoo-in. Maybe you're the most deserving, courageous human being ready for a big break, but that's not usually enough. Whatever you're hoping to give or get—a job, love, or a contribution to a cause—the marketplace isn't interested. That is, *unless* you've got something of value or interest to offer.

Hard work and initiative do get you noticed. When a receptionist notices that you've stopped by three times to have a few words with the manager in charge of hiring, your repeat appearances can at least be a conversation starter. Similarly, those assets will help you calm your nerves and eventually move past the gatekeepers. The experience that comes from hitting the anvil of effort may also connect you with knowledge that will be of interest to prospective employers.

When I was new on the job at Dean Witter, initiative and creative ways to hit the anvil were what paid off. That meant starting at the bottom—"smiling and dialing," as I referred to the grueling numbers game of cold calling. I hit the anvil so diligently, my right index finger is permanently bent to this day.

On a recent business trip to San Francisco, I happened to be in the financial district crossing the street when a young woman called my name. She explained that she was just starting in the brokerage business and wanted to know only one thing—"Why two hundred?"

I knew exactly what she meant. Why did I set such a ridiculous daily minimum goal for how many calls I had to make before the clock struck 5:30 P.M.? The real reason, I explained, "I was hungry." That was the highest goal that I could set for myself to improve my odds. It required me to employ discipline and economy of language and motion and to sharpen my tools with the use of my five Cs (see Lesson #1 for a reminder). By cutting down on coffee, not taking bathroom breaks, not chitchatting needlessly, I was being the best at doing the job that was at the lowest rung of the ladder.

That's my interpretation of hard work—doing your best, whatever you do. Again, it may seem so basic as to be stating the obvious. But if you really want to be noticed in a crazy competitive environment where you've got a stampede of thousands or more vying for the same thing that you want, the most obvious attributes may be what allow you to stand out.

Initiative was what brought me to the attention of Gary Shemano, an important mentor and friend from my early days on Wall Street. A business and golf guru, and CEO of the Shemano Group, Gary was a general partner and managing director of Bear Stearns & Company in San Francisco when I met him in the mid-1980s. Often, I'd see him on the trading floor of Dean Witter visiting one of the women in our ranks who I'd assumed was his stockbroker but who was actually his then girlfriend. One day Gary introduced himself and gave me his card. When I followed up, the first thing he said was how impressed he was by my initiative. Word was that I was the first to arrive in the morning and the last to leave at the end of the day, and that I observed the heavier hitters to learn how they mastered what they were doing. This was, of course, my following the lead of Will Rogers—who liked to say that he went to school with every man who ever talked to him.

Gary not only had noticed my work ethic but also valued it enough to make the case for me coming to his firm. In frankness, he expressed his feeling that I needed to be pushed in a way that my current bosses didn't know how to do. As soon as I accepted his offer, Gary began his mentoring from the start, saying that he saw major potential but I had to see it, too, and that there was a lot of work ahead of me. Even so, he convinced me that I could scale the heights, saying, "This is your time to shine, Chris Gardner, your time in the sun."

As he would have told me himself, the easiest sale to make is to another salesman. When he followed up by asking me to name a starting draw, I thought of the highest monthly amount that I could at the time—five thousand dollars. He agreed so quickly that it was clear I should have asked for more. Even so, I was over the moon. Chris Jr. and I moved into a picturesque San Francisco apartment closer to a terrific day-care center and a short bus ride to the office. Incredibly, the bus stopped just outside the door of our apartment.

Gary later admitted that he had to do a lot of persuading to convince the other powers that be at Bear Stearns, namely Marshall Geller, that I was a wise investment. But once Marshall signed on, he, too, became a mentor. Both Marshall and Gary, with completely different styles, were integral to my development back then and continue to guide me to this day.

I hope you have a similar recollection of a time when hard work and initiative may have helped you catch a break that you didn't specifically pursue. In those instances, you might have learned something along the lines of what I did—that every now and then, instead of chasing an opportunity, the game comes to you. Of course, that happens only when you're prepared. And sometimes when you've hit that anvil to the point of feeling that it's all futile, you may have to change your approach. What's more, we all have to adapt what we know to make it more effective.

The first thing that challenged me at my new firm was its approach to improving the odds of the numbers game, still with initiative but adding components of efficiency, R&D, networking, and innovation. The Bear Stearns mantra was—*Don't work harder, work smarter.*

When I left Dean Witter, the brokerage where I'd gotten my first break and learned the fundamentals in a straightforward, traditional business atmosphere, the move to Bear Stearns was a quantum leap to a very different power structure, where it seemed that everyone was playing at the top of their game. Gary Shemano told me from day one that I would have to do that, too. "This isn't a democracy," he explained. "It's a meritocracy." He then added, "You're in the NFL before your time. Strap it on tight."

If you find this lesson and its variations compelling, take the initiative to embrace your time in the sun, your opportunity to shine. And then you, too, can and must strap it on tight and push yourself toward excellence.

LESSON #21
Core Strengths Forged on Your Anvil
KEYWORD: *Confidence*

Right after initiative, the next tool you've got to be prepared to pull out of the toolbox, sharp and ready to put to use in any situation, is confidence. For effectively navigating the marketplace, confidence is your go-to resource, as well it should be.

There is no doubt that confidence is one of those intangibles that can take individuals much further than the skills or experience on their résumé indicates they will go. Whenever I hear highly successful folks describe how they convinced others to give them their first break, often they'll admit to blowing the interview or audition but sailing on through because there was something special—a core strength that compensated for other shortcomings—that others recognized.

In every walk of life, I see a similar confidence from certain people who have yet to attain their aspirations. But they still command an assuredness that comes from within. It's a brightness in their eyes, an expression of curiosity to know and learn more, a willingness to ask questions and to listen, a level of composure that may be beyond their years or world experience.

In contrast, I also hear from folks who are mortified at how they can't catch a break and will readily list how many times their lack of confidence sabotaged an opportunity. They'll describe what they said and did wrong, as well as what they forgot to say and what they failed to do to make a positive impression. When the next situation arises that involves any uncertainty—whether it's a job interview, a blind date, a presentation to potential clients, even a social engagement that takes them out of their comfort zone—they make matters worse by worrying about how unconfident they are.

So where does this intangible quality known as confidence come from? This is a question that has been of great interest to me over the years as I've observed individuals who are considered world class at what they do—heart surgeons, music maestros, and international financiers who move and shape global economies all in a day's work.

When you watch those individuals, you'll notice they exhibit a level of confidence that is supersized, often larger than life. They appear to have a level of focus that is more intense than everyday folk can muster. They have presence and control not only when they're in their element, but also in everyday settings—walking down the street, grocery shopping, hailing a cab. When they walk into a room, you notice them and how they move like tigers, as if they're about to pounce. They may not say a word but just seem to dominate the space.

There was a time when I assumed these superconfident people were that way because they were born with added doses of self-assured, self-possessed qualities. Yet in my conversations with many individuals who have attained levels of mastery, that assumption has proven wrong. And what I've come to discover, through this very lesson that core strengths can be forged on ordinary anvils of all kinds, is that confidence is definitely an acquired resource.

How do you acquire it, then? From basic common sense and paying attention, I'd have to say that it comes from practice, training in your area of expertise, and, yes, from hitting the good old anvil of hard work at whatever you wish to be confident in. When you step out of your element, a building block for developing confidence comes from the entitlement you embrace to do so. When you go knock on doors, for instance, it's up to you to claim the right to do so. As you may well know from your experience, the marketplace isn't in the business of rolling out red carpets for everyone. So you have to believe that you've got something special to offer, giving you as good a chance for acceptance as anyone else, if not better.

The need to entitle yourself, I should add, was first made evident to me by my mother—who steadfastly insisted that my worth wasn't tied to pedigrees, degrees, or registries but was rooted in the core of who I was as a person. By her example, once again, I saw that what she brought into a room with her sense of quiet strength and power of presence was so much more impressive than any paper credentials. The other person who embodied that kind of confidence was my beloved uncle Henry Gardner—the youngest of Momma's three brothers—who died in a boating accident when I was eight years old.

Uncle Henry didn't just have authority. He had command! Not merely strong, he was bold, and, as far as I could tell, he didn't have an ordinary cell in his body. As a boy who struggled with the "no daddy blues," I saw Uncle Henry as the closest to being a father figure that I had. I was inspired by the strengths I admired in him—from his impeccable grooming and outstanding personal style, to the adventurous spirit that guided him to see sights and places in his travels around the world. Besides the fact that the women were crazy about him and that he had introduced me to the music of Miles Davis, Henry Gardner was the King of Cool.

When he was taken from us much too young, I decided to carry on the family tradition in his memory and run with my own sense of style and cool as far as I could take it. When I was eight years old, the die was cast for me. Clearly, I was going to have to attain a decent enough living to afford the expensive tastes that I developed as a result! Not that everyone in every pursuit has to dress for success. But for me it became a must in keeping with the philosophy of another hero, President John F. Kennedy, who used words to the effect that it's not just important to do good, you've also got to look good.

On the world stage, looking good can help to draw attention to your vision and your good deeds. In the marketplace, looking good is one way to boost confidence—if that's your thing, too.

Another effective way to appreciate core strengths that you might not see as such can come from the use of your three As—authority, authenticity, and autonomy—knowing yourself, being yourself, and choosing for yourself. At every stage of my professional growth, whenever I was reaching for opportunities that took me out of familiar areas of expertise, the three As helped me find a measure of confidence that put prospective employers, bosses, and clients at ease. On a few occasions, I can recall trying to act as if I knew more about something than I really did, attempts that fell flat. As time went on, I learned that it's much better to say, "No, I don't have a ready answer for you, but one of my strengths is research and finding the top people who can provide solid answers to important questions."

As a rookie in any venture, of course, it's typical to believe that you've got to do the razzle-dazzle to win the day. Now that may be effective if you really are spectacular and can back up your show with ability. But it can also come across as trying too hard. Plus, in your effort to demonstrate that you've got the qualities that you think are being sought, you may reveal your weaknesses instead. As any experienced card player will tell you, when in doubt, it's a winning game plan to lead with your strong suit—or the best cards you've got in your hand to play.

The three As, again, are useful for evaluating those cards. With knowledge of yourself, an ease in being yourself, and the choice you make to reveal assets, interests, or even hobbies that others might not have requested, you can often take charge of an otherwise disadvantageous situation. Those unique strengths might not be on the help wanted listing or in the description of responsibilities for that promotion you hope to get, but when you show up with confidence in other capacities, minds can be changed.

I received a long e-mail from a young mom who had been away from the workplace for ten years. She described a series of job interviews for secretarial work that hadn't gone well. Every time she was asked if she knew how to use a particular kind of software or had relevant experience for the position being filled, she tried to explain how her skills as a mother of two teens and a toddler could be applied. No one seemed to be listening. In her "last resort" interview at a law firm, she told the human resources director that though she might not have prior experience or desired skills for the duties, "I sincerely want this job and I know that you will not find anyone willing to work harder with more attention to detail and a desire to do well than me." The confidence and sincerity with which she made that statement turned out to be twice as meaningful as the qualities she lacked.

I'm not suggesting that you walk into every job interview, business meeting, or workplace setting with the intention of only promoting yourself. Nor does being confident mean being brash or pushy. Literally, it does mean that you act "with faith"—in yourself and in others to recognize that you can be counted on to deliver the goods, whatever that means in that context.

In applying this lesson about honing core strengths on all kinds of ordinary anvils, you also don't want to forget about those pursuits that give you joy outside of the marketplace. Think for a moment about an activity, hobby, or passion that you've pursued regularly. It may have nothing to do with what you do for a living—like my love for style—but it fuels your overall sense of confidence. Do you read voraciously? Do you write a beautiful letter? It can be your humor, your neatness, your love of Mom and apple pie, or your knowledge of obscure *Star Trek* episodes.

Confidence builders for the marketplace come from an array of outlets that simply make us feel great. The trip to the gym is a common way to boost endorphins and well-being. Yoga, I hear, is amazing for fueling a sense of composure and confidence. Maybe being out on a boat fishing or hunting in the woods empowers and energizes you. Maybe you feel like a million bucks after you get your car washed and take it out for a spin. Do you tango? Are you a golf or tennis fanatic? Are you in your personal heaven on weekends when you garden? Retail shopping therapy does it for me.

Some might view these as hobbies, but don't tell that to those of us who are passionate about how we choose to spend our free time and how we derive confidence from those pursuits. These signature activities aren't merely for winding down after a long day. They're forms of meditation for many people I know, ways to be creative in their own workshops with their own anvils. Many of my busiest, most driven colleagues who work at top levels of business, government, medicine, law, and elsewhere, not necessarily in artistic fields, are cooking fools! They can rustle up feasts that could compete with top chefs. Most of them were taught the basics in their homes, right along with washing dishes and scrubbing stovetops.

I once had the pleasure of watching Quincy Jones—the legendary musician, composer, and producer—cook a turkey burger. He approached this other creative outlet with the same flair seen in his musicianship—blending herbs, spices, texture, and color with a methodical, painstaking attention to detail. It was like watching Picasso paint.

How about those of you who hit the anvil of home decor and design? When you can turn any old barren space into a beautiful, inviting environment, that's downright enviable. Or how about those of you who are masters of fixing stuff around the house? I have seen some of my friends' workbenches that could house a small factory. The happyness that is gained from doing something that raises energy and well-being in one area almost always spills over to the challenges in other areas.

Moral of this story: confidence is a transferable strength.

When you feel like a million bucks, whatever you do to feel that way, the marketplace responds positively. Something that I started doing years ago—when I moved to New York City in the mid-1980s—is treating myself to a shoeshine whenever I'm on my way to do business. For me, that feeling of sparkling from your toes to the top of your head is a confidence blast. I recommend it to anyone who would like to join with me and follow in the footsteps of my uncle Henry—still the undisputed King of Cool in my book. You can do so without developing the serious shoe issue that I've acquired. You also don't have to insist, as I do, that you can only wear shoes that have been shined that same day.

Not long after my move to New York and acquiring this habit, I went in search of the ultimate shoeshine and found the best of the best on Fifty-fifth Street and Seventh Avenue. For many years I thought it was my best-kept secret, too, until one beautiful autumn day in late 2002 when who should walk in and sit down on the shoeshine stand next to me but the hippest dude on the planet—the Emperor of Cool, Tony Bennett.

In his midseventies at the time, he hadn't lost an iota of the good looks, charisma, and talent that made him such a heartthrob in the 1950s and early 1960s. Much of the public knew that he had kind of disappeared with yesteryear in the rock 'n' roll heyday of the later '60s, '70s, and '80s. What not everyone knows is that in those years, following marital and financial troubles, Tony Bennett hit a downward spiral and almost died in 1979 from a cocaine overdose. Instead, he orchestrated the most amazing comeback, going back to his anvil of core strengths—the style, passion, and musicality that allowed him to sing anything and make it his own. With the help of his two sons managing and producing, he came roaring back to the top of the charts, conquering the music awards, rolling like the rock star he truly is.

I couldn't resist striking up a conversation with him about anything, everything, and nothing. Shoes done, shining almost as bright as the moment, before heading out the door, I turned back and asked Tony, "Man, when are you gonna slow down?"

Without missing a beat, he smiled and said, "Why should I?"

Confidence, baby!

LESSON #22
Wizards Begin as Blacksmiths
KEYWORD: *Transferable Skills*

Anvils? Blacksmiths?

You might be thinking something along the lines of what I've been asked by several friends and family members: "Hey, Chris, what's up with all this talk of hitting the anvil? Why the fascination with blacksmiths?"

I usually explain that it's not all that far-fetched for someone who grew up, as I did, in a steel town like Milwaukee with the hum of industry all around, with its ample waterways for powering the mills, foundries, and other metal and ironworks. In my mind, the blacksmith has always been the everyman or everywoman who represents the hard work ethic I saw in people all around me—whether they worked in the steel business or not. The attitude wasn't just *Do it!* but rather *Do it and enjoy it! And get good at it!*

Out of this atmosphere, I grew up with an appreciation for tradespeople and the different levels of skilled labor, as well as the many stages needed for developing skills. This was evident not just at the steel mills, but in all the local industries—the brickyards, breweries, tanneries, meatpacking plants, and automotive factories. Every place had its own structure and stages of production, but generally I understood that no matter what specialized skill you might attain, everybody had to start at the bottom, becoming familiar with basic nuts and bolts—that is, turning raw materials into finished goods. Along the way, you could move on to proficiency, either staying at that rung or developing a specialty. That, too, could become your highest conquered level of skill, or you could move further by diversifying and finding methods of innovation, and eventually you could arrive at mastery.

Long before I knew what a blacksmith did, these various industries allowed me to see the general steps to mastery that could be pursued regardless of the endeavor. Eventually I also discovered the coin of the realm for ascending those steps: transferable skills. Before I had come to learn that term, that capacity was something I was already using in my everyday pursuits.

As I began to see how knowledge and skills can be transferred, not only in the working world but through the stages of growth in general, I finally decided it was time to do some research about the stages of mastery that are relevant to blacksmithing. For starters, I learned that the job requires proficiency in the use of the three necessary tools of the trade: 1) the fireplace or furnace in which to heat the iron or other black metal (hence the word *blacksmith*) to be forged, (2) the anvil on which to hit the iron and shape it to its desired dimensions, and (3) something to use for hammering and hitting the metal. Other steps are involved: learning how and where to obtain the ore; doing research in metallurgy and alloys; analyzing composition of the elements; studying the chemistry of temperature change needed to trans-form the metal's molecular structure; figuring out the physics impacted by the size of the hammer and its force and speed. This all comes before the blacksmith markets his or her wares and promotes his or her excellence.

I learned something else that was even more relevant to my interest in the subject. It seems that except for the last century or so, the village blacksmith was valued as the most important craftsman in town, more integral to the marketplace than all the other tradespeople. Without the products made by the black metals that he forged on his anvil, all forms of transportation, construction, and commerce ground to a halt. Even the horses couldn't walk without their "lucky" horseshoes fitted by the local smithy. It was no accident that in most town squares, the blacksmith's shop was at the center of the marketplace. All the ven-dors, buyers, travelers, merchants, high-society folks, and commoners would stop by for services or to catch up on gossip, goings-on, and the weather. It served the same purpose as the corner barbershop or local bar of different eras—with the barber, barkeep, or smithy being sought out for advice.

All of that only raised my regard for the blacksmith and his anvil. Upon further reflection, it turned out that the image may have first been inspired for me by the books of Greek and Roman mythology that I ate up as a kid. From somewhere back in my memory banks, I recalled that the blacksmith in the myths was also the master tradesman to the gods and keeper of the horses, and he was endowed with powers of magic. It turns out that in *The Sword in the Stone* and other tales of King Arthur and the Knights of the Round Table, Merlin the Wizard was a blacksmith as well as a magician. Moral of this story: aspiring wizards who wanted to transform common metal into powerful swords had to labor long and hard as apprentices. No advancement to mastery could take place without time spent in the fundamentals, hitting their anvils.

As much as I knew this intuitively, I really didn't appreciate its importance or the value of this transferable skills lesson until I was an apprentice under the Wall Street wizards (the "Masters of the Universe" as they were known in the 1980s) who mentored me. True teachers, like Gary Shemano, occasionally reminded me to take a closer inventory of what I already knew before tackling something new. For example, if I was going to be approaching clients with long-term investment strategies for retirement purposes, Gary would make sure that I had a frame of reference for doing so. Well, in that case, I could recall my work at a nursing home where I took care of the elderly and saw the concerns of their families up close. In fact, as I looked back on my employment history, for the first time I was grateful for the diversity of experience that could be applied to my efforts to be successful on Wall Street.

This revelation inspired me to come up with an alternate to the traditional job résumé, which typically only lists the name of the employer, position, and duties specific to that field. My idea was to create more of a worksheet that could outline the portable knowledge, marketplace skills, and life lessons that could be applicable to other fields and positions. It's an idea that I've used for myself and have recommended for anyone who is facing a sharp learning curve in a new field. As a planning tool for interviews—that is, not something you hand to a prospective employer—whether you're doing the hiring or hoping to be hired, this transferable skill worksheet is also a wonderful reminder to bring up strengths that would otherwise go unnoticed.

Take a look at my version of an in-house résumé that you can emulate should you need or want to familiarize yourself with your abundance of transferable skills. I've listed my employment history that came before I went to work on Wall Street and can assure you that every bit of it has been valid as I've moved up in my field—from blacksmith status to conquering the fundamentals, paving the way to mastery.

Field and Position	Duties and Compensation	Life Lessons	Transferable Skills
Restaurant business *Dishwasher*	"Humping the Hobart"—minimum wage	You have to start somewhere. If you quit, be diplomatic or you won't get your last paycheck.	Always respect the work of folks who do the most thankless jobs.
Nursing Home *Orderly*	Emptying bedpans, caring for elderly; minimum plus.	There's always demand for supplying kindness, care, and respect.	If you learn from the best, you'll become the best. Hospital operations and procedures.
Inland Steel *Steelworker*	Loading dock, maintenance; union entry level w/ benefits.	Best practices mean everybody wins when everybody wins.	Hitting the anvil. Labor and management relations. Industrial protocols.
The U.S. Navy *Medic*	Naval training, medical clinic, hospital services—wound care, patient transport, surgical support, proctology. Military pay w/ benefits.	Initiative and excellence increase demand for what you can contribute. Also: "Join the Navy, See the World" may mean only North Carolina.	Time organization, respect for hierarchies, rules, and an intro to demanding superiors. Medical, scientific protocols. How to use humor in matters of life and death.
Shipping Industry *Night watchman*	Security for retired naval ship. Top hourly wage. Part-time while at VA.	When there are rats, don't deal in cheese.	How to know your limits.
VA Hospital *Research lab director*	Laboratory R&D, overseeing scientific tests; coordination of personnel; written analysis of data for scientific journals. Paid by research grants.	All the confidence you will ever need comes with knowledge of what you are doing. The marketplace will pay a premium for that.	How to follow and lead at the same time. Inner workings of institutional, medical, and scientific fields. Intro to writing and publishing.
Medical/Scientific Supply Distribution *Sales rep*	Outside sales. Salary plus commission.	Love what you do or find something else that you do love.	The importance of the tools of the trade, basics of supply and demand.

When you do this kind of inventory not only to land a job in a new arena but also when you're trying to ascend a ladder in your field, it can provide you with very helpful guidance as to where you are in your pursuit. Do you need to push yourself to the next level? Do you need to gain more proficiency? Are you in too much of a hurry? The latter question is a reminder to pace yourself because being in too much of a rush may mean having to repeat or relearn a lesson later. This can be very costly in terms of opportunity, not just money, and most of all in terms of time. After all, you can always make more money, but you can't always make more time, and opportunities can never be re-created.

When you do decide that you're ready to push yourself but are intimidated or unsure about skills that you lack, you may want to consider a piece of wisdom that I learned from Gary Shemano not long after I started at Bear Stearns. Gary taught me many things but perhaps none have been as transferable as his suggestion for how to overcome the feeling of being intimidated when contacting high-powered, important people. The key, he said, was to never be afraid of calling someone you think is bigger than you—as long as you can offer something that is of interest to them.

His advice was given around the time that I'd been trying to get a Mr. Nelson Hunt of Texas on the phone. My goal had been to establish a dialogue that I hoped would lead to a business relationship. The Hunts had allegedly been attempting to corner the world's silver market, and my goal was to compete for a portion of the brokerage transaction that promised to be huge. I knew it and so did every other broker on the street, since it was no secret what the Hunts were buying. All in the same chase, we eventually got to the same place: nowhere.

And then one day, for no particular reason, I called and left a message for Mr. Hunt regarding a company called Holly Sugar, not expecting anything different to happen. Later that same day, my assistant interrupted a sales meeting to inform me that a Mr. Hunt was on the phone for me!

After I ran to take the call, the first thing he said to me in his thick

Texas drawl was, "Is this Chris Gardner? Did you call me about some sugar?"

We established a dialogue and though I didn't actually get a chance to do business with Mr. Hunt, I had put Gary's advice to the test and it had worked. I had come up with something that was of interest to him that no one else had found. This was pay dirt. From then on, whenever I was feeling unsure about going after the heavy hitters that everyone else was chasing, I did my research to find something of interest that hopefully no one else had uncovered. The ability to connect with individuals deemed impossible to get on the phone thus became a major transferable skill that I use to this day. In fact, a short while after my success in getting Mr. Hunt on the phone, I was able to make contact with J.R., another Texas oilman, who took my call by accident— thinking that I was someone else. On that same phone conversation, he ended up buying fifty thousand shares of "whatever you called to tell me about," sight unseen. At fifty cents commission per share, that was a $25,000 profit for me. It was the largest transaction I'd ever made to that date, not to mention a significant boost to my ranking on the totem pole.

The lesson *Wizards begin as blacksmiths* can be applied not only to push yourself when you're ready to move to your next level, but also to know when you may need to slow down. As I learned through a rude awakening or two when I arrived in New York City, full of myself and ready to blast off to the top, I still had more fundamentals to conquer before being ready to do that.

As you apply this lesson and put your transferable skills to use, don't hesitate to ask yourself at different points where you really are in your journey to mastery. If you're starting out, know that the time you invest as a blacksmith will pay off soon enough and later on. And if you've reached wizard status at whatever you do, don't forget to stay grounded in what you learned back at the beginning. Maybe that's a secret after all.

LESSON #23
Are You Bold Enough to Go Back to Basics?
KEYWORD: *Resilience*

For all the financial and economic woes that we've witnessed in recent times, I'm a firm believer in the resilience of the marketplace. Even more important, I have faith in the capacity for resilience that's available to each of us—as this lesson is here to emphasize.

Not too long ago, I went to a social event attended by several colleagues and friends from the financial field, many of whom were dealing with personal and professional challenges they'd never experienced before. It was fascinating to hear how for some it was the best of times and for others it was the worst of times. Some were toasting to new, exciting prospects while others were drowning their sorrows.

Now, I should point out that I am not a drinking man. That was a decision I made at a young age. Growing up, I witnessed the destructive influence of alcohol on my stepfather, as well as on other folks in the neighborhood where I lived. The choice to abstain from alcohol— not as a teetotaler but as a part of who I chose to become—has had its challenges but mostly has brought many positive dividends. In the business world, where meetings and deal making often take place over drinks, it's put me at an advantage sometimes to be the only person at the table who is clearheaded at the end of the night. It's also helped me sharpen my listening skills—which is never a bad thing.

So there I was at this cocktail party, possibly the only person not drinking, when I heard an entertaining earful from a complete stranger who was upset with me for causing him to quit his job in order to pursue happyness!

Instead of staying in the financial field, when the industry was starting to change, he had decided to reinvent himself and do something, as he said, "to serve the greater good." The problem was that it was turning out to be so much more difficult than anything he'd done before. Back in the good old days in the rat race, he was a CPA working for a national accounting firm, making lots of bucks. Now he had hung out his own shingle helping nonprofits with their financial books, and he had started his own effort to raise money for a job-training program working with individuals impacted by poverty and low education levels. He couldn't believe the many obstacles that kept being thrown in his path. "And you know what's wrong?" he asked. Before I could say a word, this guy said that he read somewhere that if he started giving more of himself to others, he'd be happier. So far, he said, it was turning out to be harder than dealing with the most grueling IRS audit!

"You want to go back to being a CPA?" I asked, not sure if he really wanted me to say something or if he just wanted to rant.

"What and give up my dream?" he replied with a laugh. And then, with a drunken hug, he thanked me!

It turned out that as hard as he was working, with less money and time than he ever had before, the autonomy of running his own show was more fulfilling than anything he'd previously done. His complaint, and it was valid, was that, in many respects, when he decided to become an entrepreneur and strike out on his own, he was forced to go back to square one and start with basics that he'd surpassed years earlier.

Now it was my turn to thank him. His story enabled me to recognize one of the most critical marketplace lessons of my career. It comes with the ever-useful question you can put to yourself whenever you're contemplating change or a different path of growth—*Are you bold enough to go back to basics?*

Not a day goes by that I don't hear from several different individuals who are intent on finding meaningful advice for how to launch their own business or major undertaking. The three most frequently asked questions that I hear in this connection include the following: (1) What made you decide to start your own firm? (2) What was the one thing that helped you build a multimillion-dollar enterprise that started in your apartment with only a ten-thousand-dollar investment? (3) How long did it take before you knew that you were really going to make it?

My answer to the first question about opening up my own firm takes me back to the moment when I left San Francisco and arrived in New York—and had the same mind-blowing, rocket-blast liftoff of energy as when I stepped onto a trading floor for the first time. No longer was it—*oh, yeah, this is where I want to be!* Now my focus was on learning from the Masters of the Universe who ruled Wall Street with blazing powers in the 1980s, so that eventually I could borrow from their knowledge to do my own thing. Somewhere in my daydreams the vision of having my own firm—with my name on the door and all—must have cropped up early on. But for every practical reason, I knew that such a pursuit would have to come much later.

Meanwhile, I began to see this immense galaxy of opportunity that only a few fearless innovators were chasing. That's where I really wanted to be. Plus, I saw possibilities for going ahead of their curve and pursuing revenue streams for investment that had been attempted but not at the scale that I envisioned.

Was I ready to go test the waters and find out? Hell, no. That was, until the day, much to my shock, that I was fired.

Though I should have seen it coming, I didn't. Here I was, a rising star, working my way up in the ranks of Bear Stearns, but instead of toeing the company line by promoting the packages that I was supposed to be selling, I had bigger ideas. Independent money managers, middlemen and -women, were dominating in the arenas of wealth management and institutional investment strategies for pension funds and the like. There was no reason that I as a stockbroker couldn't compete with the money managers and work directly with institutional clients. Or so I thought. After the fact, I should have realized that my employer would not relish my dreams of reinventing the game on Wall Street or veering from the company program as enforced by the chain of command. So when my immediate supervisor fired me for not sticking to policy, I shot back, "You can't fire me. I'm gonna go to see Ace."

Going to see Ace Greenberg, the chairman and legendary CEO of the maverick phenomenon Bear Stearns & Company, what was in those days one of the most profitable private partnerships on Wall Street, was the equivalent of going to go see God. Since God wasn't in that day, the great and mighty Ace was in charge. I found him sitting among the rank and file at his familiar seat on the trading floor, from which he rose to escort me into his office and hear me out. He was sympathetic to my vision—and passion—but in the end he had to back his guys in middle management. "You can't serve two masters" was his fundamental message. That was the deal. But when he showed me the door, Ace didn't close it completely. Actually, his last words to me were, "The road is long."

At the time, it felt as if I had been exiled from the only home I'd ever known. Only later did I perceive what a gift that was. Today, I think of Ace Greenberg as the prime example of someone who is both a journeyman blacksmith who has never stopped hitting the anvil, and a true wizard. As a matter of fact, it is well known that in his spare time Ace's favorite anvil is working on his talents as an amateur magician. From what I can tell, the word *amateur* is a definite misnomer.

Not to gloss over the reality, let me go on record when I say that back in 1987—or anytime!—getting fired sucks. But it can be a blessing in disguise. In my case, it was not only the means that got me to stop digging my potatoes (Lesson #6) when it came to opening up my own shop, but it provided me with an additional and necessary lesson about resilience.

Perhaps you've had opportunities to access this priceless resource on your own. You might remember when you surprised yourself at how resilient you really were. Or how willing you were to go back to lessons you learned much earlier. On the other end of the resilience spectrum, maybe you freaked out over the prospects of starting over again, reinventing yourself, or changing your way of life. In each of those scenarios, you most likely were forced to make a serious choice about which way to go next. You could have opted to get up, brush yourself off, and return to the path you were on. Or you could have challenged yourself to go in the James Brown direction of "Papa's Got a Brand New Bag."

After some memorable soul-searching, I chose the bolder, much more uncertain route of change. I could have joined another firm and toed that company's line, but I decided to strike out on my own.

This brings me to the second question I'm so often asked regarding how it was possible to start a business in Chicago in the competitive business environment of Wall Street with only ten grand of capital going in. For one thing, I didn't know that it couldn't be done: ignorance is bliss. Additionally, I brought with me the resourcefulness that came from nearly a year of being homeless, being a single parent, and starting my career at the same time. If anything prepared me for lean days ahead, that experience and many of the life lessons learned in the process were central to the early survival of my firm.

Nevertheless, I need to add a disclaimer for entrepreneurs thinking about going solo—like the guy who drunkenly complained about obstacles never anticipated—which is that for all my training, I picked the worst @#$^&* day in history up to that date to open up shop. My very first day of business was none other than October 19, 1987, aka Black Monday, the very same day that the Dow nose-dived 508 points, a devastating drop that, at the time, rocked financial markets across the globe.

Talk all you want about adversity building character, this was not my idea of a good sign. But there I was. So, hitting the anvil with my stack of business cards and my telephone, I reminded myself every day of the old lessons that the cavalry ain't coming (see Lesson #3) and that baby steps count, too (Lesson #5). As frugal as I was with the start-up money that had been given to me by one of my most generous mentors, pretty soon it had dwindled to almost nothing. It was time to reach out to another potential investor. On the day of our appointed meeting, for reasons that I don't remember, I forgot one of the most basic marketplace rules: *be punctual*. Ironically, I'd mastered that one years earlier, to the point that I was sometimes overly early rather than not being on time.

To my own dismay, and that of my prospective investor, I arrived in his office twenty minutes late. He did what I would have done in his place. He turned me down. He said, "Son, if I can't expect you to be on time, I can't expect you to make timely decisions with my money." From that day forward, I have worn a wristwatch on each wrist, to make sure that I never forget the time or the basics that are as important now as they were when I was starting out.

Not only that, I now make it a habit to be aggressively early—fifteen minutes at the least—to appointments. I've discovered that folks will, if possible, see you earlier than planned. That has proven so successful, I have recently taken to padding in thirty minutes extra when I'm en route to a meeting—which gives me more opportunities to connect to individuals who may wish to tell me about their pursuits. No rush, no anxiety—just enhancing the potential of making friends before needing friends.

None of this was in the works yet when I arrived late to that memorable meeting. At that point, I was in full-blown survival mode. Since my five-year-old son and baby daughter were staying with relatives while I arranged living quarters and set up shop, I had all the incentive in the world to make good on my new venture so that we could be reunited. Failure wasn't an option. If it meant scrimping and saving, no problem. If it meant making do on oatmeal, so be it. Besides, who needs food when you can boil oats and water? But then, as things started to inch forward, I came home to a five-day pay-or-quit notice on the door.

Well, I'd handled a cash flow shortfall before, so I wasn't worried. But before I could call someone, move some things around, and buy some time, my phone got turned off. Just to repeat—there's a five-day pay-or-quit on the door, no real food, no sleep, oatmeal running low, and my #!$%!?? phone gets turned off!

This was what I'd call "think fast" time. A stockbroker with no telephone? How does that work? It doesn't! In thinking fast, I had to go through my mental Library of Resources, pull out every bold memory of something that I'd done or learned before, or that I had heard about someone else doing.

In the process, I remembered hearing a story back when I was at

Dean Witter and was given some fantastic pointers from a much respected broker by the name of Gary Abrahams. As someone who embodied boldness, Gary had motivated me at the start of my career just by the way he walked into the room and commanded attention without saying a word—simply with a disarming smile, piercing eye contact, and impeccable, razor-sharp attire and grooming.

Having done very well for Dean Witter, Gary was sent in the late 1970s to develop business in the Las Vegas area. Instead of hanging out a shingle and waiting for customers to come to him, or going after clients who were doing business with other brokerages, Gary did something much bolder. For a broker of his stature and for most brokers, it was almost unheard of. He had noticed out in the Las Vegas suburbs that there were big million-dollar homes being built, which was then a fortune. So he decided to get out and meet the buyers by going door-to-door. Nobody at the senior levels of the competing brokerages was going door-to-door, but Gary Abrahams did.

Instead of seeing that as something that only a rookie would do or as below him, Gary put on his best blue suit, looking like more than a million bucks, and went out to hit his anvil by knocking on doors and introducing himself to the owners who had just moved in. I never forgot hearing that story and how he shook their hands, handed them his card, and explained, "I'm new here in town with Dean Witter and I don't know if I could ever be of service, but keep my card in case, and if I ever can be of assistance in any way, I'd love to talk to you." That eventually led him to create a massive amount of business in Nevada.

As I recalled that story some years after hearing it, there was no question in my mind but that I had to deal with the fact that I had no telephone in the boldest possible manner by following the example of Gary Abrahams. First, I put on my best and only blue suit, then went out and knocked on doors. In Chicago, in the wintertime. Without appointments. I went and showed up in the offices of every viable contact on my list. Just about everyone welcomed me in. I was able to pitch a retirement plan at a fund director's office, then reviewed options for growth with pension fund administrators at a couple of corporate head-quarters, and toward the end of this process I went over to see some of the principals at the City of Chicago who were open to what my exper-tise could do for them. Every meeting was productive, each concluding with a nod and a request for me to follow up soon. Instead of embar-rassing myself by having folks call only to discover that my phone had been cut off, I had actually improved my prospects by making personal contacts with my potential clients. Nobody seemed to think it odd or beneath me that I was showing up and knocking on their doors. No one else on Wall Street was doing that, so I was well ahead of the game.

Within one day, boldness and the basics led to payoff, giving me time in the interim to scramble and do whatever I needed to do to get the phone turned back on. Business began to slowly build, and pretty soon I was off and running. Resilience had won the day.

Flash-forward to the present day for a moment. Picture my reaction as I'm walking over to a book-signing table after finishing up a speech, when suddenly I spot Gary Abrahams. A little bit older, a little grayer, even in retirement he was still unmistakable, except that this was the first time I'd ever seen him without a suit. Even so he was just as regal. As a crowd gathered, I was finally able to publicly express my gratitude for what he had inspired in me twenty-some years earlier—not without shedding a joyful tear or two, as did Gary.

The moral of that story and of these back-to-basics lessons is that the marketplace rarely turns a blind eye to boldness. It also reminds me that the sweetest successes can be those that demanded more of us than we knew we had in us to give. And on that point I should finally answer the third question that began this lesson—when was I able to breathe easier and believe that this start-up of mine was going to make it over the long haul?

Well, I have to say that the most exciting milestone for me was about two years into the endeavor when I bought my first fax machine. In those days, that was becoming one of the tools of the trade that everybody had already turned into a verb. More and more, I'd been hearing things like, "Hey, can you fax me a contract?" or "I'll fax you my info," and I couldn't keep running down to use other businesses' fax machines forever.

Once I brought that baby home, every time I heard the electronic fax sound go off, I would celebrate. In fact, as my staff grew, we would all cheer; and I'd be the one crowing the loudest. That's been a mainstay of my business, as it has flourished—that we celebrate the small and large victories.

What's your version of a fax machine? What milestone will let you know that you're making progress? If it doesn't come to mind readily, think back to earlier milestones that you've celebrated. Much to my delight I was reminded of the power of the fax machine when a letter arrived not long ago from a gentleman who recalled meeting me when he was with the National Association of Securities Dealers. He had been on hand for one of the first audits—another milestone for my fledgling company—and could remember "books and records up against the wall" and how every time the fax machine went off I turned to him and his colleagues and pointed out, "You hear that? That's the sound of money coming in!" What gave me the biggest smile and hugest belly laugh was how he went home and told his wife that same night that he ought to come and work for me, since I was undoubtedly on my way.

That's the power of a milestone that signals success not only to you but to others. It's whatever allows you to do your version of Kool Moe Dee and ask everyone, "How you like me now?" It's whatever lets you sing "Hallelujah" and "Praise the Lord" your way.

To this day, I refuse to give up the office fax. Sometimes, when great goals are met and deals are closed, I have even been known to throw confetti and dance down the sidewalk.

You can too. And don't forget the parade! Why not?

Oh, and there is one advisory I should tack on here about how to engage the power of resilience using one of the three As—*autonomy,* the capacity to choose for yourself. My objective in that choice was simple: to be my own boss in a business that I loved. It was something that I loved so much I would have done it for free (and did for a while). And I should also mention that I agree with whoever said, "You're not an entrepreneur until you've had to make payroll out of your own pocket."

Wherever you are, if you're bold enough and resilient enough to go back to basics, you're probably ready to venture out where you've never gone before. If you are considering veering off on that road less traveled for yourself, my further advice is that doing it your way, on your terms, requires the recognition that your ass is on the line. Not so much your money, but your energy, passion, joy, dreams, and desires. Are you ready to do that while taking the long view, understanding that success will come and go, that you'll be down and up, flush and strapped? With the ebbing and flowing, are you prepared to be constant with your own oceanic persistence—being your own tide that rises and falls, comes and goes, moving forward, backing away only to come forward, again, again, and again?

Are you that bold?

LESSON #24
Supply and Demand Ain't Rocket Science

KEYWORD: *Marketing*

Everybody's selling something.

That is another stone-cold rule of the marketplace that's been engraved on clay tablets since the invention of language. You probably are well aware of this truth, but it's important to consider again, especially whenever you gear up to launch a new venture or even a new attitude. If you didn't learn it when you were growing up, or managed to tune out media marketing and messages, or decided to stay above the fray, it has probably gotten to you anyway. Maybe it came as a rude awakening or as something that you heard before but didn't want to believe. Or it could have come as a reconfirmation of what you already knew. Anybody who earns part of their education on the streets knows this rule backward and forward. From the alleys of the 'hood where I grew up to the meaner sidewalks of the bigger cities, to Wall Street, up and down Fifth Avenue and onto the Champs-Élysées, the laws of supply and demand are no different—everybody's got their hustle. When I say "hustle," I'm not suggesting any kind of con job or folks trying to put something over on others. I mean that they're working hard to provide whatever they've legitimately got to offer on the supply side of the equation—goods, services, charm, intimidation, religion, politics, information, hope, motivation, challenge, and so forth.

Let me repeat myself, and this you can take to the bank: *everybody's selling something.* That's the essence of this lesson, *Supply and demand ain't rocket science.* It has applications from the cradle to the grave, and answers numerous questions about how to make your way in the marketplace—whether you're starting out or you're already on the Forbes 400.

What you're selling could be, and often is, something lofty, revolutionary, and unique—an idea, a vision, a dream, or a transformational, practical solution for a most pressing issue. Even the saintly Mother Teresa, who dedicated her life to healing and lifting up the poor, sick, and homeless, had to become a brilliant saleswoman to raise money and awareness for the cause that was so much larger than herself. She had to put on her best blue suit and go knock on doors to sell others as to why they needed and wanted to contribute to her cause.

Her story first caught my interest when I learned that her journey to become beatified by the Catholic Church—as "Blessed Mother Teresa" after her death—began early in her life in Albania when she made the choice to serve God as a missionary. To find what she referred to as "the call within the call," she traveled thousands of miles with several stops before she came to Calcutta and spent a year of homelessness herself. Through that process, she was given permission by the Vatican to establish her own missionary. From those beginnings, Mother Teresa started with thirteen members of her own order in India. Established in 1950, it grew into a global charity with more than six hundred missions that today house schools, orphanages, and hospices, serving the most needy citizens of the world. To make that a reality, she had to be a businesswoman, too.

As a fund-raiser, Mother Teresa had to figure out what exactly she was selling that would get the attention of her prospective contributors—clearly and concisely—but most of all, she had to find something compelling about what was in it for them. She could make her case for the dire need of the poor. Or she could make a case for why her funders might need to help her. To do that, as in all successful marketing matters, she had to know her audience, as we all must learn to do, regardless of our pursuits.

Mother Teresa explained how this worked by often telling the story about how a chairman of a multinational company came to her to say he was interested in buying a property in Bombay for her. But first he asked, "Mother, how do you manage your budget?"

Mother Teresa's response was to ask who had sent him to meet with her.

He admitted, "I felt an urge inside me."

Mother Teresa told him, "Yes, other people like you come to see me and say the same. It was clear God sent you, just as he sent the others, and they provide the material means we need for our work. The grace of God is what moved you. You are my budget."

This example is a reminder that even if you are not in any form of sales or marketing per se, you're selling something. And if you do claim the title of salesman or saleswoman, you shouldn't have to apologize for what you do. Every pursuit must be marketed, if only to yourself. That rule is woven into the fabric of society. We're all selling something. You sell, I sell. Or, like my mentor Marshall Geller once said—if you're not selling something, then you ain't in the game!

Let me quickly add that by the laws of supply and demand, if everybody's selling something, then everybody is buying something, too. If not, life as we know it would come to an end, and the world would stop turning on its axis. The application is that the more you practice wearing both your buying and selling hats, the more you sharpen all your skills. In short—the better buyer you are, the better seller you are. Vice versa. The more you recognize what appeals to you as a buyer, the more you'll know what you've got to offer as a seller—that is, what's in it for your customers.

Back in my early days of cold calling, one of the first things that I learned was not to try to talk someone into buying something she or he did not want to own. Instead, my R&D was to find out what the potential buyer was already buying. By the dictates of supply and demand, I could increase likelihood of making a sale by following a simple adage—*Sell 'em what they're buying.*

You can turn cartwheels and somersaults letting folks know how great your product is, but if you're selling oranges and they're buying apples, you're at a disadvantage. So you procure some apples, and now you're in business. But wait, they're buying produce from someone else. Why should they buy your apples and not your competitor's? You then go to your well of resources and assets that you offer on the supply side and hope to increase your chances of getting a piece of their apple business. Yet again Uncle Joe was a step ahead in teaching me that if you made friends before you needed friends, they'd be the first to try your apples.

There's a second part of this lesson, which is what we learn from supply and demand about what to do with all those oranges you've got sitting around. The question you want to ask is—*who is already buying them?* Once you answer that, you need to find out *where* the orange buyers are. That's the other twist on supply and demand—you gotta *go where they are.* You get up and go to where they're buying what you've got.

So, as you can see, supply and demand really isn't rocket science. Except now comes the application of the lesson in real-world terms. In the early days of launching my own business, these laws weren't so clear-cut. For one thing, I was just me going up against vastly more established names and brands. So what could I do from a marketing standpoint that could be compelling to folks who never heard of me? I started with what I had in my hand—my name—and then added another fictitious name that had its own appeal. Actually, I borrowed the last name of one of my business heroes, Marc Rich. With no connection to him actually, the result was Gardner Rich & Company! To me, it gave the feeling of a brokerage that was classic and established, yet hip. Luckily, no one ever asked to speak to my partner, Mr. Rich.

The more challenging concern in terms of supply and demand was that Gardner Rich & Company (me) had the crazy idea to grow wealth for underserved individuals and communities—which included African American individual investors, minority-owned and -run businesses, educators, union members, and government employees. The mechanism for that was to cultivate the market that would create the demand. It all came down to educating the decision makers at the institutional level about why they needed me in addition to the vendors and firms they were buying from. In those days, the people with the power of the purse who oversaw pension funds and the like went through money managers—the intermediaries—who dealt with the stockbrokers and investment analysts. I believed it would be advantageous to the shareholders to bypass the money managers and buy direct—from us guys who were doing the actual trading—for a couple of reasons. My expertise was one reason. Even more important, I cared. The personal connection to teachers, union workers, minorities, and community organizers came straight from my background. Through my actions and how I communicated, they understood that their business was important to me.

Perhaps you've faced a similar situation when you were pretty much evenly matched with your competition as you vied for the same sale, job, or opportunity. What gives you the edge over your competitor when you're each good at what you do? At certain levels of the different industries, it's often the case that everyone is qualified and reputable. Much of the time, though not always, the margin of victory goes to whoever shows they care the most about the potential client or the business in question. But how do they know who cares the most? Marketing! Getting in the door in Chicago meant overcoming the attitude "Don't bring me nobody who wasn't sent by somebody."

Fortunately, the idea to not go through the money managers appealed to my prospective buyers. In practice, it would require going against the grain in a major way. Because there was no model for me to duplicate or replicate, no map or path to follow, that gave me only one option—to start whacking, to blaze my own trail and never look back. It would work, I knew, if I conquered the first hill fast enough; because as soon as word got out, I knew that the followers would arrive. By their nature, the imitators were just going to where the buyers were and doing what they saw working. The trick was to have changed the game by the time the followers arrived.

By the time everyone turned around and realized what we were doing, I had enlisted my first two institutional clients—the National Education Association and its more than 3 million members and 1.5 million members of the California Public Employees Retirement System.

Nobody could believe it. How had such a thing been possible? Well, I would explain, it wasn't rocket science. Marketing 101: Know your audience.

However you choose to apply your own lessons about how the laws of supply and demand can be used to your advantage in the marketplace, don't forget that the best audience for checking out your wares is you. If you were a stock, what kind of an investment would you be willing to make on yourself? If you were a prospective employer, what do you bring to the table that would be of interest to you?

If you feel that the marketplace just doesn't get what you're trying to sell, switch hats and go shopping. You don't have to buy a thing. But in the process of seeing what's out there, you might be inspired to see what's moving where. And that's the beauty of this lesson that the marketplace is never static. Neither should you be!

LESSON #25
Truth Is a Hit

KEYWORD: *Authenticity*

Every now and then a marketplace lesson comes along that defies conventional wisdom and turns all the other rules and laws upside down on their heads. Such was my experience when I started to test the waters in public speaking. At first, following what I knew of supply and demand, it seemed to me that the market was glutted and that nobody was out crying in the streets over the lack of enough public speakers. On top of that, many heavy hitters at the speakers bureaus advised me that before ever taking my show on the road, I would need to consult with acting and media coaches, speechwriters, and even wardrobe experts. Wardrobe experts? Me?

None of this interested me in the least, not to mention the fact that I loved my day job and planned on keeping it. But doing my R&D, I decided to hear what the experts had to say. The input was valuable, yet the more I thought about the suggestions that were being offered, the more uncomfortable I became. The mere idea of coming across as canned, rehearsed, or packaged made me miserable. Then I remembered reading a quote by George Wallace, the former governor of Alabama, that gave me a starting place. Yes, I know that the two of us never had much in common, but that didn't mean that I couldn't learn from him. The point that I recalled him making about effective communication was that you have to keep your message so low that a goat could get at it. Lowest common denominator.

I was also given terrific advice from the brilliantly gifted Bebe Winans, a gospel singer, actor, and minister, who insisted that the only thing that counted in any public presentation was to come from your heart and to only speak on what you are truly passionate about. Something else to keep in mind, he added, was the fact that the audience was hearing everything for the first time. Just remember, Bebe said, "They're new and it is true."

Between those two very different individuals and their wisdom, I was able to employ another one of the three As—*authenticity*—and just be myself, dispelling the need to live up to any artificial marketplace image of what an aspirational speaker should be. Three years later, I'm happy to report the essence of this lesson—*The truth is a hit!*

The original teacher of that lesson and the source of those words is the legendary Berry Gordy, founder of Motown Records. When I first went into business for myself, he was one of the only role models I could find who had proven that when it comes to selling to the general marketplace, *it's not about black or white, it's about green.* From his earliest days in the music business, Berry Gordy was the first person to ever defy those who believed that supply and demand would prevent buyers in the white market from buying records made by black artists.

When Gordy published his memoir, *To Be Loved: The Music, the Magic, and the Memories of Motown,* I jumped on an airplane and flew to Detroit for the launch of his book tour. It was important to me to stand in line for as many hours as necessary to have my book signed, simply so I could shake his hand and say, "Thank you."

The independent music business was in its infancy in 1959 when Berry Gordy borrowed eight hundred dollars from his family's investment savings club to produce his first record. Within three short years, he and his fledgling company had taken that running start and, without any precedents, were consistently hitting the top of the charts—with everyone from Smokey Robinson, Stevie Wonder, Marvin Gaye, and the Temptations, to Diana Ross and the Supremes—until Motown had come to dominate the culture of the times. And for many Americans, the music became the soundtrack of our lives.

From a marketing standpoint alone, how does that work? How did they do it? One of the ways they defied the odds, Berry Gordy wrote, was as a team made up of the best of the best from all divisions of record making and all ethnic backgrounds, unified by passion born out of living with "rats, roaches, soul, guts and love." They also broke through thanks to a Gordy guiding principle that authenticity—everything that makes you *you*—is something that audiences hear and embrace because "The truth is a hit."

He meant that on many levels. It was partly his version of "tell it like it is." When Motown was starting out and struggling, for example, Gordy complained that everybody else was writing the same old tired love songs. Why not do something different? He decided to start with the truth about what was most on his mind—the need for cash flow and hits to support his growing company and family. Such was the thinking that led to his 1960 chart-topping single "Money (That's What I Want)," recorded by Barrett Strong.

It was outrageous in that era to be so up front about wanting money more than love, but it came from a place of humor and truth, and turned out to be a transformational hit.

Berry Gordy was also emphatic about creative authenticity across the board, insisting that if something real and true was happening in the grooves of the vinyl records, the public at large was going to relate and embrace the truth, too. "The hits are in the grooves" was the A&R motto. But even before laying down the tracks, Gordy continually reminded songwriters to tell true stories from their lives. Whether it was Smokey Robinson's "Tears of a Clown," Norman Whitfield's "Papa Was a Rollin' Stone" (recorded by the Temptations), or Stevie Wonder's "Living for the City," the truth of those emotions that came from real-life stories made for supersmash hits—around the globe.

Gordy was such a stickler for authenticity that when he received a phone call from Marvin Gaye in the early 1970s and heard that Marvin wanted to do a protest album for his next project, he was sure that it was a big mistake. He tried to persuade Marvin to stay in his successful groove with the soulful, romantic songs that had been surefire hits for him—"Stubborn Kind of Fellow," "How Sweet It Is," and "If I Could Build My Whole World Around You." Marvin refused to listen, insisting that he didn't care if his new, more serious work didn't sell. Yes, it was different, but no less authentic. Berry Gordy later said that Marvin taught him a new version of his own lesson when they released "What's

Going On" and it became an anthem song for a generation and an album with songs like "Mercy, Mercy Me" and "Save the Children" that came to define Marvin Gaye more than any other work he did.

Berry Gordy also demonstrated the principle that truth, in terms of honesty and integrity, made good business sense—a maxim that has been proven correct for me time and again. The most telling thing about his memoir was that the title he chose came from one of his first hits as a songwriter, before he had founded Motown. The song, "To Be Loved," recorded by Jackie Wilson in 1958, revealed the essence of Berry Gordy, before any of his major success had arrived, and gave the most authentic reason for his motivation to make music: "To be loved, to be loved, Oh what a feeling to be loved!"

Following Berry Gordy's example, we all can be inspired to see that there is everything to be gained from honoring the truth of why you've chosen your particular pursuit of happyness. That's what was discovered by a retired military chaplain whose work was brought to my attention. After leaving the military, he decided to continue to do God's work by ministering to the dying and their families in hospice care settings. When he wrote a book to share his unique spiritual and practical approach that had been so effective in his work, he faced extensive rejection from agents and publishers. No matter how many times he changed his manuscript to be like the other books out there—following all the marketing steps recommended at publishing business seminars—he couldn't find an opening in the marketplace for what he had to offer. Finally, he realized that he had strayed from his purpose to speak from his heart and expertise, and to give comfort and guidance during one of life's toughest passages. He then rewrote the book in keeping with his authentic approach and his truth. The kicker? The chaplain got an agent who sold his book to a midsized publisher, and he signed a deal for a follow-up book to boot. In the meantime, when he asked for advice about public speaking, I assured him that he already had all the right stuff.

This lesson is one of those that lots of folks find somewhat obvious.

You most certainly have been advised in your life at different times about the importance of being yourself. Maybe you tossed it off as overly general. If so, it may deserve a second look. What about those times when you've got to stand up and make a presentation, even at work or in another familiar setting, that somehow makes you break out in hives just thinking about it? You'd be surprised to know that some of the world's most famous performers panic over the idea of public speaking. If you can remind yourself to come from your heart, your soul, and your truth, you will not only get past the nerves but you'll be a hit!

If the idea of being yourself still seems simplistic or overstated, I need to mention that a lot of us who find ourselves on unfamiliar turf try out of reflex to be somebody else to fit in—acting out an almost cartoon version of who we think we're supposed to be. There are the rocket scientists who don't have an urban bone in their bodies but try to be rap stars. There are the hip-hop baby moguls who suddenly want to quote Nietzsche. And then there are the women who are twice as smart as all the men around them who try to dumb themselves down. That makes no sense. Women are so naturally powerful, in their gifts of intuition, patience, and persistence, it has surprised me how they sometimes shortchange themselves by pretending to not be so bright, but then play up their sex appeal or feminine frailty. Besides, when it's authentic, I believe that smart is the new sexy!

I'm asked often what to do when there seems to be absolutely no demand for the thing that you're selling, as heartfelt and authentic as it is. At what point should you throw in the towel and admit that it's not what the marketplace needs or wants?

My answer is that the marketplace doesn't know squat. Example? I've got two words: "Pet rock."

Who ever needed a pet rock? Nonetheless, the inventor and marketer of pet rocks, advertising executive Gary Dahl, had the authenticity and originality to come up with it; and he became an overnight millionaire with a product that was all the rage for one six-month Christmas selling season.

How about that Rubik's Cube? Of course, I have a great personal affection for and connection to the machinations and challenges of the Rubik's Cube. But thirty-some years ago, nobody in the world was clamoring to buy a mind-bending puzzle to twist and agonize over its billions of combinations (a quarter of a trillion according to our research). That didn't stop Erno Rubik, a Hungarian-born sculptor, architect, and university professor who had developed it back then. Within a decade, the authenticity had been such a hit that over 100 million cubes had been sold, with many more times that since then.

Erno Rubik certainly didn't set out to invent something that nobody needed or to create a product that would sell in the hundreds of millions. What guided him was his fascination with the use of space, a multidimensional design with moving parts, and how those dynamics impact human beings. Nobody needed another puzzle until he came along and added his version to the mix.

Unfortunately, Rubik didn't cover his assets and never made a dime from his invention. Of course, that's another lesson. On that score, when you invent something that is the essence of you and your brand, you may pardon my French when I tell you that if you don't pee on it and mark it like a dog, I pity poor you. Rubik lost out on any profit because he didn't mark his creation with a copyright to make it his own.

Even so, the application of this marketplace lesson still holds: truth wins.

LESSON #26
Learn the Ropes First, Then Conquer Rome
KEYWORDS: *Discipline/Character*

What are employers looking for? This is a subject that comes up in many settings.

The top attribute most named by employers is passion. That's the coin of the realm. Folks know when you've got it or not. It comes from who you are, and it can't be bought, sold, taught, or acquired. It's like the color of your eyes. After passion, a number of different assets come up that many employers find valuable. Foremost on my list after passion are the related qualities of discipline and character. Although recommendations and education are indicative of the potential for those attributes, for a truer picture, while interviewing candidates I listen to the kinds of questions a prospective employee asks me. That tells me a lot about someone's level of curiosity as well as his or her potential to get the most out of on-the-job training and that person's willingness to learn the ropes.

Let me give an example. In 2004, I had the opportunity to interview three candidates for two positions at Gardner Rich & Company. The first candidate was very impressive—with an Ivy League bachelor's degree, terrific grades and scores, no direct experience in investment but with strong recommendations in related fields. The second candidate hadn't been to college and had no experience but had been raised working in his family's retail business and had actually invested some money in the stock market to start his savings for college. The third candidate was ideal on paper—top business schooling and a versatile work background including a stint at a prestigious brokerage firm, plus he was the son of a business associate.

During the interview process, the first candidate asked how much phone work was involved in the job? Clearly, he wasn't crazy about being on the phone. That should have been my first clue. Nonetheless, I hired him on the basis of his recommendations only to find out that he couldn't overcome his fear of taking calls or making them. I offered to teach him the ropes, but he couldn't get past his nerves. He had a future in research but not in an area that we were involved in. He gave his notice without having to be let go.

The third candidate was not shy in the least. No matter what I asked him, he had all the answers. Then it became apparent that all of his questions were ways for him to drop all the big names in the business world that he knew. When I mentioned that, yes, I knew so-and-so, it turned out this young man didn't know him at all. He was much more interested in perks, company travel, and, basically, how soon he could have the corner office.

The second candidate, the youngest of the three, won me over in the interview by asking if I had heard about a new tech stock he'd been reading about. Of the questions that I asked him, if he didn't have an answer, he would say so and ask me to clarify what I had meant. I hired him on the spot. That was Sal (Salvador Guerrero), who has been with the company ever since; he not only had the discipline to learn the ropes from the start but no sooner would I explain something than he would be off and running, putting it into action before I had to ask for that next step. I have seen the strength of his character through that discipline time and again. When we offered to put him through college and business school, he deliberated seriously and then came to the conclusion that he could learn as much where he was.

The lesson to me in recognizing how much I value discipline and character today is remembering myself at earlier stages when those concerns weren't always priorities for me. Like everyone else, when I was starting out I had my eye on the rock stars of the industry, and my intention was to get where they were, as fast as possible. Thankfully, the structure of the marketplace prevented me from doing that without first acquiring the knowledge needed to ascend to the next place. As it so happens, that structure is ancient, going back to the seafaring days when commanders of sailing vessels had to make sure that new recruits were trained correctly to know how to tie the different knots and how to tell which ropes lifted which sails. There was a precise order for learning the ropes, such that if the sequence wasn't followed, the ship would not sail.

Along those lines, when studying what it is that causes a career to run aground or to float, often you can see what important steps were taken and which were ignored. In hindsight, I'm grateful that I had mentors willing to tell me to pace myself or not to be too cool for school, and to avoid shortcuts so that I could get to that corner office lickety-split. I also had the benefit of watching how the fast-track mentality sank some very talented, promising individuals. I think of the excesses of the 1980s, in particular, when a lot of folks definitely went overboard. And those who didn't get taken down either had some discipline or were just fortunate.

I'd venture to say that in many industrial accidents where human error has been involved, someone or a group of people tried to take shortcuts. In the financial world, many of the booms that turned to busts were the result of get-rich-quick schemes that skipped steps and that should have been obvious to smarter people. You can see that in the crash at the end of the 1980s, the Enron debacle, the dot-com bust, and, indeed, in the dynamics of the subprime mortgage fiasco that contributed (among other factors) to the global economic meltdown of recent times. With a wanton disregard for consequences, Wall Street perpetuated the "HIV of finance" that has now infected the central nervous system of the global economy.

Not everyone got caught up in the free-for-all that was always a disaster waiting to happen. There were many cooler heads, like those of us in the smaller financial services companies, community banks, and other more self-contained business entities that stayed out of the bad debt betting game by minding our knitting. We kept pounding the anvil of business that we knew, and had the discipline to avoid the temptation of "get rich quick." Not so with our counterparts among the supermarkets of the Wall Street financial institutions, where greed and excess trumped sound fiscal judgment. To put it bluntly, they were pigs. How? Why? Well, it's as simple as observing that your competitor is dealing in high-risk products, gaining market share and earning enormous amounts of money, and choosing to get in on the same game. The rationalization is that if you don't offer your clients the same or even "better" products, you'll be at a strategic disadvantage. It takes discipline and character to say, "No thank you, I'll stick to the anvil," and to deal with the consequences if you lose some of your clients who want in on that action. When you've learned the ropes and come up the hard way, it's easier to recognize the pitfalls of what could happen—and did happen—when the bill came due and there was hell to pay.

Of course, there are ambitious step skippers in every field of endeavor—those folks who don't want to stand at the back of the line, pay their dues, and work their way up, and some who think they're entitled to take the shortcuts.

While it's true that nepotism is not dead and buried in the market-place, I've also seen the downfall of those who've been brought up to take over the family business but who didn't want to learn the ropes. Maybe you know that person who wants the frills but not the responsi-bility of being in charge, guys or gals with that silver spoon who assume because they've been around and picked up on the lingo, as well as the policies, they've got it down and know all they need to know. Ships of state have been sunk and businesses have been ruined when captains have taken over before proving themselves seaworthy.

No doubt we've all met those fast-trackers and hotshots who fly up in the ranks of whatever they pursue with drive, charisma, and an unrelenting will to win. They're impressive, attractive, and dangerous when they have not spent time learning not just how to get ahead but what their values are and what they stand for. Talent is dazzling, but if individuals aren't grounded in a sense of discipline and character, their ride is destined to be short-lived. We've all seen the extreme cases of burnout when the sports industry throws massive contracts at rookies, not giving them time to learn everything they need to mature, to heed the advice of others. The pressure of having all that attention, freedom, money, and fame—sometimes before barely stepping onto the playing field—can be overwhelming.

Michael Vick, formerly number 7 of the Atlanta Falcons, who went on to wear a different number as an inmate at a correctional facility, is a most unfortunate case of not learning the ropes and applying the dis-cipline of a world-class athlete that is required for becoming a world-class person. That would have come if he'd been willing to learn from his own trials and errors. It would have helped if he had entrusted himself to the guidance of others who could have let him know that athletic skills, without qualities like decency, integrity, and character, do not a happy life make. I believe he would have been spared his demise if he had learned that decisions in life must be pursued with the same discipline applied on the field. There is something to be said as well for having the discipline and character to cut loose from the folks, no matter who, when it's apparent that they're going nowhere on their own. Perhaps his career might have continued to progress if he had broken those toxic ties that bind. End of that story.

Although you, too, can probably find as many outside examples as I've offered for why it's important to first learn the ropes and then go conquer Rome, I hope that you'll apply this lesson for yourself. We hear so often that it's not how often you fall but how fast you get up. I also think that it's not how fast you get to the top but how much wisdom you attain on the way. With discipline and character, you can savor the true fruits of success.

As an entrepreneur in charge of where my ship is headed, I like this lesson in particular because it's a reminder that our victories, large and small, belong to everyone onboard—like Sal. Only the errors and faults belong to me and me alone. I own them. I accept and use them, and learn from them. And then I let 'em go and set 'em free in order to sail further, higher, faster. In the words of Dr. Maya Angelou, "And still I rise."

LESSON #27
Who's Who at the Office and in
Your Spheres of Influence?
KEYWORD: *Networking*

Besides being uncaring and unwelcoming to newcomers, the marketplace is crazy. It will turn any activity under the sun into a game you can play for money. In fact, all those fun games that we used to play as kids—you know, the ones like kick-the-can and hide-and-seek—can either be good training or accurate predictors of how you'll play the game as you make your way through the working world.

It turns out that an earlier lesson, *Who's who in your 'hood?*—which focused on trust issues (Lesson #16)—gave me portable knowledge in understanding the power of relationships in most every working or social environment that I've encountered. Indeed, trust, good faith, and general all-around people skills are essential ingredients in business dealings, negotiations, and especially for playing the vitally helpful marketplace game known as networking. Interestingly enough, when you have taken the time to identify key players in your early life's history, you may find it easier to identify who plays important roles in this expanded version that I call *Who's who at the Office and in your spheres of influence?*

Whenever buying and selling are involved, I've learned from this process that it's helpful to research the "Who's Who?" of the other party or parties in terms of chain of command. It's valuable to know who has the buying power but also who is second to that position. Frequently, that number two person can be your best ally. The working environment of an office also says a lot about the personnel. Just the way that you can get a vibe walking into someone's house about whether the family who lives there is functional or dysfunctional, the same can be detected in the workplace. There are sometimes even familial roles— like the father figurehead who only shows up to act like the boss or the mother of the office who really wields the power and makes the decisions. Of course, the gender can be the other way around, too. In the office setting, you might also spot some of the same stock characters you used to know back in your 'hood—the bully, the nerd, the hotshot, the nosy neighbor, the villain, and the wise counselor.

I'll bet that if you think of your current or recent work settings, you know exactly what I'm talking about. You might even consider that just as people are in your personal life for a reason, many individuals with whom you have mainly business or professional connections are also in your career journey to offer meaningful lessons to you. So that's a simple way to play the office version of "Who's Who?"

My uncle Joe Cook, who walked on foot from Mississippi to Wisconsin, first taught me about the importance of networking with his oft-quoted philosophy, "It's always best to make friends before you need friends." As a kid I took that to heart and started applying it at an early age. Fortunately, this wasn't a challenge, as I genuinely like people—and not just some people. I like people. Period.

Anyone who knows me will attest to that and can also tell you that I have a thing for remembering names. This isn't an innate capacity. Rather, it's a special interest that I've cultivated. Names are beautiful, distinctive, and personal, so I learned early on that remembering someone's name was a way to show respect to a fellow human being. And if I can remember the names of your mama, baby, and dog, too, I will! In the marketplace, whether selling or buying, using someone's name can help level the playing field. Many times I'm asked by someone who works in a service capacity, "How did you know my name?" Then they remember the name tag that they're wearing! Nobody wants to be treated like a nonentity or an extra on a movie set who plays the role of "woman in a crowd" or "cop #2." Everybody has a name.

If you feel that you lack people skills or don't know where to begin practicing the art of networking, start with the name game. Ask people their name, look them in the eyes, and shake their hands. And tell them your name. This is one of the oldest marketplace rules of the game out there and it works.

The other benefit of playing the "Who's Who?" game for even the most practiced of us, as I've learned, is that if I keep my ears open and pay attention to my instincts, I might discover something valuable. I might discover someone who'll be a friend, an associate, an introduction to a matter or person of interest, a partner, an employee, or an intern. Or that person might be connected in some way to someone else who might be all those things. That person might even be a pillar of an entire neighborhood—what my mentor Marshall Geller called a "sphere of influence."

When Marshall first introduced me to that term, it was long before such marketing strategies as networking had become popular, and way before social networking like Facebook and MySpace had come into being. Marshall gave me an example of who in our office was already in league with spheres of influence—including a vice president of the United States, the head of a state pension fund, plus individuals with stature and connection to more spheres. How could I do that, too? There were no specific steps to take. Marshall Geller had merely pointed me in the direction and suggested that I pay attention.

When learning the fundamentals of the marketplace, many folks get stuck even after they've done the work of reaching out to meet people outside of their familiar circles. They have a cell phone full of names and numbers or a shoebox full of business cards, but they don't know what to do next.

So, how do you grow your success with initial contacts? You stay on it. This all goes back to the lesson of hard work. You have to hit the anvil, do the follow-up, write the thank-you card, remember details, and remember names. Let me repeat: stay on it. If you're selling something and you want to beat the competition or introduce a product that you're excited about, that extra kindness, interest, and caring that you show may be the difference.

I heard a story about Donald, a real estate salesman in California, who was the only one left standing in his area after everyone else ran for the hills when the market started to soften. He had built his network of clients by making friends first, then cultivating relationships, checking in from time to time, attending their church suppers, their kids' Little League games, and patronizing their businesses. When it came time for those people to sell or buy a house, he was their go-to guy. Donald understood that when everybody is offering basically the same expertise, that added amount of caring seals the deal. And those clients tell a friend and they tell a friend. And so on.

A struggling accountant in New York back in the 1980s did something similar when he went around to all the comedy clubs and picked out the comics he thought were going to be big stars. He made each of them a deal: if he did their taxes for free, when they made it big and earned some decent money, they would hire him to manage it for them. Today he is one of the most sought-after business managers in the entertainment industry.

Whenever you're playing the game of "Who's Who?" it's a reminder to do more than develop marketplace relationships that may be mutually advantageous at some point. Of course, that's a terrific fundamental of networking and doing business in general. But the next step, all the more important, is to get to know who those individuals and business entities are. If you're preparing to become trading partners— whether you're buying or selling, representing or consulting, collaborating or competing—the more you know about a potential client's track record, the better the agreement you'll make together. The ability to trust and to be trusted is as crucial to business dealings as it is to personal relationships.

Networking teaches many lessons at different stages. I've certainly learned from several mistakes when I didn't follow my hunches or when I was naive about the "Who's Who?" of a particular venture. One episode in particular taught me about a component of networking and marketplace relationships that should be addressed by anyone who wants to play to win at the game. I'm referring to the expectation that whenever someone has scratched your back, you're going to be called upon to scratch theirs.

To put it more politely, when you ask someone for a favor—an introduction, a freebie, a string pulled on your behalf—you're going to owe a favor back and it can sometimes be called up at a time and place not of your choosing. That was made very apparent to me several years ago when a well-established financial institution was balking at paying my firm—for services and profits rendered—and I decided to bring in some juice in the form of a high-powered individual who carried more weight than we did at the time.

Even though my instincts told me that I should fight my own battles, I made no headway when I appealed to the chairman of the board of this outfit that owed my firm money. He shrugged me off. With that, I decided to let him know that I had connections and that I was going to be pulling strings through my network of who's whos. So I said to him at a conference meeting, with all the defiance I could muster, "Have you ever met Johnnie Cochran?"

"Uh, no," he said.

"Would you like to?" I glared at him.

Let me quickly add that I didn't know Johnnie Cochran or have any famous legal guns in my corner. So I asked a high-powered community leader whom I knew through other activists if he would help me seek justice and come with me to a showdown with those who had wronged me. When we arrived, I was ready to rumble, but he took the lead on my behalf, rose above the fray, and smoothed everything over; we left with the agreement that I'd receive 60 percent or so of what was owed to me.

It didn't occur to me that I had much in the way of a return favor to offer, although I was certainly in his debt. Not too much later, however, the bill came due when he asked me to provide some favorable quotes to the business media in regard to a financial venture he was spear-heading. I was happy to do it, but when articles ran linking us, I was stunned by the reaction from several of my clients who assumed that I was partnering with him and decided to take their business elsewhere. Unbelievably, I turned around and saw that I'd lost more than 50 percent of my accounts. I had to take a close look at what had just happened and whether the benefit that his favor had provided me was worth the loss when the bill came due. Or, as I refer to this moment of revelation: *Sometimes you gotta ask yourself, is the juice worth the squeeze?*

The networking analogy here is to think of that orange that you know is going to give you juice, but at what cost or at what amount of squeezing? So if someone represents the juice—a person who brings excitement, celebrity, and energy to your cause, or who can open doors, pull strings, and provide leverage for you—you must ask yourself how much of a squeeze that will entail for you.

At times the juice is definitely worth the squeeze. I've been amazingly blessed by those who have favored me with the greatest gifts of their wise counsel, sound advice, and strong support. Though they don't operate by a system of quid pro quo, they know that when and if I can offer the same to them, I do so or will do so in a heartbeat—at whatever the effort required.

My last advisory that goes along with lessons learned about networking and business relationships has to do with loyalty. I'm referring to the team that works with me every day, above and beyond the call of duty. In terms of winning marketplace games, the individuals on that team are the most valued players in my who's who at the office and in my spheres of influence. The trust and loyalty toward one another that we have cultivated over the years, together, has been a key part of our growth that we've sustained even in tougher economic waters.

You may have a team of your own that you feel similarly toward. If not, the entirety of this lesson may be just the encouragement you need to start identifying the "Who's Who?" among your support system. You might even consider these individuals as your primary stakeholders—from loved ones to allies or associates who benefit from your success directly or indirectly. It may be old-fashioned to ask what good is success without others to savor it with you, but I believe it's part of the equation of happyness. As you shift your thinking and your language from words like *me* and *mine* to an emphasis on *we* and *ours,* the juice you get from that effort will definitely be worth the squeeze.

LESSON #28
It Takes as Much Energy to Bag an Elephant as It Does a Mouse

KEYWORD: *Focus*

The essence of this lesson is very simple. In a nutshell, it teaches that you do not have to be an entrepreneur to think like one. That message had particular resonance for me when I was asked a question during a

Q&A session at a conference for cafeteria workers in my early days of public speaking. Many of the questions asked that day had more to do with the arc of my personal journey than the specifics of what I do for a living. So I was surprised when a woman who was probably in her early sixties strode up to the mic and asked, "How would you describe your management style?"

Well, that was a subject that I'd addressed before, but I hadn't expected it to come up in this setting. My assumption was that perhaps she was a supervisor and was looking for advice for the workplace. It turned out that, no, she was a line worker, rank and filer. Nonetheless, she was interested to find out what she could learn from me to apply to her work and to other areas of her life. Since she had read many books about business management and effective leadership strategies, she was curious as to what guiding principles or philosophies I used to inspire and motivate employees.

As I gave my answer to this impressive question, I found myself becoming inspired and motivated. What a gift for every child or teenager who slid their tray across her cafeteria line to be able to have someone like her keeping an eye on them.

My job as the head coach of my team, I explained, is to keep the focus. The power of focus, without a doubt, is often our most overlooked natural resource; when tapped, it has the strength to move mountains. So my other job as head coach is to help the members of my team identify their strengths and focus on them. And on an overall basis, I aspire to keep us focused in general. On what? On opportunities rather than challenges. Purpose rather than perks. Pursuit rather than pace. To maintain focus and marshal all of our forces to adopt a big-game mentality, the philosophy and slogan I developed was *It takes as much energy to bag an elephant as it does a mouse.*

In marketplace terms, this reminds all of us not to sweat the small stuff, to establish priorities. It's a gauge for how to use time wisely. After all, if the bigger goals end up taking the same time as the smaller ones, why not go big? Focus is also about concentrating your energies individually and collectively, about having an intensified presence in everything you do, and about how you come roaring onto the field with your power and drive. All those aspects of focus, I believe, were pivotal in Gardner Rich & Company's success at going big. And as we grew, with pockets of activity happening in multiple offices, this approach has helped unify our efforts that could otherwise drain us or pull us in too many directions.

The lesson keeps teaching itself as we continue to grow, setting a tone and an energy level throughout our operations that make the atmosphere more fully charged. Applying our interoffice motto even further, at one point I decided to strategically place bold reminders of elephants around the office—in a wall-sized photograph of a majestic African elephant, small statues, even screensavers.

When I related these details at the cafeteria worker conference to the very focused woman who asked the question, I could see by the way she nodded her head that she immediately understood the principle as a management style and as something she could apply for herself. At the same time, I recognized that not everyone in that audience had the same reaction. And that's okay, too. I hoped that, kind of like the punchline of a joke that doesn't hit you until you're halfway home, this was a lesson that could sneak up on folks later on.

The power of focus is something that has interested me not just as the CEO of a company but as the CEO of my personal pursuit of happyness. I think that it's fair to say that there can be a downside to the hyperfocus that many of us big-game guys and gals have in work-related matters. I'm the first to admit, not proudly, that beyond my personal commitment to my children, I've sacrificed the time and energy needed for sustaining long-term personal relationships. I'm working on it but don't want to sugarcoat the downside of focus or pretend to have much wisdom to offer in how to better balance the needs of work and home. In fact, with my travel schedule, whenever anyone asks me where home is, I have been known to answer, "United Airlines."

For anyone who seeks to be in a role of power and responsibility, there will be times when a big game mind-set may lead you to ponder the proverbial question, "Is it better to be loved or feared?" After much deliberation, I've finally learned the answer for myself: It is better to be loved—because if you are feared, you can never be loved. But when you are loved, you have nothing to fear! Such is my focus.

However you choose to apply the opportunity to focus your energy on what matters most to you—elephants rather than mice—in your career, your health, your peace of mind, your relationships, or any undertaking in which you seek out the best of yourself, I do have one piece of advice. Through much pain and deliberation, I have learned that when you choose to focus your every molecule on a pursuit, you have to sacrifice somewhere. With all the demands of your time taken up by many equally important matters, only family rules. Everything else can be sacrificed, but family is nonnegotiable, especially children. The bottom line for me is that all that other stuff is negotiable but not my son and daughter, who moved back to Chicago to be with me, not long after my company was up and running.

Besides the fact that Chris Jr. and Jacintha help me keep my focus on my life priorities, they also keep me grounded and humbled as a parent. Being my mother's son, I do put a premium on education and make every effort to participate as much as possible in their school activities—communicating with their teachers, staff, and yes, absolutely, the thoughtful, entrepreneurial, nurturing cafeteria workers who are part of the proverbial village raising all of our kids. I've also tried to include my children as part of the extended family of my company and to share some of my marketplace lessons with them. Case in point? Report cards. The key to doing well, as I told both of them when I wasn't pleased with their grades one year, is "Focus!" Oh, and I didn't fail to mention that it takes as much energy to get an A as it does anything below that.

Let me add one more note about this lesson as it applies to parenting. To my knowledge, there is no pursuit that is as humbling, challenging, rewarding, and frustrating as that of becoming a successful parent.

Many years ago, I was given great advice from a teacher who was offering suggestions for the best ways to respond to the upsets that come along with having adolescent children. She said simply, "Pick your battles." That, too, has been another spin on this lesson, and it has helped me to focus on loving my kids and being there for them. Sometimes focus is just that simple.

LESSON #29
Share the Wealth

KEYWORD: *Community*

Not long after I went into business for myself and set up shop in Chicago, I was taught a major lesson about how I could give of myself to others and make a contribution to the community at large. Up until that time, I had wrongly assumed that only someone financially very well-to-do could achieve the status of a real philanthropist.

My revelation came after a series of failed attempts to procure appointments with some of the most successful businesspeople in Chicago. Now, I understood that, hey, I was the new kid in town and these folks already had their top-tier investment professionals they were most likely content to keep giving their business to. My agenda at that time, however, was less about selling them my firm's services and more about asking for ten minutes of their time so that I could learn from their vast expertise. My interest wasn't only to find out how to navigate the Chicago business world, but also to discover how the success of Gardner Rich & Company could enrich the community. After all, if I was going to reap profits from local soil, I would want to replenish the ground that made the growth possible. In my logic, since many of these individuals were self-made and were probably once in my shoes when they launched their endeavors, they would be only too glad to share the wealth of what they learned.

Unfortunately, I was naive. Many of these very busy high-powered, self-made individuals didn't know me from Adam, and they didn't have ten minutes to spare. Undaunted, I showed up in many of their offices, where I introduced myself in person; and I received an abundance of great advice that I value to this day. But there was one gentleman who was a holdout. Not only that, but he was surrounded by a team of gate-keepers whose sole purpose, it appeared, was to tell me no.

Following my best playbook, after weeks of phone calls, I headed over to his headquarters to introduce myself in person but was stopped by the downstairs security guard. No one would be allowed to ride up the elevator to the executive suite unannounced. Of course, that made sense. So I asked the guard to call up and announce me. The answer came back directly from the top, from the head honcho himself, "Not available."

Feeling let down, to say the least, I decided to blow off some steam and go for a stroll in the neighborhood of Chicago's financial district with its tall, gleaming fortresses of power and success. I walked and walked, thinking about how I could choose to respond positively to the rejection I'd just experienced. The farther I walked, mulling over the situation, the more that I noticed the scenery start to change as I wandered into poor, forgotten neighborhoods there in the shadows cast by the towers of industry. On those streets, I saw reminders of myself—single parents, struggling, some who were possibly among white-collar or blue-collar working homeless or between places to stay. I saw young men and women who were no different from me when I was first starting out in the business, no doubt in search of opportunities to work hard and hit their anvils, while learning the fundamentals of their pursuit. And that's when I made one of the most important decisions of my adult career.

It came to me in a flash that as soon as my company was situated and secure, my door would be open to anyone who wanted ten minutes of my time. What had been a disappointment turned into the inspiration for where my headquarters was eventually located—in the heart of the financial district, on the ground level, and with all glass windows, too. If I couldn't be accessible to share my lessons for success with others, that wasn't success.

The revelation that sharing the wealth is about so much more than money was liberating. I decided that if I could make a contribution of my time to offer advice, I didn't have to wait for people to come calling on me. Instead, I created an internship program at our office for high school students to learn about Wall Street and financial literacy. Our policy is that we will pay tuition to college for those interns willing to work and learn consistently for two years, while maintaining their grades. By investing in the potential of young people of different backgrounds and neighborhoods in Chicago, my company benefits from the opportunity to put resources we've gained back into the soil. We also have discovered that many of the students who have gone on to college and then found work in the business world end up becoming clients and affiliates. Just as they have been mentored, they naturally go on to mentor others in their pursuits.

Let me recommend to fellow entrepreneurs and marketplace executives that if you haven't yet explored the benefits of being a mentor to give it a shot. The gift of your time to encourage someone who was once in your shoes will be repaid to you countless times over. The pride that I feel when a mother calls me after attending her son's or daughter's graduation from college after he or she interned at Gardner Rich & Company is more thrilling than I can describe. I'm also over the moon every time someone walks up to me on the street and says, "You don't remember me, but you gave me ten minutes of your time fifteen years ago," and then that person proceeds to tell me how he or she was able to make possible the impossible, and was now sharing that same wealth with others.

You may be a philanthropist already—giving to your community with your time and/or your wallet—and you know well how gratifying it is when you have the opportunity to give something that you once lacked and had to seek for yourself. If you have never considered the fact that you have wealth to share, the most immediate way to apply this lesson is to look at other contributions you could make that have nothing to do with money.

Then again, there's nothing wrong with putting your hard-earned cash where your heart is when you've got it to share. Back in my rookie days when hitting the anvil meant cold calling and then warming up leads for the more seasoned stockbrokers to close, I never forgot those few guys and gals who dug into their pockets and bought lunch for those of us on the front lines. I decided to pay that forward when I started to make some bucks. Years later, I still receive notes from Wall Street success stories who remember the hundred-dollar bill as well as the thumbs-up that I gave them way back when. "If you only knew how much I needed it at the time," they'll tell me. But of course I did know, having once been there, too.

Another way to share the wealth is to be open to others about the struggles that you have overcome to reach a high level of success— which is sometimes the most encouraging and inspiring thing you can do for those in the midst of their struggle. A fine example of that is my good friend Glenn Beck, the conservative radio and television talk-show host. We don't always agree politically, but I have immense respect for him as a person and for his generosity of spirit. A devoted family man, Glenn has openly talked about how he overcame a very difficult child-hood, and he has long championed several causes that were important to his empowerment. Whenever I'm reaching out to friends and col-leagues to contribute to a charity or organization that I believe in, Glenn is someone I can always count on to give generously, happily, and without a desire to be acknowledged for it.

One of my close colleagues, who happens to be Jewish, once told me that according to the tradition in which she was raised, there are eight levels of charitable giving. At the lowest level, your arm is twisted into writing a check. At the next to the highest level, you give gener-ously and anonymously, and the recipient doesn't know who gave the gift. But the very top level of sharing the wealth isn't about handing out money or material goods. It turns out that the greatest wealth you can share is when you give someone a job or do something to create an opportunity for that person to find employment, because you are preventing poverty from happening in the first place. Included in that practice is funding for education, which is vital to job creation. Along those lines, I am a committed proponent of providing scholarships to individuals in all underserved communities, along with grants to honor educators—who are heroes in every community.

Whenever you question what resources you have to share, as I once did, this lesson is a reminder that the smallest gift of time, consideration, kindness, advice, or direction that you give to one person can truly have a ripple effect that lifts the well-being of the entire community and of the marketplace. That's how we can all improve the general economy, believe it or not. Indeed, the wealth of knowledge and innovation will need to be shared, now more than ever, so that we can strengthen and revitalize our ailing sectors. We can and we should.

Yes, there may be those who want to hoard what they have, behaving as if it's a dog-eat-dog world and believing that you have to bury the competition to be a success in the marketplace. But new trends suggest those attitudes aren't working and are changing. Signs indicate that business alliances will soon act like old-fashioned trade guilds so that companies can work together to share the wealth of new technologies, boosting business for everyone. My friend Jonathan Tisch calls this new paradigm "cooperatition"—a blend of *cooperation* and *competition*. My belief is even more basic—everybody wins when everybody wins.

Sharing the wealth and caring about the community where you live as well as the global community is not complicated. It can be applied however you choose. Give what you've got. And don't wait. Start now. Right where you are.

Four / Your Empowerment Zone

One can have no smaller or greater mastery
than mastery of oneself.

—Leonardo da Vinci

An Introduction to Lessons #30 to #37—Life-Changing Lessons for Mastery

We all have our moments. Some have called them "aha" moments or peak experiences. Others describe their moments as major epiphanies that change their thinking and their lives. They recount almost an out-of-body moment that takes them from a place of "seeing through a glass darkly" to a new clarity and vision. What seems impossible in one moment suddenly becomes possible in the next.

My understanding is that these moments occur for all of us at significant stages of our growth when we are ready to change. So many of us find ourselves at the wall, when we've been hitting the anvil with all our might, wondering when we're finally going to break through to the other side. These moments open the gate and often seem to occur in a heightened state of awareness—as though in a quick visit to what I call an empowerment zone. They may also be sparked by teachers who are empowering or by the right lessons at the right time.

When I recall those kinds of turnkey experiences from earlier in my life, they stand out in my memory as learning breakthroughs—

brought about by life-changing lessons that enabled me to go further, faster, and higher. I remember them vividly as attention-getting moments, almost as if the universe was tapping me on the shoulder in a big way, presenting opportunities that required a new perspective.

Well, that's what's on the menu right now for this fourth type of lesson that we're about to unveil as we examine the life-changing moments that may have happened to us previously, or to others, or may have yet to happen in our lives. These are the lessons that take us to our next levels, after we've hit the anvil in our pursuits and are ready to learn the ropes of mastery—in whatever venue we dare to seek it.

There was a time in my life when I thought that it was only me who dreamed and dared to be world class in an arena of my choosing. Boy, was I wrong. Judging from the overwhelming interest that I hear from individuals of all ages who define their pursuit of happyness as a desire for mastery, I know for a fact that it's not just me. And that has made it incredibly inspiring to travel to so many distant and out-of-the-way places where I've met people who already know that it takes as much energy to bag an elephant as it does a mouse. They're playing at the top of their game, reaching for greatness, often against the odds, not resting on prior achievements or being satisfied with the status quo and the material trappings of success. They're reaching past what they even know they can do—to be world class at it and to be about something that adds value to the fabric of society.

I've witnessed many different interpretations of mastery—from those who work to achieve mastery in a particular venue, career, project, or art form, to those who have a focus to become world-class parents or world-class friends, to those determined to be world class for causes greater than themselves, or those whose quest is to simply be world-class people. Some I've encountered have dared to pursue mastery over an extraordinary challenge, whereas others have made the decision, once and for all, to attain mastery in a particular area of their life—like their finances, health, or their relationships. I've met superstars who have achieved greatness in one notable arena but are pushing themselves into entirely new pursuits. I've met a lot of people who are self-made masters but nobody's ever heard of them—and they don't care!

What do they all have in common? Well, for all their differences, my take is that all of these individuals have reached a level that has allowed them to enter their own empowerment zone. They know how to get into the heightened state of being in which masterpieces are created. It's the same zone that five hundred years ago enabled Michelangelo to give birth to his vision for the Sistine Chapel and then bring it to life. It's the elevated ring in which the champion Muhammad Ali floated like a butterfly and stung like a bee. In fact it's the zone in which every world-class athlete fires on all cylinders, summoning every molecule of energy to perform at the absolute highest level of physical ability in his or her sport—and at the precise, exact moment when the athlete needed to.

Your empowerment zone might be a state of mind that you only visit on occasion, when you have heightened moments of awareness and inspiration. And it might be how you aspire to live all the time— with all of your faculties working together at optimum capacity and at peak performance. I'm talking about hitting your stride, your life's groove. Not only in one area or with one project but across the board: triumph to triumph, glory to glory. You're not going with *the* flow but you're *in* your flow. Let me revise: you *are* the flow. The word for that perhaps is actualized. It means that you've pushed past limitations to your highest good, grabbed hold of your innate powers, and have actualized your potential.

For most of us mere mortals who choose not to stop growing, though it means stumbling, falling, getting back up, and then elevating our aspirations once more, we may not take up permanent occupancy in the empowerment zone. In my lifetime, I've met only a few individuals who can claim mastery at the highest of levels, who live in that space most of the time, and who never cease to amaze me because of that. And even they have bad days yet manage to stay connected to that voltage all their own; and they retain focus with general flow and direction.

Let me also add that whenever I meet anyone I've admired for being world class in even just one area, I'm in awe. It doesn't matter if they also happen to be all too human in other areas. Never was this truer than when I finally met the very person who had inspired my desire to one day attain mastery at something. In fact, he had first inspired me to want to be him one day. Yep, that's right, I'm referring to the incomparable Miles Davis.

Set the date to be somewhere in the high-flying 1980s in New York City on what happened to be a dark and stormy night in Greenwich Village. As the limousine I was in pulled up to a curb in front of a club called S.O.B.'s, I caught a glimpse of someone familiar looking as he was strolling up to the car and thought that I recognized him as Miles Davis. Nah. It couldn't be. Just then there was a knock on our window. When we rolled it down, sure enough, there was Miles. All he said was, "You got a phone?" Tongue-tied in front of my idol, I said yes, of course. The limo had a phone in the back. The next thing I knew, Miles Davis was sitting in the back with me and my date, talking on the telephone with someone else. When he hung up, instead of thanking me, he reached into his pocket and buried his nose in a bag of what looked like some serious contraband, snorted good and loud, and then split. Not one word. No "thank you," or "nice to meet you, have a good night." Didn't he know who I was? His passionate devotee and greatest fan? Hell, no! And he didn't care.

Miles Davis once said something that defined mastery for me in terms of being in a class all his own and continuously pushing further, with others only trying to duplicate, impersonate, and replicate. He was as unfazed by followers as he was by detractors. "I am so far ahead of these"—(insert expletive here)—"that when they finally show up, I'm gone."

Sure enough, the minute he jumped out of the limo, before I even saw him get in his car, he was gone.

Was I disappointed? Was I crushed? Hell, no. That was Miles Davis. He existed in the flesh. He had just borrowed my phone. I was over the moon! He was as eccentric and excessive as I imagined he'd be. And nothing would ever take away from his ability to make music that had the power to change the energy in a room—to alter the atomic structure of the atmosphere.

That first time I heard his music come on Uncle Henry's record player was one of those life-changing lessons for mastery that made me want to be able to do that, too, one day. Even though my pursuit eventually took me in a direction that may not seem to have much to do with playing the trumpet or with the rule-bending game of jazz, that moment paved the way for future possibilities.

Many individuals who have become exceptional at what they do refer to moments early in life when they envisioned themselves reaching a level of greatness that perhaps wasn't obvious in the cards that were dealt them. I have corresponded with an amazing woman named Amy J. Cheney who described the passion for books that was her be-all and end-all as a child growing up in a challenging home life, and how her earliest dream was to one day impact others as powerfully as her favorite authors were able to do. Instead of becoming a writer, however, she sought mastery as a librarian.

Today, Amy is a superstar in her field with her own library program for promoting literacy to teenagers in juvenile hall lockup in Oakland, California, near my old stomping grounds. Not only does she inspire youth to read with a passion and find the tools for empowerment to change the direction of their lives, but she also manages to compel every top author in the nation to come and speak or read to the kids. She simply won't take no for an answer. If she wasn't such a master librarian, she'd be a knockout on Wall Street. More important, the literacy and responsibility programs she has promoted have reduced recidivism dramatically—keeping kids out of the system for good, instead of coming back and then moving on to worse.

When I wrote to Amy to ask how she carved out this rarefied position for herself and what lessons helped her find it, she wrote back this thoughtful e-mail:

For so long, I hated my work. And now I've found that I can do something that I absolutely love. What happened? It turns out that all my past jobs were preparing me for this one. I had no idea at the time. Now I can look back and see that getting up at 5 am to prepare produce displays when I worked at the farmer's market was preparing me for the hard work of arranging a special library out of nothing—and I use a hand-truck for boxes of books (instead of produce) all the time now. I can see that working with the inmates at the jails and prisons and on Death Row gave me knowledge of books and the system, and now provides me with a degree of credibility with the youngsters. It's all good. It was all in place all along. Now my passion to serve the youth flows forth easily and I find my job fun, creative, and happening effortlessly all the time.

No doubt but that Amy has drawn from many of the lessons for mastery that are relevant to any and all who want to enter their own empowerment zone. Such lessons are what's on tap for this chapter:

#30 Amy has embraced, as we can all choose to do, the resource of **risk** in reaching for the ring of being world class at what she does.

#31 Like her, we can apply such resources as transferable skills whenever we decide that goals and thinking alike can stand some **reinvention.**

#32 As all masters like Amy know, achieving the heights of success at what we do is sometimes determined by the intricacies of **timing**—a resource to be honed.

#33 With changing landscapes and economies, like her, we must all seek to master the need for **adaptation** of our pursuits that is central to **survival of the fittest** no matter what we do.

#34 As Amy or anyone can tell you, **balance** between practical concerns and audacious dreams is a lesson you must keep learning on a daily basis.

#35 Here is a lesson about **worth** that comes to those daring enough to challenge worldly views of it.

#36 As Amy's example reminds us, when our personal success is tied to the **contribution** we can make to causes greater than ourselves, we're in the empowerment zone.

#37 Finally, the ultimate lesson for mastery is how our **vision** can be shared for the greater good.

One other note that I'll make about the lessons coming up, as you'll see, is that they often require us to combine earlier lessons learned—but in new ways. They allow us to change our lives by changing our game. It's not just about going ahead of the curve, but about drawing the curve—using every color in the crayon box. Don't worry, there are rules, but only those you dare to create.

LESSON #30
Seek the Farthest Star

KEYWORD: *Risk*

"Why Wall Street?"

Not only is that a question that I hear all the time, but it was exactly what everyone around me demanded to know way back when I first set my sights on pursuing mastery in that arena. From wanting to be Miles Davis, to a passing fancy about becoming an actor, to setting forth for several years on a path toward a possible career as a heart surgeon— why the quantum leap to making a place for myself at the upper echelon of business and the stock market? Actually, what inquiring minds wanted to know was, "Gardner, what the hell are you thinking?"

Was it simply because of the feelings experienced that day when I stepped into a trading room and knew that I'd found my button and could feel the passion with all the bells ringing, whistles blowing, and fireworks telling me that this was where I belonged? Not completely. That was one of those attention-getting moments for sure. But the actual life-changing choice that came from out of that moment was the decision to go for it—which required me to immediately veer off into unknown territory for this improbable pursuit. In one second I was a guy standing in the middle of all that excitement thinking—*Gee, I'd love to do what they're doing here, I get this, I feel this, but, man, there ain't no way*—and in the next second, I was a different person standing there thinking, well, *why not?*

Though I didn't know it at the time, I had made up my mind to seek the farthest star. Indeed it was the least likely pursuit that I could have undertaken at the time, given that there was absolutely no evidence I could be successful at it. After all, I had no previous experience. I hadn't even worked in a stock brokerage mailroom, I had no college degree, to say nothing of an MBA, and no Rolodex of high-rollin' contacts. But I had the ability to see the possibilities—that is, the *"why not?"* of it all—which has turned out to be what I consider to be the first requirement for mastery. It's about seeing upsides and downsides yet taking the risk anyway to go for the gold.

Think for a moment, if you will, about how you deal with risk in your current pursuit, as well as how you have dealt with different forms of risk in the past. If you have never been afraid to put everything on the line for your dreams, more power to you. Except, that is, if you keep ending up in the same place as where you started. There is such a thing as being addicted to risk and risky behavior, which is not masterful in the least— and can be highly destructive. But if you tend to be more risk averse than not, you would be in the vast majority of folks today who are better at seeking their farthest stars in theory rather than in reality.

Ironically, experts in several fields suggest that part of the problem many have with taking risks comes from the pressure being placed on everyone, starting with our kids, on winning at everything. Perfectionism, it turns out, is not a stepping-stone to mastery. It's probably more a means for developing an ulcer. In every form of education, students need to feel safe so they can learn and win—to have a feeling of control and find arenas in which to excel. They also need safe structures in which it's okay to fail. The experience of failure not only teaches how to succeed the next time, it is the only way to combat the fear of failure.

In many adults, fear of failure prevents us from taking risks— necessary in all meaningful pursuits. What we need to be learning is that it's okay to fail but it's not okay to quit. Overcoming fear of failure isn't our only stumbling block. Alternately, fear of not winning or fear of losing out to someone else may force us to take a risk that doesn't turn out well. It could be argued that the rampant greed and excess in the Wall Street meltdown came from such bad risk thinking.

Needless to say, not all risks are created equal. Experience can help us to learn which ones are which. What about those folks who have no problem taking risks or incurring failure but are concerned about going overboard and not achieving actual goals? If you see yourself in that bracket, there's an interesting theory that may apply to you. I've heard it said that some of the risky behavior, inability to stay on task, and lack of impulse control, or traits that are observed in individuals considered to have ADHD (attention deficit/hyperactivity disorder), were once the most valued attributes in our ancestors' days of living in hunter-gatherer societies. If you were the hunter, you had to have a certain quest for danger or risk when you were going out to get dinner for your family. You had to be a little dreamy to imagine how you were going to be the big hero and conquer the prey, but you also had to be alert to distractions in case a predator in the vicinity decided you looked good to eat. And when it came to conquering, if you controlled your impulse to defend yourself—you'd be dead.

This is all to encourage you to see the different facets of risk and to see the role it has played in your life. Then you can ask yourself what you'd be willing to lay on the line for whatever it is that represents your farthest star. When you're traveling from familiar ground toward your empowerment zone, what are you risking—the regular paycheck, the creature comforts, the applause that may not continue anymore? Ain't no shame in identifying what the risk is—and giving yourself credit for the choice you're making. Once you've accepted the risk, you are ready to have your moment and embrace the steps that will be required for you to go to the next level. Risk is the essence of seeking your farthest star. And if you're not sure you've really got the right stuff to make it all happen or that maybe you're just deluding yourself, you can count yourself human.

What's the difference, then, between those who are crazy enough to dream of blasting off to outer space and those who actually land on the moon? Again, there are no single silver bullet answers for achieving mastery, but a critical piece will always be taking that big risk—as I learned from a conversation with Quincy Jones about how he felt when his arrangement of "Fly Me to Moon" for Frank Sinatra became the first song ever played in outer space. It's common knowledge that pursuing a career in music doesn't come with any guarantees. Yet look at the rewards.

Another critical piece for achieving mastery is training in the fundamentals to be able to handle the risk at the highest levels. I remember watching a *60 Minutes* segment in 2006 that featured Neil Armstrong, who made the point that preparation and the rest of NASA (National Aeronautics and Space Administration) were most responsible for the success of the mission. He also spoke about John F. Kennedy's declaration in 1961 that within a decade the United States would win the space race against the Soviets by flying an astronaut to the moon, touching feet down on its surface, and then returning that person back home to Planet Earth safely.

The risk to even declare the mission at that time in our history was astronomical. Tragically, as we know, President Kennedy was assassinated in 1963 and couldn't live to witness the triumph that he'd inspired a nation to make our journey toward. But even without his leadership, there was no turning back. After an investment of twenty-four billion dollars along with the passion, focus, drive, determination, and mastery of four hundred thousand members of the team, NASA was ready in only eight years—two years early. Every step of the way, especially the failed ones, was necessary for the moon landing to even stand a chance.

In the process, Armstrong barely survived test runs that were near fatal. His skills and nerves of steel in making correct decisions each time were the saving grace.

In the *60 Minutes* piece, Ed Bradley recalled the famous shot of Neil Armstrong giving the thumbs-up to the crowd when he, Buzz Aldrin, and Michael Collins went to board the rocket ship on that memorable July morning in 1969. Bradley noted that he had never seen anyone so confident. The response was not what I expected. "Yeah," Armstrong said, "but a little bit of a sham, I admit. You know, the reality is, a lot of times you get up and get in the cockpit, and something goes wrong somewhere and you go back down. So, actually, when you actually lift off, it's really a big surprise."

This was a small aha moment for me that confirmed what I've always felt about seeking the farthest star. Like Armstrong said, the reality is that whenever you take a risk of any size and climb up into the cockpit of your rocket ship, it may fail. You may never even achieve liftoff.

Of course, we've all heard Armstrong's words spoken as he first touched his foot onto the moon—"That's one small step for man; one giant leap for mankind." For anyone old enough to remember the feeling of watching on television as he spoke those words and then looking out at the night sky in our own backyards, I can report that it was mind blowing and life changing. But it was something that Armstrong said in the interview with Ed Bradley that told me more about what he saw when he walked where no one ever had been before. Thirty-seven years later, in describing the lunar surface, he recalled, "It's a brilliant surface in that sunlight. The horizon seems quite close to you because curvature is so much more pronounced than here on Earth. It's an interesting place to be. I recommend it."

Remember those words as you take your possibilities out of the same old state of wishing and hoping for one day. Ask "why not?" With that to urge you on, go seek your farthest star. Go find it, step foot on its brilliant surface. And come back to tell us what you found.

LESSON #31
Seeing Ghosts, Reading Signs

KEYWORD: *Reinvention*

Everywhere I go these days, I meet individuals who have risen to the top of their game, yet who are coming to terms with the reality that either the rules have changed or the game itself no longer serves them. These are individuals who by choice or necessity have decided to reinvent themselves and their lives. Some describe it as thrilling and others as terrifying—like walking a tightrope without a net. And, indeed, the lesson for mastery that I've had to learn is that reinvention can be a high-flying, daredevil act that requires a keen awareness of both opportunities and the hazards of going after them. The honing of that awareness is what I mean by the name of this lesson—*Seeing ghosts, reading signs.*

My first inklings of this dual awareness began with my mother, who would notice me daydreaming and ask me if I was "seeing ghosts." In fact, she encouraged me to push my imagination beyond the everyday. She would say that it didn't matter if nobody else saw my dreams, as long as I was seeing them with the eyes of my soul. At the same time, Momma wanted me to pay attention to the practical pitfalls that might accompany the pursuit of those possibilities—to read the signs.

If you can recall those moments when you chose to reinvent yourself, you'll remember the feelings of excitement mixed with uncertainty that the process stirs. You might be at that place even now. If you're not in the reinvention mode, you may still be interested in options for reinvention that may be just what you need for where you are—that is, if you dare.

The scary aspect of reinvention can best be explained by an old Gypsy curse that I never understood until I became a parent. The worst thing you can say to someone who has done you wrong, as a Gypsy, is to wish for that person, "May your child go to the circus!"

The point is, of course, that we as parents want to protect our children as best we can from the dangerous forces out there, of which there are plenty. It's not just the unsavory characters who are associated with circus operations. The fate you most fear is the peril of your kid having to be up on a tightrope; swinging on a flying trapeze; performing dare-devilish feats of strength, magic, and lion taming; or being part of a freak show, all in front of roaring crowds who may turn on your child at any time. And if he or she falls, gets hurt, gets eaten by a snake, or plummets to his or her demise, the roaring crowd will gasp and shudder, but it'll forget your child the minute a replacement shows up. Even more horrible is the curse put on the heads of your children to have to sing for their supper or to have to depend on the kindness of strangers when their tightwire act loses its appeal.

But, of course, this story of the Gypsy curse focuses only on the pitfalls of running off to join the circus, so to speak, or what is required to follow a dream that is beyond the realm of imagination for anyone but the dreamer. The gift of such a pronouncement can also empower someone to reinvent an ordinary, predictable life and make it into an extraordinary one.

To offer the most obvious and spectacular example that comes to mind, I must take off my hat to Will Smith, who sees ghosts and minds his signs, continually upping his pursuit at every level. He has reinvented his game at every turn, from recording artist and triple-threat singer/dancer/actor, to comedian and television series star, to becoming the number one box office feature film superstar in the world. It happens that he also works at being the world-class father, husband, and person that he is. And he's continually looking for ways to reinvent his imagination and passion to reach further still—as a producer, story-teller, and activist for causes that matter to him.

Will credits his ability to pursue opportunities and avoid the pitfalls of fame by staying grounded in his work ethic—which was inspired by his father. Will has shared several stories with me about lessons learned from his dad, a bricklayer. My favorite is the simple, powerful advice he gave Will and his brother about excellence and focus on the job, telling them, "Forget about the brick you laid before. Forget about the next brick. Focus on the brick in your hand that you're laying right now."

That philosophy also explains how it's possible to reinvent yourself and attain mastery at something new, as long as you focus on laying that brick in your hand to the absolute best of your ability.

Reinvention doesn't necessarily require you to alter who you are or pursue a brand-new career path or title. It may be that you stay on your course but seek a new and improved method of pursuing your same dream. You might choose a new destination. Or perhaps you fall from your perch but then find a new reason to make the climb back up. Maybe what you are reinventing is your facility for problem solving— kick-starting your imagination to look at new possibilities while engaging your practical know-how in different ways.

This, I'm certain, is one of the processes that will lead to the next great revolution industry. Case in point? Cars. True, there have been financial interests that have resisted new technologies for manufacturing automobiles in America. But I believe that somewhere in a garage in some small town in the United States, a guy is playing around with a new gizmo that's going to alter how we look at transportation—not to mention the production of the next generation of cars as we will know them. This is a guy or gal who throws away the old playbook and says, "What if?" The ingenuity and industry of our human resources right here in this country are making that possibility a reality, even as you read these words.

Whenever I'm asked for counsel about the process of reinvention, especially by those who've weathered the shock of having recently been fired or downsized or who can't see positive possibilities for themselves, I refer to an experience of mine that occurred back in the 1980s—it was in conjunction with being fired by Bear Stearns for not toeing the company line. In trying to decide whether or not to seek work at another major brokerage firm or to branch off on my own, as I eventually chose to do, I had to reinvent my definition of mastery. And I didn't let go of the earlier version very easily. In less than five years, I had come up in the ranks—all the way from not having a roof over my head to living and rolling like a rock star. Was I really ready to cash in all the chips and go do something that was going to require me to go back to basics and, yes, start from near nothing?

Then again, as I thought about the signs of the free-for-all that was happening in that era—the megamergers and massive amounts of money changing hands along with the high-cost lifestyle that was all about bigger, better, and best—I suspected that it might be as good a time as any to reinvent myself, even without a net.

So there I was in the midst of uncertainty, sitting alone in my apartment in Harlem round midnight with thunder, lightning, gunshots, and gloom all booming in the background, and I had one of those moments of altered awareness. While wondering if I should go back to hitting the anvil as I had been or do something completely different, I suddenly heard a voice from out of nowhere speak directly to me. It said only one word: "Change."

I didn't immediately assume that this was the voice of God, although I have no other explanation. My higher power clearly understood that I had stopped seeing ghosts with the eyes of my soul and that I needed to change, to reclaim that ability, and also to reinvent my pursuit. Fine, I thought. It was time to change. But to do so was going to require that I change my thinking.

In the past, whenever choosing a new undertaking, I had always been able to find an example of someone who had done it and who represented what world class meant in that venue. But there was no one who had done what I had in mind at that time—to start my own company and dare to compete on my own with the major brokerage firms, and reinvent the rules by sidestepping the well-established money managers in going after institutional clients. For me, without any proven precedent for what success or failure was going to look like, or any net if I fell, that was akin to getting up on the tightrope.

The person who encouraged me to go for it, no matter what, was one of my most important mentors, Barbara Scott Preiskel. She dared me to see possibilities for changing not just me but my industry. That became my new definition for mastery—being a force, making a difference. Those were ghosts that I began to see, at the same time that I saw signs that said to go for it. Ms. Preiskel's only words of caution were not to read too much into initial indications of success or failure, but rather to let the process unfold. No better reassurance could have been given to me.

Ms. Preiskel was someone who had the ability to elevate your consciousness simply by her presence. When I first arrived in New York City and was intent on upping my education by learning from the best in a variety of fields, I started calling her office in the hopes of introducing myself. After a year, Ms. Preiskel finally agreed to meet me, and we hit it off from the start.

Ms. Preiskel was the second African American woman ever to graduate from Yale Law School and went from there to become one of the greatest legal minds in America, as well as someone who famously broke many barriers for women and minorities over the course of her seventy-seven years. At the Motion Picture Association of America where she served for two and a half decades, ultimately as general counsel, she was considered to be the driving force in promoting higher representation of minorities and women in movies, and fighting portrayals of negative racial stereotypes.

When exhibitors in the South refused, for instance, to show films with black actors and actresses in lead roles or that had story lines that challenged segregation and other kinds of racial prejudice, Jack Valenti, the head of the MPAA, would fly Ms. Preiskel to the various state capitals and have her testify to the legislatures. He recalled later, "Inevitably, she'd charm their socks off and if there was venom in the air before, she quickly filled the room with her sweet and elegant personality and flawless logic. The air turned fresh. The southern legislators fell all over themselves congratulating her. They just melted." The lawmakers then put pressure on the exhibitors to allow the films to be shown. As a result, a sea change in public perception took place.

After leaving the MPAA, Ms. Preiskel took on unprecedented leadership roles on numerous corporate boards—like General Electric,

R. H. Macy, and the Washington Post Company. She then turned to nonprofit work, using her boundless energy for causes of education, women's economic advancement, arts and culture, diversity issues, and her personal favorite, Tougaloo College in Tougaloo, Mississippi.

Ms. Preiskel was much more than a mother figure to me, and she had a much different style from Momma's. But as a mentor, she pushed me just as hard and gave me a law degree's worth of lessons to boot. One of the best negotiating skills she helped me to cultivate was how not to be intimidated when feeling outpowered. Very simply, she explained how you don't walk into those situations without bringing some sort of ammunition to back up any statements you might need to make. "Remember, you don't have to throw the brick," she would caution, "but sometimes you may need to show the brick." That has been indispensable for not missing opportunities in negotiations and for clearing up potential conflict.

Over the years, I learned and absorbed so much from Ms. Preiskel that I grew to be like her on many levels. Clear, subtly forceful, and unwavering, she taught me how, in all matters, to respect the process, play it all the way out, and then be prepared to write my own ending.

Even in her last days, which came much too early in 2002, when she was seventy-seven years old, as she lay in the hospital with leukemia, Barbara Scott Preiskel was fully present, passionate about asking me how I was and wondering what she could do for me, and where was I headed next. Her beautiful family and throngs of friends who adored her would come to the hospital to see her, and she would comfort each one of us, never complaining to my knowledge.

When Ms. Preiskel passed, I had been mourning the loss of my mother some years earlier, and even though I had been so blessed to have the two of them as mentors at different stages, the world didn't seem as welcoming a place without both of them in it anymore. Then again, their wisdom and cherished counsel is never far from my memory.

The loss of loved ones, as we all will face at different times, regularly turns our thoughts to our own mortality. It can be an opportunity or a challenge to question whether we're making the most of the precious time we've been given. Are we living up to our potential, seeing ghosts with the eyes of our soul, and paying attention to the signs that give us meaningful guidance? It's true that our time will come and that others will miss us when we're gone, but did we do everything possible to make sure that it mattered that we were here?

You can apply this lesson about reinvention by asking yourself the same questions. Is it time for you to go out and defy the Gypsy curse by getting up on your flying trapeze? Why not dare to be a force in your world, to make a difference? Raise your stakes and your definition for mastery. Now go for it. Take Ms. Preiskel's advice and respect the process. Let it play out and be prepared to write your own ending.

LESSON #32
Opportunities, Like Pancakes, Are Best Served Hot, but Sometimes You Gotta Set the Table Before You Can Eat

KEYWORD: *Timing*

As you probably know about me by now, I'm not a person who waits for strangers bearing surprise gifts to come up and knock on my door. As is our theme, I believe pursuit is best fueled with action verbs that put us in charge and that allow us to do the knocking. But every now and then, unforeseen opportunity does arise, and it can be a life-changing lesson when you must decide how to respond. In those instances, timing is everything. Do you wait? Do you pounce? Do you use that opportunity to gather and build more of the same?

Well, to dramatize my answers, I have a story about timing that can be applied to many situations when something of interest and potential value is offered to you. Let me preface this story by saying, these were opportunities that come once in a blue moon and that I never expected. Back in 2003, I was approached by Lynn Redmond, a producer, on behalf of Barbara Walters and 20/20, about doing a segment on my life.

Though I never viewed my year of being homeless and a single parent as something that defined me, by that point I had made the choice to speak publicly about my journey from being among the working homeless to becoming a successful entrepreneur. The more forthcoming that I was, the greater awareness I was able to raise about the issue of homelessness and its causes. Still, I wasn't eager to talk about that very difficult period on a prime-time newsmagazine show. Nonetheless, what Lynn described was a very respectful approach, and since my desire was to reach a wider audience in the right way, I had to remember the old adage—Don't look a gift horse in the mouth. Or there's my version—*Opportunities, like pancakes, are best served hot.* The timing was right. I said yes, and I was more than pleased with the outcome.

One of the first signs of confirmation that I was on the right track had come in a hand-delivered note to my office from a single mother of three, a victim of domestic violence, who had been living in her car with her children, in the dark of winter, and working full-time during the day while her kids attended school; at night they all slept in their blankets and clothes in the car. By some chance, she had seen the 20/20 story and it gave her the courage to seek out information about a shelter where she could stay until she got back on her feet. That was all I needed to hear to know that sharing my story could empower others.

But I was not prepared for the onslaught of interest and offers that arrived almost instantaneously after the segment aired.

"Good morning, is this Chris Gardner?" were the first words spoken to me by an unknown caller on my cell phone very early on the day following the airing of the piece.

The guy was smooth to the point of alarming, clearly a successful veteran of show business and a partner at one of the top Hollywood talent agencies. He knew his stuff, I could tell, and I was impressed that his agency represented some of the "biggest names" in the industry. "Nothing happens that we don't touch" was how he described their access to the heavyweights among actors, directors, and writers, and their relationships with the studios in green-lighting movies. They would provide soup to nuts, he said, with all the potential he foresaw for my interests—publishing, film, television, speaking, merchandising. Unbelievable.

Was this an opportunity that should be seized at once? I couldn't tell. So I made him an offer. I was on my way to Maui and if he could get through security and into the Red Carpet Room at LAX at the appointed hour when I was arriving to make my connecting flight, I would sign with him.

"Done," he said. "I'll see you there."

In my head I was thinking—*Hey, I'm not believing any of this stuff, why shouldn't I sign, go to Hawaii for a well-earned time-off with my lady, and see what happens when I return?*

When I caught my first glimpse of the agent, he looked like he was right out of central casting, everything he sounded like on the phone. Smooth, cool, dapper, and tight. We met, shook hands, and just as effortlessly as this whole process had begun, he produced the contract. In a very happy mood because I'm heading off on vacation and this seeming opportunity has landed in my lap, I asked for his pen. He patted his pocket and grinned sheepishly, not finding one, as if it was no big deal.

Whoa. No pen? No !@+% pen? Mr. Smooth Operator, "nothing happens in this town that we don't touch," Mr. "we represent the biggest names in show business"? Seeing my reaction, the guy began to frantically search for a pen, begging everyone in the vicinity to produce one for him. Nobody had one. It must have been pen-eating Day of the Locust in L.A.! But it was too late anyway. All the red flags in the world were waving for me. The karma police had chimed in. How was he going to represent me when he didn't even have the most basic, essential tool of the deal maker's trade?

Needless to say, I did not sign. My lady, chief of the karma patrol, agreed that something as little as not having a pen was reason enough to pass. "He was the wrong guy" was her take.

I never regretted my decision, including the next time when I heard from him with a sour grapes call to me after it was announced that I'd signed with Escape Artists, the right production company to tell my story, and that Will Smith would play me. His unenthusiastic spin was, "Well, I hope you got a percentage of the budget." I wasn't fazed; I told him that I appreciated his concern and that I'd see him at the premiere soon—all of which happened, impossible and unlikely as those odds were.

Now this story has two morals. One of them I already knew—that if you catch me butt naked on a desert island alone, I've got a business card and an ink pen somewhere! In other words, if you are going to play at the top of your game, don't be sloppy with your fundamentals, your tools of the trade. Otherwise, you won't be eating your pancakes.

The other lesson was one of timing for me in this whole process. The truth is that I had a lot more R&D to do before I was ready to appreciate and put to use the opportunities of telling my story on a public scale. This was going to take me back to asking questions, reading whatever I could get my hands on, following my gut, and educating myself on the "who's who?" of several new arenas that were totally foreign to me.

In fact, my failure to do all my homework almost caused me to blow the opportunity that presented itself when I met with the key people at Escape Artists. They were giving me their visions for the movie and talking about the impact of this heroic story when I made a big point of saying that it should have the tone of an everyman or everywoman story. The example I mentioned was *Forrest Gump*—a story of a hero who didn't set out to be one, a regular guy who found himself in extreme circumstances. Everyone nodded, except for one producer who said nothing but looked at me strangely. After the meeting, he followed me out and said, "Oh, by the way, my name is Steve Tisch. I produced *Forrest Gump*."

There was nothing for me to say or do, other than to vow to do a much better job from then on of research and development!

And fortunately, the opportunity with Escape Artists brought to fruition a film that went beyond anything any of us could have imagined. The time, energy, collaboration, and many lessons learned in the process were all required so that the table could be ideally set for me to do what I'm doing now—in passing on direction that has guided me over the years and allowed me to savor the feast that is my life.

In almost every venue where I speak, I am asked how the story that I'd been hesitant to discuss for many years had wound up on the big screen. As I recount the details to others as I have here, my point isn't that something along these lines can happen to anyone. In fact, most people in Hollywood have emphasized to me that it almost never happens as it did for me. Somehow, all the elements of timing clicked.

Yet I also believe no matter what your endeavor, when you're open to possibilities that can and do show up on your doorstep, all the elements of timing can click for you, too. Think about how aspects of my unusual story may have played out in your life. Can you remember when you seized the day and grabbed onto an opportunity that was hot? Can you remember when you had to accept that sometimes you have to set the table before you could eat? If you can do both, you're harnessing the art of timing even as I write these words. If you've been one to look gift horses in the mouth or to deliberate too long on an opportunity that cooled too quickly, that's your cue to be on the lookout for those wonderful meetings, pieces of advice, and offers of interest that could pop up anytime. Or, if you've been in too much of a rush and haven't enlisted your own karma patrol for helping you deliberate more thoughtfully when you should, that will tell you to employ timing by letting the game play itself out before you jump in.

Whenever I'm accused of being lucky, I dispute that notion. But what I have mastered is timing. And so can you.

LESSON #33
Stay Open, but Don't Wing It
KEYWORDS: *Adaptation, Survival of the Fittest*

If you love to laugh at the movies, you may recall the outrageous characters that Mike Myers masterfully created in the three *Austin Powers* films. In that case, you may remember that in the second movie, *The*

Spy Who Shagged Me, the archvillain Dr. Evil sends his lackeys back in time to steal Austin's mojo. Hilarity ensues, Austin eventually gets his mojo back, and all's well that ends well.

But in real life, I'm sorry to say, sometimes folks lose their mojo, or allow it to be stolen, and can never find it again. Some of my colleagues who've scaled the highest heights of success arrive at a point where they have nothing to energize them enough that they can't wait for the sun to come up so that they can do their thing. No mojo, no nada, kaput.

Maybe you've felt something along those lines or have had a friend or colleague confide about having trouble rousing passion like he or she used to be able to do. We're referring to passion for pursuit, of course, those times when you need to rediscover the real mojo that gives you your power to drive. When you've been a tenacious fighter, undaunted by challenges, a master of hope and resilience, it can be natural at times to find yourself in a proverbial rut. Maybe you've come to a standstill for no reason, or feel that you're phoning it in, or that nothing matters anymore. In such cases, you may be required to throw out all your preconceived ideas of what happyness and success used to be for you. You don't have to wipe the slate entirely of your past accomplishments, but you will have to revisit the drawing board for what's next.

The quest to reclaim lost mojo is not as funny as it sounds. It's actually critical for survival of the fittest and is dependent on your power of adaptation. That may mean you'll have to retool your best-laid plans or throw out some stale ideas. You don't have to scale back your dreams, however. In fact, rather than downsize the scope of what you're doing, I have learned, it's your time to broaden your horizon and grow. The operative means of doing that is essentially this lesson—*Stay open, but don't wing it.*

In the early 2000s, I came to a place where nearly all of my original goals for my company had been met. Many choices faced me. I could stay at the top of the game in the profitable niche that I'd found and continue exactly with what I was doing. I could reinvent my pursuit altogether. Or I could build on my foundation, staying with it, but at the same time adapt, evolve, and grow—personally and professionally.

One of my musical heroes, Carlos Santana, provides us with a famous example of the power of creative adaptation. He has never lost his distinctive sound but has constantly evolved artistically, adapting to changes in the global music marketplace and surviving cultural changes to become among the fittest. Santana—who defined the term "world music" before it existed—came to America from Mexico with his guitar and started where he was, playing on street corners for change. After he burst onto the scene at Woodstock in 1969, his musical growth produced almost a decade's worth of classic hits that could be identified from the moment you heard three notes from his guitar. When he basically peaked in the marketplace by the end of the 1970s, much of the public moved on, even though Carlos was still at work creating and releasing records. Most of the music business and his fans wrote him off as having made his mark, unaware that his musical virtuosity and spiritual exploration were leading him to an evolution that no one could imagine. It has been noted, in fact, that in 1990, no label wanted to sign him. But nine years later, those who had an opportunity to do so must have been kicking themselves because Carlos Santana rose up from the ashes of "where are they now?" with *Supernatural,* a masterpiece that had grown out of musical collaboration with contemporaries like Eric Clapton and mostly younger artists who were up and coming in their genres—Dave Matthews, Wyclef Jean, Rob Thomas, and others. The album won every possible award, sold 25 million copies, and catapulted Carlos back into the stratosphere and then further than he had ever been before.

Santana reclaimed his mojo not only in his musical artistry but went further still, expanding his horizons to include creative expression as a painter, clothing designer, and entrepreneur. He has coupled those efforts with a commitment to social justice and a world-class agenda for solving our most dire issues. Of particular interest to me is his work with an alliance of artists in investing resources for a revitalization of

South Africa—a cause close to my heart. Instead of pointing fingers at others to carry the load, he has taken a leadership role in pursuit of his vision of global transformation through music. To some, that might seem a true stretch. Not to Santana, who believes that music allows us to grow and evolve through the basic act of experiencing sound, which he says "rearranges the molecular structure of the listener!"

In adapting to changes in his industry and in the world, Carlos Santana didn't choose to wing it and just put any old music he could make out there, hoping to rest on the laurels of his former glory. Instead, he chose to be open to the input of other musicians, younger artists, and global concerns.

You can apply the approach of Carlos Santana to where you are now if you're looking to reconnect with your mojo. No need to wing it and hope that you'll find your beat again. You can simply stay open to ways that your molecules can be rearranged. Listening to music, as an application of this part of the lesson, may be just the medicine for doing that.

When I made the choice that it was time to reach for another distant star and to raise the bar for myself, what revved up my passion was a concept that I would eventually identify as conscious capitalism—based on the principle that wealth is created individually and globally by investing in developing economies and new technologies, within ourselves, our communities, and our world. Not for philanthropy but for profit. Uplift people, uplift their economies—and everybody benefits. For some time, this idea was far too broad and general for it to be anything more than a big dream without a specific plan.

That started to change, however, through the course of conversations with very knowledgeable individuals who were involved in the movement to end apartheid in South Africa. Every time the subject came up, I felt a kind of rush and quickening of interest. A logical proposition popped into my head somewhere along the way. Since it was the pressure from labor unions and civil rights organizations in cities here in this country that started the ball rolling, through the power of their pension funds and the like, why couldn't it work in reverse? All those corporate entities that had been putting capital into the system understood that pension funds would no longer invest with them as long as they were doing business in South Africa. They got the message and pulled out. That's how the walls came crumbling down. But now that South Africans had political freedom, my question was what good was it without investors bringing outside capital to restart the engines of economic freedom and opportunity? It occurred to me then, from common sense, that those very same companies should be welcomed back to postapartheid South Africa, and that the same leadership who put pressure on businesses to leave should be involved in the reinvestment process. In my estimation, South Africa had the potential to be the Hong Kong of Africa, and if this kind of endeavor was done right, it would be.

The minute I mentally saw the possibility, I had one of those life-changing moments when I knew that this was something that I could do—and had to do. This was going to be my Sistine Chapel. The naysaying began almost at once. Now everyone who'd ever suspected it was sure that I had to be crazy.

What became the Gardner Rich Pamodzi South Africa Fund I, a first-time private equity fund, faced enormous hurdles, not the least of which is that it's in an emerging market. Since the terrain is far from a proven commodity to most investors, much of our time was initially spent educating our potential stakeholders as to why it would be profitable for them and positive for the world. Challenges notwithstanding, at this writing, after four years, we are on our way to raising a billion dollars of investment. We have built the scaffolding and are starting to paint.

One of my early forays on this pursuit came with my first trip to South Africa, a crash course in staying open without winging it. I had come with an agenda to assess the viability of a unique product in addressing the dire demand for decent housing. Gardner Rich had an opportunity to market low-cost prefab panels that, when assembled into a home, would maintain coolness in the summer and warmth in the winter. The real gold was that the prefab panels could be made in South Africa in factories that could be built in the nine provinces—thus creating jobs and helping to develop community wealth. The opportunity had fired up my mojo and I was sure the South Africans with whom I was working would be receptive.

But before I'd even arrived, I heard some murmuring about how this wasn't going to work, although there were no clear reasons as to why. Normally, I might have chosen to stick closely to my plan to close the deal on the prefab panels. Instead, I realized that I needed to stay open to hearing what the objections were and then to adapt once I met with the government officials and trade union leaders. It occurred to me that once I saw the whole field, I could become aware of other, equally promising opportunities.

Once in South Africa, as the meetings commenced and I presented the plan, I heard a resounding "No." The reason behind that no was: "The white man had bricks. We want bricks." The objection to the prefab panels, in spite of the potential for job creation, was a cultural thing, not to be discussed. End of story.

How could I successfully refute years of thinking a certain way? And, more to the point, why should I? So, staying open, but not winging it, I have continued to go back to the drawing board many times. What I've discovered in the process is that letting go of one detail in the big picture—like the prefab panels that didn't work in the grand scheme, for whatever reasons—made way for better, bolder possibilities that were obscured until then. After four years, we're close to unveiling the results.

As out there in the impossible stratosphere as this pursuit may seem, it wouldn't have been possible if not for this lesson that I encourage you to test for yourself. Take a reading of your mojo. Are you satisfied? If so, fine. If not, raise your game, dare to pursue your life's work—and do so with a readiness to adapt your plans, when needed, on the fly.

That brings up another application option you have for this lesson, one that is much more basic than having to retool your whole apparatus for pursuit. You might just need to update your hairdo. Perhaps you want to choose to take another route when you travel to work every day.

If you want your molecules rearranged, maybe all that you need is to listen to some different tunes for a change. Sometimes, being open is as simple as that and is just the ticket for getting your mojo back.

In the pursuit of mastery, I also think of this lesson as a reminder that when road conditions demand, we may need to switch gears without switching course. Early in my company's development, for example, there were two individuals I was intent on meeting. One was Henry Kravis, the leverage buyout billionaire whose private equity firm, KKR (Kohlberg, Kravis, Roberts), was at the top of every "who's who" list on Wall Street. The other person was responsible for the buyout of TLC Beatrice, one of the single largest buyouts of the 1980s. That was Reginald Lewis, a Wall Street phenomenon, and the first African American to buy a company worth a billion dollars. Certainly, Reggie Lewis had inspired and raised the bar for me, so I focused my plan on meeting him first. It stood to reason that he might provide an introduction to Henry Kravis as well. Both had their main offices in the same building on West Fifty-seventh Street in New York.

For months on end, I called the office of Reggie Lewis and had no luck whatsoever at getting him on the phone. Finally, I decided to go over and knock on his door, introduce myself, and establish a rapport. His gatekeeper was an alligator trained in military efficiency with a drill sergeant's mouth. She not only chewed me out for arriving without an appointment but then escorted me out the door, through the lobby, and into the elevator. Two floors down, the doors opened and into the elevator steps none other than Henry Kravis. A little bolt of lightning hit. A moment. My gears shifted so I could adapt to this new opportunity. Game on.

I had perhaps three to five minutes for an elevator pitch in which to introduce myself and let Mr. Kravis know why my company had something of interest to offer to him. Survival of the fittest meant adapting to this moment. Before stepping out of the elevator, he invited me to call on him anytime. Adaptation!

But don't just take it from me. Whenever you look at examples of those who have attained enduring happyness and lasting passion for life, people you may know personally or individuals you admire from afar, notice how they've adapted to change at different stages of their pursuit. You'll see someone who is open, curious, questioning, and available to new input all the time. Yet they're grounded at the same time. They're not winging their way from one peak to the next, but rather they're anchored and secure in who they are and why they are. Their mojo isn't pushed or over the top, but it's infectious and disarming nonetheless. That's survival of the fittest.

If you don't see your passion at a similar level, go find the Dr. Evil who stole it from you, get it back, and retool your mojo if need be. If you don't, and the proverbial parade starts to pass you by, whose fault will that be? And finally, as our world changes, our individual and collective survival will depend on how we do or don't adapt. Choose accordingly.

LESSON #34
Mo' Money, Mo' Options, Mo' Problems
KEYWORD: *Balance*

Perhaps the most humbling pieces of correspondence that I receive come from individuals who aspire to attain their own "rags-to-riches" story (or "bags to riches" as I've joked at times) and who ask me most sincerely to invest their life's savings for them. A single mother with four children wrote to tell me that she was running two businesses she started—a janitorial service and an Internet site that sold her products—while managing to work full-time as a nurse. Her aspiration was to cut back her hours on these jobs to spend more time with her kids, theoretically by reinvesting her savings in the stock market. Talk about mastery of multiple pursuits! That's the kind of entrepreneurial spirit that corporations should be hiring for executive status. Moreover, her desire to invest is certainly cause for applause in my book. My advice to her as well as to you, if you are similarly inclined, is to take smaller, incremental steps toward getting to know the stock market.

As is the policy of my firm, we are unable to accept such requests, since we invest for institutions and aren't equipped for individual invest-ment programs. What we do advise to anyone who wants to invest wisely is to explore mutual funds or investigate forms of professional asset management. But, more important, use your time to become financially literate before you invest your money. You can empower yourself by learning how to use every tool in the financial toolbox that is applicable to your needs and objectives. Unless you have a passion to do the R&D in the stock market yourself, I encourage you to seek a licensed stockbroker who has come personally recommended by some-one you know and trust. It may mean paying a small fee or percentage to that broker, but that will be money worth the expense. And if you want my two cents about the kinds of stock that you and your broker should be examining, it's no secret that for at least the next decade, I have two words for you: new technologies.

I'm also asked about credit card consolidation and other kinds of debt reduction offers. Again, go through accredited experts who have proven themselves to be trustworthy by someone you know. Visit your local library to see what books on managing your own finances will assist you in doing your own research. The folks at the reference desk may not only direct you to helpful reading materials, but they may also know of community classes or lectures that are typically free to the public and offer sound money management advice.

Although this lesson doesn't address specific ways to make money in the stock market, or how to develop a budget you can execute, or how to shake off that monkey of debt from your back, it does deal with something of concern to individuals of all ages and backgrounds, and at almost every financial level—the pursuit of mastery over money.

It's important to make the distinction between pursuing money for money's sake, and pursuing mastery over the role that money plays in your life. Three questions can be very helpful to ask, to keep your rela-tionship to money real: (1) Does it control you or do you control it? (2) Do you work hard for the money (like Donna Summer sang to us)? Or do you let your money go to work for you? (3) Does money represent the cavalry that you've been waiting on, or is it only one resource in your pursuit of happyness?

Of course, I can cut to the chase and say that in the best of all worlds, you would hope to be in control of the role that money plays in your life, and that it should definitely go to work for you as opposed to you being enslaved to it. And, above all, it should never be seen as your ultimate salvation or even as a cure for what ails you when your problems seem to all be money based. Needless to say, all of that is much easier said than done, no matter where we fall in the economic spectrum. What's required, more than anything else, is finding a sense of balance.

That's why this lesson was a life changer for me on the road to mastery of that balancing act.

The first installment of the chain of many events that led to my moment of realization in this lesson took place back in San Francisco midway through a year of being on the street with my son, six months into my first year as a stockbroker. Around that midpoint, I can remember how the weather suddenly changed, from gorgeous autumn days and nights to weeks of cold rain that wiped out options like sleeping in the park or taking Christopher for walks at the beach to play. As I've often said, I don't know where I'd be today if not for the discovery of Reverend Cecil Williams, Glide Memorial Church, and Mo's Kitchen—which was housed in the basement of the church—as well as the overnight stays in the homeless hotel run by the church. Whenever I stood in any of the lines, whether it was for a meal at Mo's for me and Chris Jr. or waiting in the line at the hotel to find out whether there would be a room for us that night or not, I had to count my blessings for having those lifesaving options.

As if it were yesterday, I can also remember thinking that there was going to come a time when our situation would be different and we'd have ample money for resources galore. The belief that most sustained me was telling myself, out loud, as often as I could—*One day, in the not so distant future, I won't have these problems anymore.*

You know what? I was right. So was my all-time favorite rapper, the late great Notorious B.I.G., who told the God's truth about balance in financial matters when he wrote "Mo Money Mo Problems," a song and video released after his untimely death. "I don't know what they want from me," he wrote. "It's like the more money we come across, the more problems we see."

So let me ask you—have you ever imagined that money was going to solve all your problems? If so, you must have eventually come to the same conclusion that I did when I learned, over time, through trial and error, that although money serves many needs and does indeed provide you with options you didn't have before, it also creates a whole new slew of problems that you never could have imagined. If that crushes your fantasy that money is going to make all your dreams come true and your sorrows vanish, or if your definition of happyness is tied to the accumulation of money, this may not be what you were hoping to hear. But it is a significant stepping-stone on your way to finding balance in mastery over money.

Before I really understood Biggie's refrain, I had the opportunity to experience how mo' money does in fact produce mo' options. My year-long experience of being one of the white-collar working homeless taught me well that every dollar earned moved us a step closer to putting a roof over our heads. With the financial advancement that followed, of course, we were able to thrive as our surroundings and our lifestyle improved. Some of those improvements were necessary, others were important, and some options were luxuries. It was unquestionably empowering to go from pressing my nose up against the glass of all those places that barred me from entering—not because of race or class but because of the notorious "place-ism" that didn't connect me to those inner sanctums—to being someone who had the option to walk in, sit down, and invite others in to join me at my table. Those are options money can bring.

Similarly, for anyone who has seen the movie *The Pursuit of Happyness* or read the book, you'll know that it was Bob Bridges's red Ferrari that caught my attention and that led me to ask him what it was that he did for a living. The car became a symbol for me of what was possible.

It represented the empowerment of having the option to buy any car that I wanted. And so, when the day came that I was able to own and drive one of those babies, it was a milestone, without a doubt, a time to celebrate, throw the confetti and the parade, and then get back to work. At the same time, the power to believe that it could be an option one day was the life-changing part of the story.

That's portable knowledge. If you ask yourself whether you could have the option of doing, having, or being anything, and your answer is yes, then you've got this part of the lesson down. You understand that money is only a means, not an end. You recognize that it's a useful measure for the marketplace, not the be-all to success. You've already got a handle on financial balance.

What about Biggie's emphasis on the problems related to money? First of all, you don't have to be a rap star to learn that the minute your income rises at a certain healthy rate how quickly your expenses rise exponentially to blunt any profit you could have anticipated. It's not just your own excessive desire to have those options you wanted when you couldn't have them. Even if you're disciplined in keeping yourself in check, you can be sure that before you've actually made some decent bucks, the feeding frenzy will begin. All of a sudden, friends, relatives, former associates, and strangers you passed on the street years before will come crawling out of the woodwork to spend your money for you. Everybody and their brother, as well as their pet poodle, will remind you constantly of everything they did for you once upon a time and go on and on until all you can do is say, "How much?" As generous as you want to be, you'll have to learn to say no, and that won't make you beloved.

That's only the beginning of grasping the double-edged sword that gets swung with this lesson. Again, one of the reasons that some of us downplay our aspirations in terms of our larger goals is the jealousy and downright hatred it provokes in others. Seeking your farthest star may have nothing to do with money, but it will still cost you. It may be that you're leaving an abusive relationship or breaking a cycle of dependency. It may be that you're taking on the status quo. You might be crazy enough to think that you can create a new paradigm for the engines of industry and commerce around the world. Whatever it is, the more empowered you become, the more you may be resented. Be prepared for push-back and be prepared for problems. Be prepared to spend a lot of time alone—which is okay, too.

And if you're still just thinking about the toys, what you'll learn, as I discovered much to my surprise, is that you won't necessarily have the time to enjoy them. It is true what they say, that time is the ultimate luxury—which is why a quiet night at home watching a classic movie with folks I love is as enriching to me as a resort vacation.

This life-changing lesson for mastery, again, is a reminder that the closer you come to reaching that farthest star, the crazier things will get. At your zenith, all of that will multiply and amplify. And the odds heavily favor that it's going to involve folks close to you. In any pursuit of happyness, I recommend that you highlight these words. You may not want to believe that anyone you know would be jealous or feel entitled to your options, but you should expect it.

None of us are immune to the reality of *Mo' money, mo' options, mo' problems*. Standing back in that food line when I was thinking about how riches could take away all my problems, who would have known that after crawling out of the gutter with a baby tied on my back to become a self-made entrepreneur and contributing citizen of the world, I would also become the first man in the history of the United States to have a complaint of racial discrimination filed against him by one of his own relatives? That is true. A member of my extended family was given a job in my company and wasn't doing the work. Upon being dismissed, my relative's reaction was to sue and claim racism! Preposterous and baseless, yes. Painful, absolutely! And it cost.

The saying that no good deed goes unpunished must have been applicable as well, but that was all it took for me to fully digest the expression *Mo' money, mo' problems*.

Once I put both sides of the equation together, I had an epiphany. It was finally possible for me to answer those three questions and say that I wanted to control my financial resources, to have them work for me, and that money was neither the problem nor the cure.

The practical application has been to maintain balance between desired financial growth and the cost of doing business. That has been a reminder to keep focused on the work at hand and to reinvest the lion's share of profit back into the business, minimizing excesses all around, and to share the wealth by investing in socially conscious organizations that emphasize education and job creation.

Let me emphasize that there ain't no shame in the game of marking your success with a symbol like a red Ferrari or any other option that the fruits of your labors might bring you. And as you expand your belief in your possibilities, so, too, can you expand your income. I'm also big on the old-fashioned advice many of us learned growing up—spend less than you earn and pay as you go. If you set the rules and adhere to them, that's another way to gain the advantage in the power over money. It's useful to also have a stated policy in regard to your personal financial affairs, which you can create with your C-5 complex, making it clear, concise, and compelling so that you follow it with commitment and consistency. What's more, such a document may diminish the problems of misunderstandings when partners or family members have differing ideas.

My last suggestion as you seek your balance when it comes to mastery of money is to remember the earlier lesson to learn the ropes first and then conquer Rome. That's the real strategy for rags to riches.

LESSON #35
Money Is the Least Significant Component of Wealth
KEYWORD: *Worth*

At a conference for an association of small-business owners, which included freelance artists and entrepreneurs involved in an array of interests, I had a memorable exchange with a fellow named Dave who stood up and introduced himself as a "fifty-year-old recovering surfer dude." He went on to say that up until three years earlier, he had never considered himself a success by any measure. Then push came to shove when he lost his "bill-paying job" along with the family's medical benefits, at the same time that his wife had a health crisis and couldn't work. Dave said that he had never been forced to step up to the plate. Now it was time. Even though he didn't know what he could do, his motivation was to show his young sons that he was going to try.

Instead of thinking on a modest scale, Dave accepted the challenge at hand to make a bold plan for how he wanted to live the second half of his life. He invested in equipment to start his own carpet-cleaning business and found out off the bat that he was a born salesman. The busier he got, the more energized and focused he became. If he could build a business and enjoy it, why not investigate a second pursuit along the lines of some of the direct marketing programs he'd been hearing about. In three years both businesses were booming, and he was having the time of his life. How had it all been possible? Dave explained, "I started to read. Anything and everything. Ten, twenty minutes a day to start. Before that, I'd never read a book in my life."

As the result of reading, Dave decided if he could change something as basic as his own literacy level, he could change from someone who felt unsuccessful to a person worthy of being successful and empowered. His life-changing lesson for mastery came from the realization that success was nothing more than doing the little things that unsuccessful people don't do. Many of his examples were the ways we all learn the fundamentals of hitting the anvil: giving that extra amount of care, following up on leads, making five more phone calls than the amount required, staying on top of the details.

Now that he was starting to make some real money, his question to me was, "What's the one thing I should know that people who aren't wealthy don't know?"

My answer was stated in the form of a lesson that took me some time to learn and that has been emphasized to me by every master I've ever met—*Money is the least significant component of wealth.*

Dave understood immediately. In fact, I could tell by his smile that his worth had nothing to do with the balance in his bank account or how much he was pulling down a year.

Let me be quick to add that not everyone in that room or elsewhere gets it. Interestingly enough, whenever I receive correspondence about how useful this lesson has been for someone, I will note that the individuals are often prominent in their communities or have attained some of the other components of wealth that are more significant than money.

Young audiences aren't big on this lesson, and I don't blame them. They've been raised with the get-rich-quick-or-die-trying mentality that isn't just in the 'hood but is everywhere. My argument whenever they wish to debate me about the value of money in determining worth is to look at every kid in the room and ask, "How many of you know any retired drug dealers?" Of course, that's an oxymoron because drug dealers don't retire. They either die or go to jail.

Although this lesson has been transformational for me, it took a while to learn. The teachers of it were Christopher Jr. and Jacintha. My son comes out with some pretty dazzling pearls of wisdom now and then, but the absolute most priceless gift he ever gave me that I never forgot was the night when he was about two years old, back in Oakland, and I was giving him a bath by candlelight because the electricity had been turned off. Cash had gotten low and I was late on the bill. Even so, that night I was the wealthiest man in the universe when he said, quite out of the blue, "Poppa, you're a good poppa."

My daughter is so much like her grandmother, my mom, it's uncanny. Often she will say things in almost the same intonation as my mother. Every day she and her brother remind me that family, for me, is the most significant component of wealth. And time, as we've already seen, is also a luxury that I dearly treasure, an asset to be used wisely and prized. Other resources that I value in myself and that give me worth are passion, focus, oceanic persistence, and many of the very assets that have been revealed by numerous life lessons. Pursuit, as you probably have discovered by now, helps us to value those assets even more.

Again, this isn't to be naive and say money doesn't matter. To the contrary, it's the dominant means of exchange in the world, a useful measure and standard, and the usual means for providing those *options* we discussed elsewhere. Anyone who tells you that money doesn't matter at all probably has never had to go hungry or worry about where they're going to sleep that night and how to pay for prescriptions, transportation to work, or clothes to keep them warm.

We all deserve to receive respectful compensation for our work and our contributions. But if money becomes the only barometer for wealth and worth, we will never master an appreciation or use of all our other valuable assets. As the least significant component of wealth, money is still and has always been a unit of measurement. It should never be a measurement of the worth of your life.

A practical application of this lesson that has been helpful for me is to substitute the word *resourceful* for wealthy. It can be eye-opening to reconsider how, yes, money is only one resource among many, and when compared with the others, it's the only one that is easy to replace when it's lost. To take this application a step further, you might also want to explore the always useful tool of the PBS.

No, this doesn't mean watching more television, even if it is educational.

The PBS, or personal balance sheet, is traditionally a two-tiered or two-columned ledger that quantifies your net worth by listing your gross income, savings, investments, and other material holdings, from which you subtract your cost of living and what you owe, short and long term. It's an accounting of your assets less your liabilities. Ideally, the plus side of the ledger will be greater than the minus side.

Some years ago, economists began to recognize how balance sheets showing a company's net worth in fiscal terms alone were not coming close to providing investors with a sense of the company's real value in terms of intangibles—those assets and liabilities that can't be measured by tangible, quantitative numbers. Other than on-site visits and gut reactions, we had very few ways to assess such intangibles as human resources.

A company that wasn't ringing up the numbers yet might still be a gold mine of innovation, intellectual property, strategic partners, powerful brand concepts, corporate values, and reputation. As a result, some have developed the use of a "balanced scorecard" that includes profits but also attempts to create market values for intangibles such as socially conscious practices that positively impact the community and the planet.

To apply the lesson that money is the least significant component of wealth, you may be surprised at what you'll discover by creating your own version of a PBS to consider the assets and resources you most value. You can list accomplishments and even undertakings that you dared to pursue, whether or not they succeeded. You can list challenges and obstacles overcome, along with life lessons you were savvy enough to keep as part of your worth.

Maybe your professional work ethic is an asset. Maybe you are a gold-medal-winning parent. You may want to remind yourself of areas in which you've attained mastery that you don't value enough. What about character, discipline, resilience, instigation, and other resources that make you proud of yourself? You can list any of the five Cs or the three As. What about your reputation for kindness, humor, and flexibility, and your unique point of view? What about your natural resources? You could have a million-dollar smile or the style of someone who looks like a million bucks. How about your eyesight or your powers of observation? Are you a good listener? If you know that you are where you are right now because you drove here, then you have power that is a thousand times more valuable than dough.

All of these intangibles are resources that can infinitely enrich you and lead to lasting growth. If you, like me, find that you have been blessed by the opportunities to teach, to pass on your life lessons, to share your story, and to inspire others to dare, dream, and do, make sure you write those things down on your PBS in big bold capital letters.

Now bankers may not buy into this accounting. But they're not riding too high on the authority scale these days, so who are they to assess your value?

Take it from me and from Dave. Worth is in the proof of your actions, the sum of your choices, the success that you believed possible—even before you mastered it.

Yes, it's true that not all those assets on your PBS will be acknowledged by a banker—unless, that is, the banker is you. There we have our bottom line: that only you can determine your true worth.

LESSON #36
Conscious Capitalism: A Personal and Global Primer
KEYWORD: *Contribution*

The mastery of the pursuit of happyness is a mysterious and challenging subject. You won't be surprised when I say that it's provoked many questions that I've sought to answer over the years. At the top of that list is a question so ancient that it was probably asked back in the days of cave dwellers when our human ancestors started fighting over who had the better cave. It's the question of why the cave dweller with more and better stuff wasn't necessarily the happyest. Cut to modern day: examples abound everywhere that the guys and gals with the most money are usually not the happiest either.

What is it that defines those who are the happyest? That question has also probably been asked as far back as when prehistoric humans looked around and saw that odd, happy individual who had the least amount of stuff—except for something he or she had created messing around with sticks and stones, a little valuable commodity later known as fire, which, of course, led to the first-ever community barbecue and picnic.

What that happyest person had attained, in my own opinion and that of other experts on the subject of mastering happyness, was a sense of contribution. The fire was undoubtedly created to better the chances of survival of that individual and family. It also went on to contribute to the survival of humankind.

That is the premise of *conscious capitalism*. It rests on the belief that each and every one of us can and should have (1) the opportunity to create value for ourselves and (2) the opportunity to add value to the world. As a business paradigm and as a structure for personal growth, it works along the same lines.

As for how this life-changing awareness was first presented to me, I have to give credit to a handful of mentors who have been among the greatest movers and shakers of our times and who have attained mastery while changing the games in their respective fields. Each of them taught me in different ways that socially conscious use of capital can be more powerful than all the other forces combined that may rise up to defeat it. They also gave me wise counsel at different times to stay connected to core values, lest I lose focus. Most of all I learned that true contribution is always a two-for-one.

William Lucy may have taught me that more than anyone else. He also demonstrated to me that you never want to underestimate someone with a background in engineering in their ability to help you expand your global vision and strategy. Not that Bill is one of those traditional square-thinking engineers who are so unfairly maligned for collecting spare parts to build nuclear reactors in their extra time, but his analytical brilliance has a way of sneaking up on you and everyone else. The founder of the Coalition of Black Trade Unionists, Bill built it from the ground up when he launched it in 1972 to become one of the most powerful labor organizations in the nation, with over fifty chapters and going strong. He's the former chair of the Council of Institutional Investments, and for thirty-five years he's been the secretary/treasurer of the AFSCME (American Federation of State, County and Municipal Employees), which serves 1.3 million members. For me, he epitomizes the blacksmith who has ascended to the status of wizardry.

Knowing and learning from Bill Lucy has been a blessing for me for many reasons. As mentor and mentee, we connected on many levels, not the least of which was the fact that his father had split early in his life. He understood what it meant for me to have been raised without a dad, and he gave me encouragement at times when I was trying to break through to the next level but hadn't figured it out yet. Though we didn't speak much at all about the tragedy he had endured in the loss of his son many years earlier, the subtext was there, and I admired him even more for his courage in committing himself to causes larger than himself after something so devastating.

I learned about how he held himself above the fray in one instance when I accompanied him to a rally at a convention center where he was going to be giving a keynote address. As for myself, I certainly did not stay above the fray. There are only a couple of things in the world that can set me off and transform me from a basically down-to-earth, peace-loving, God-fearing man into a major asshole—if you'll please pardon the term. One of those things is the question, "Where are your credentials?" Even worse is when that question is put to someone who happens to be one of my most valued mentors, as well as someone who should be globally recognized for his many contributions.

Unfortunately for the convention center security guard who unwittingly asked that question of William Lucy, even blocked our entrance and asked for some form of identification, I started into a tirade. Bill shot me a look that told me he could handle the situation. But more to the point, Bill Lucy didn't need to part the masses and have them cheer his name. He was about something bigger than being recognized.

I learned from Bill Lucy, through his firsthand account, about the labor issues regarding making a decent working wage that Dr. King had come to address in Memphis, in the same speech he gave about the Promised Land of dignity for people of all races. It was also from Bill that I was able to understand the working components of how he and other labor leaders fired up the movement to pull money and investment out of apartheid-run South Africa. Of course, all of this was inspiring and fascinating, especially as I began to hammer out ideas for how to bring back the investment needed to instigate the flow of capital for job and wealth creation there and here in America.

Bill's advice on that front and for solving such problems as homelessness and poverty has always been to look at those issues from a fresh perspective. He has often said, "Chris, before you can fix something, you have to understand how it was built." He has also reminded me that systems of the status quo aren't necessarily built logically. So if you want to defeat them, introducing logic is not always a winning strategy. Organization of human resources, ingenuity, passion, timing, adaptation—all of those capacities, employed individually and collectively, are important.

More than teaching me that we each have the power within us to uplift ourselves and others at the same time, Bill Lucy demonstrated by example how we can do that. What I learned from watching him was that whenever he has felt called to action, his willingness to put himself in tough situations was never preceded by the question, "Should I?" Where he can play a meaningful role, no matter what the odds, his question is always, "How can I?"

If this empowers you to look around yourself right now and see opportunities where you can make a contribution—or do more than you already are—then you already have the basics of this lesson down. If you have recognized the benefits to yourself as well as to others, then you've got it mastered.

You can also take this to the next level, as I did, and employ the two steps of conscious capitalism to whatever your pursuit of happyness, personally or globally, might be. Let me emphasize that this doesn't have to be in the business world or on issues of worldwide concern. You can localize and personalize these two steps for such pursuits as empowering yourself as a person, parent, professional, or plain old citizen. The simple construction that I use is (a) create value for shareholders (including yourself, your family, co-workers, allies, associates, and affiliates, or any stakeholders who may benefit) and (b) find a way to add value to the world.

When all is said and done, inasmuch as we have autonomy over our actions, we're still all here in this together—microorganisms in this here and now as we know it, totally connected, interrelated, and dependent on the whole. And what is having fire all to yourself—or success and happyness in a vacuum? It's empty.

You may disagree with the premise that fulfillment and meaning will come from the knowledge that you're creating value for yourself and your shareholders (whoever they are), and adding value to the world. You may just want to say to hell with making a contribution to anyone, let alone yourself. So be it. You may still want to ask yourself, when it's all done, again, *Will it have mattered that I was here?*

On the flip side, you may feel that you must give of yourself unconditionally and not combine socially conscious action with any form of capitalism. That, too, comes from your right to master happyness on your own terms.

My advisory on this lesson, however you decide—or not—to apply it, is to think of that cave dweller coming up with the force of fire. The question wasn't "should I?" but "how can I?" Furthermore, there was something definitely in it for him or her, and for the rest of us. And that said, if the cave dweller could do it, why can't you?

LESSON #37
Make Your Dream Bigger Than Yourself

KEYWORD: *Vision*

This lesson is one that has lived inside of me from the time that I was young and has woven itself into the fabric of who I am. But it has only been in the last five years that I've witnessed how many ways it can be applied, thanks to the gift of meeting everyday people everywhere I go—and getting to know their stories through correspondence in the most moving details. They are living examples of what it means to expand your vision in order to *Make your dream bigger than yourself.*

An e-mail from sixteen-year-old Scott of Phoenix, Arizona, told the story of how two years earlier he and some friends decided to commit some hours to community service and to volunteer one morning a week at a homeless shelter, serving meals. "It was an amazing experience as a youth," he wrote, "to see the joy on people's faces as they received breakfast." In the process, they befriended a middle-aged homeless gentleman who had been unemployed for some time. At first Scott and his friends made small gestures, like pitching in to buy him toiletries, then purchasing him a few articles of clothing. Whenever they asked if he wanted something else, he would tell them, "I don't want to put you out." Scott recognized that he was genuinely concerned that these teenagers would end up broke and homeless, if they did too much. Then one day while volunteering at another homeless shelter, Scott came to the conclusion that they could do more:

> Homeless person after homeless person came through the line. Young people, old people, single mothers with a child, they all needed food, they were all trapped in a reality that none of us feeding them had to deal with. . . . I was thinking that we were keeping them alive, but that was it. . . . What could we do to help them get out of homelessness?

They thought of the gentleman they had befriended and wondered how he would receive their help if they offered to mentor him to "get a job, maintain a budget, create a community of support and love around him."

Scott went on to say that two years later their friend was employed, managing his own money and time, happy in his own place, and "living the life he never dreamed would be possible." For Scott and his friends, it was all the incentive they needed to create a project they call "Open Table"—using the same resources of support and coaching that had been successful in their first effort, all putting their energies into something larger than themselves. The three had continued to grow their vision and were working in partnership with other forces in the community with the shared focus to empower those who are homeless toward rebuilding their own lives.

Two aspects of Scott's e-mail have really stayed with me. First, he never needed anyone to tell him to "Be the change you want to see" or "The change starts with you." With passion, focus, and determination, he had started and he was being the change! Second, Scott helped me answer a question that comes to me constantly from folks still diggin' their potatoes when it comes to pursuing their dreams. They all want to know how and where to find a mentor. Many ask if I'll be that mentor. Scott didn't have to go looking. He chose to become his own mentor. Certainly, he may have been inspired by role models in his community and others, but he rolled up his sleeves, motivated his friends, and said, *Let's go, let's do this thing.*

If you are anything like the majority of folks that I've been graced with getting a chance to meet and know, I suspect that this is a lesson that lives within you as well and that it may have already been activated. Or perhaps it's waiting for that right kind of fertilizer to help it grow and reach forth to the surface.

Sometimes those tough and even devastating challenges that occur are what's needed to connect us to the cause of our lifetime, in order to give us the vision for the role that we can play. I've met survivors of unimaginable suffering who have told me as much, who have said that in their darkest hour the only light they could find was the belief that they could make it through so that someone else wouldn't have to suffer as they had. In that way, their dreams became so much more than themselves.

As you read these words, if you have not experienced that kind of suffering or a severe blow like the loss of a loved one, you may wonder how it is possible to bear. If you know about such a loss, you may appreciate the words that I received from a single mother who wrote to me about her struggle after losing her mother, "my rock and my inspiration," followed soon after by her young daughter who was "the light of my life." How do you respond to someone who has lost both her parent and her only child? When we are parentless, we are called orphans. When we lose a spouse, we are widows and widowers. But there is no word to describe the loss of a child. She wrote to let me know that the only thing that had rallied her spirits was to work to raise resources for medical research about the rare disease that had taken her daughter from her—so that families wouldn't have to go through what she had. The idea that she could do this in her daughter's memory was what helped her to grow her vision and to believe "there is light at the end of the tunnel."

The connection between our own suffering and the ability to have the vision to make our dreams larger than ourselves is not coincidental. No one personifies this more for me than Nelson Mandela. It was his journey that most illustrated the fact that wherever you are in life, you can see all the steps that were taken, all of the collective steps that count—and must be accounted for, accepted, and acknowledged. There is no doubt that he wouldn't have accomplished what he did—and wouldn't have changed all of us in the process—had he not lived through every challenge along the way that he faced, including twenty-seven years spent in prison.

I had the haunting and life-transforming experience of visiting Robben Island Prison, where Mandela had been sent at the end of 1962—with a life sentence—and where I was shown his prison cell. His life story flashed in front of my eyes—his childhood in a remote village, loss of his father, his promising education, his masterful legal and boxing careers, his battle to bring down apartheid, and his twenty-seven years of incarceration, eighteen of which were spent in isolation. His story amazed me then, as it still does to a certain extent, as I try to imagine what sustained him. What was it that allowed him to declare in 1975 that he believed he would one day be free and walk out of prison on his own two feet?

His vision was possible because of nothing more than the light that came into his window—a small, high square no bigger than a picture frame. All that was visible was a sliver of the world outside during the daytime hours. That was all he was allowed to see during his years of solitary confinement, before he was sent to work in the quarries and was nearly blinded by the sun there.

In 1990, after international pressure helped free Nelson Mandela— what many once said would have been impossible—he walked out of

prison on his own, baby step by baby step. How fitting that Mr. Mandela's autobiography is entitled *A Long Walk to Freedom*. Seeing that
place for myself and visualizing that moment was in itself life changing, as it has been to watch how his vision has unfolded. At so many
points, Madiba, as he is called in South Africa, could have retired and
retreated from public life, but he seems to do more with every passing
year. After winning the Nobel Prize, serving as president of South
Africa, even creating a new fashion for the men of his country to
improve self-esteem, Mandela's dreams have continued to expand to
include the formation of an international council of elders who are
focused on the most pressing issues of our times.

That work, however, is not only for our elders—one of the most
important applications of this lesson that I can share with you. With
the opportunity to grow your dream, your pursuit can become larger
than money, success, and mastery of only your arena. With vision,
you're about much more than all of that, on a higher level. Money woes,
economic troubles, and business bubbles can't defeat you when you
choose to be above those concerns and instead grow your dream to
take in others.

When I had the privilege of meeting Nelson Mandela for the first
time, what had been scheduled as a fifteen-minute handshake meeting
to share my vision for conscious capitalism with him turned into a
forty-five-minute sit-down. The two of us sat on his couch together,
side by side, and spoke of growing the dream of socially conscious private investment, job creation, and economic empowerment together—
for South Africa, America, and everywhere, in underdeveloped and
developed countries alike. The conversation, of course, was life altering, but it was his closing observations that most resonated and that I'd
like to share with you. Madiba told me that in spite of the challenges,
those of our time have all been given the opportunity and the responsibility to play a role in what he calls "the Great Generation," defined by
him as the generation that has the will and the means to do things
bigger than ourselves.

Five / Spiritual Genetics

People see God every day, they just don't recognize him.
—Pearl Bailey
Singer, actress, composer

An Introduction to Lessons #38 to #42— Spiritual Lessons for Connecting to *Your* Higher Power

In previous chapters, many of the life lessons for pursuing happyness have had a practical focus for accessing the abundance of resources that are available to all of us. In this chapter, we're going to depart from the focus on the practical and turn to a handful of spiritual lessons that have been more empowering and more transformational for me over the course of my life as a whole than anything covered so far.

Although I have touched on matters of faith in earlier lessons, I want to use this introduction to respond to the many questions that are sent to me about what religion I practice and what denomination I follow. Though I continue to be a member of Glide Memorial Methodist Church in San Francisco and see myself as a mainstream Christian who rolls with Jesus, I honor the faiths of friends and colleagues who are Catholic, Jewish, Muslim, Buddhist, and those who have other viewpoints, as well as those who don't name their beliefs. Therefore, if I had to say where my loyalty stands, I like to say "All of Thee Above."

The essence of spirituality—versus religious doctrines and denominations—is that it emphasizes the higher power that is within each of us and that connects us to one another. What we call our preferred form of showing worship or even what we call that higher power shouldn't get in our spiritual way.

You don't have to subscribe to any religious affiliation to be spiritual. Frankly, when I imagine what heaven looks like, I don't envision a bunch of souls running around wearing jerseys with denominational logos on the back. I could be wrong, but so far no one has come back to tell us otherwise. I've also considered that perhaps some religious leaders and institutions—of course not all—do damage by misrepresenting the word of the Lord or our higher power for their own purposes. This has led me to wonder what Jesus would say about how his teachings have been used. I've also said that on the day he does come back, I want to be in the front row on that great day, sitting there, surrounded by all the preachers, rabbis, reverends, and priests, when the Messiah comes out onto that stage and looks right at those who believed they were the authorities and tells them, "I didn't say that—" or perhaps "That is not what I meant!" Right there and then, I'd love to see the response from all those religious leaders. God speaking to us directly with no interpretation needed and no commission charged? And I'll be very happy on that great and glorious day to be the first to turn to those men and women of the cloth and say, "Can I have my money back?"

That's where my imagination leads me—to humor!

You know what? I think that the God I know and love would actually laugh, too. Because what I believe and feel deep down in my cells—yes, my genes, or rather, my spiritual genes—is that God's in all of us and connects us one to the other through commonalities like laughter, compassion, and love. Humor, after all, is a saving grace, endowed to us by our Maker—just like all of our other parts.

A brief background on my use of the term "spiritual genetics" is definitely in order, since many have written to me asking for further elaboration. I'd never heard that term used before until it actually came out of my mouth in answer to a question that was put to me during a newspaper interview. When those words came to me, and then through me, in the form of a concept that I'd never explained or hammered out for myself, I was frankly thunderstruck. The journalist had simply asked what it was that made it possible for me to break the generational cycle of fathers who abandon their children.

For a moment, I had started to say, well, I take after my mother. And then I thought it better to rephrase that and say I inherited that ability from my mother. But actually, as I thought about it further, I realized that it wasn't a given; it was a conscious choice. I had at some point, when I was very young, *consciously chosen* to embrace the spirit in myself that I'd seen in my mother as well. I could have as easily chosen the spiritual genetics that I'd inherited from my biological father—who was a void in my life until I met him at age twenty-eight. Or I could have become that which I saw in my stepfather, for that matter. But instead, just as my mother chose to embrace her light—rather than the dark—so did I.

Out of so direct a question from a newspaper interviewer—which, by the way, I'd been asked by others—had come a personally transformative moment. And when I began talking about my revelation to others, I could see the concept stirred something that connected them with deeper, inner truths.

The more that I've explored the properties of spiritual genetics since that conversation with that interviewer, the more I believe we all can learn from embracing the best that is within us and within our human family. As we'll be seeing with the lessons coming up, the good news is that, unlike your mother's nose that you have no choice about inheriting, we have options as to which of our spiritual genetics we energize within ourselves.

I have received a deluge of correspondence, in fact, about this growing area of interest of mine—confirming for me that the subject is as enlightening to others as it is to me. A colleague of mine confided that he had never felt any connection to a higher power until he took a closer look at how he had consciously chosen to embrace a quality within himself that was reminiscent of the fighting spirit of his grandfather who had driven an ambulance for the French Resistance in World War II. Countless individuals have shared similar stories of embracing the light from the spiritual genetics of someone they loved. Others have written to say that they felt liberated by having the option to reject the darker aspects of their own spiritual genetics.

An e-mail that was sent to me from a married couple shocked me. In it the wife introduced herself and explained that her husband had always used hateful language toward minorities and it really bothered her, but there was nothing she could do to change him—until recently. She asked him to sit down and explain what had happened. He continued the e-mail from there, stating at the beginning, "Until I heard you explain generational cycles, I have always hated N3$^&*(s." He actually censored his own racial epithet. He then went through a list of prominent, successful African Americans and celebrities who were minorities. "They don't impress me with their money or their success," he wrote. Then he said that he didn't hate me:

> There is something about you that makes me not look at your race. Maybe it's because you had the kind of relationship with your step-father that I had with my dad. Hearing that, all the hate and discomfort went away. It made me realize that we're all the same in God's eyes, under the skin, and that my ignorance was passed down to me from my dad's hatred and bigotry that got beat into me every day of my life until I left home. I remember swearing that I'd never lay a hand on my kids and, with my step-kids now, I've kept my promise. But I never thought about how his hatred could get passed on too. I want to break that cycle and make sure it ends with me. It will make me a better husband and a better father.

The wife ended the e-mail by saying that he had agreed to join a local men's softball team that he had previously avoided because of the minority membership. And he was having the time of his life!

I use this story as a dramatic example of how spiritual lessons that give us connection to ourselves and our higher power can change us at any stage of our lives, as we'll see in Lessons #38 to #42, coming right up:

#38 This man's conscious choice to let go of judgment proves this lesson's message that we are all equal on the road to **enlightenment**.

#39 In his case, and in all of ours, there is a spiritual path to **healing** that is also accessible to one and all.

#40 This is a lesson about our higher power's gift of **abundance** to which we are all entitled.

#41 For this couple, and for all of us, opportunities for **reverence** arise out of the most unlikely circumstances.

#42 And, finally, how we choose to embrace lessons of **growth** from our past and our present paves the way for our own futures and those of our offspring.

These next five life lessons represent only the beginning of my exploration of spiritual genetics, and only a sampling of how spiritual lessons ultimately reveal to us all the guidance we will ever need in our respective pursuits of happyness. Everything we've covered earlier is vital, I believe, in our journeys to become who we were meant to be. But it's the spiritual wisdom we seek that brings the blessings and that crown us with our true glory. These lessons, therefore, aren't intended to convert you to any way of thinking but your own. Hopefully, they will be nourishing, in any event, and leave you with some soul food for thought.

LESSON #38
Embrace the Best of Your Spiritual Genetics
KEYWORD: *Enlightenment*

Have you ever been thinking strongly about a question—searching for an answer that you couldn't even find a map to steer you toward—

when, out of the blue, your answer arrives? Or have you ever thought it uncanny when someone happens to come along as if divinely appointed and practically reads your mind with your answer? In those cases, you might have been startled or incredulous. Or you might have figured out that there's a logical explanation that has nothing to do with telepathy or supernatural phenomena. In my experience, the best way to make use of those moments of synchronicity is not to worry so much about how they happened but instead to enjoy the wonder. Not only that. I've also learned that those apparent coincidences can come as messenger moments—when valuable knowledge that is most needed can be obtained.

For instance, as I've recounted both here and in my memoir, *The Pursuit of Happyness,* my mother counseled me that whatever I wanted to do, I could. That was a messenger moment. When a perfect stranger happened to cross my path on the street in San Francisco and, without any specific, possible knowledge of my situation, reminded me about Glide Memorial's food program and homeless hotel just when I most needed the support, that could only have been another messenger moment.

Along these same lines, not long after I had started thinking about this idea of spiritual genetics, before I'd found the words to ask more questions, important information arrived from Dr. Maya Angelou. In connection to a conversation we were having about the devastation in New Orleans after Hurricane Katrina hit, we both agreed that the disaster revealed the best and the worst of human capacities for survival— the good, the bad, and the ugly. On the one hand, we saw the help citizens gave to one another to save lives, at the risk of their own. On the other hand, we saw those who simply didn't care and let a city drown.

"But you know, Chris," said Dr. Angelou, "we can't separate ourselves from all that is human, good or bad." She went on to say that whenever anyone commits the most heinous, unspeakable crime or whenever anyone rises to perform the most heroic act, we can't say that we are like only one and not like the other.

What I understood her point to mean is that within us are capacities to be both the sinners and the saints. In any given situation, we can choose to embrace the saint within us but not the sinner. We all have our lightness and our darkness. Our human challenge is to continuously claim the light of the best that is within us—the best of our spiritual genetics.

Then Dr. Angelou told me an astonishing story about where this concept crystallized for her. She described her discovery of the written works of Terence, a freed slave who had originally been brought to Rome from Africa, and who became a leading playwright before he died ca. 160 B.C.E. Little known today, the plays Terence wrote about 2,175 years ago went on to be an important influence for famous dramatists throughout the centuries that followed—including William Shakespeare. When asked once how he could tell stories of interest to Romans of all backgrounds, Terence explained the universality by saying, "I am a human being; nothing human can be alien to me."

Here was an instance of someone embracing the best of his own human capacities to overcome actual and mental bondage in order to pursue mastery. So, too, does Dr. Angelou's life journey demonstrate how she rejected the darkness of abandonment, poverty, rape, and abuse and rose to embrace the best of her spiritual genetics. These were her soul's lessons on the road to enlightenment.

After Dr. Angelou told me about Terence, I did some research and learned some interesting details. Amazingly, not long after being brought to Rome and given his freedom, Terence quickly made his way into one of the most exclusive literary circles of the day. Nowhere was it indicated that he knew this was to be his calling, but apparently he was a natural and soon his gifts as a comedic playwright flourished. Instead of following the prevailing Roman styles, however, Terence went against the grain and ahead of the curve, basing his plays on some of the riskier "new comedy" that the Greeks had developed. Despite all kinds of criticism that he would pollute the purity of Roman rules of classic theater, when Terence's plays were performed, the critics and the public alike embraced his uncanny ability to capture Rome at the time—from the intricacies of language to social class differences. How was it possible for someone raised in a remote village nearly two hundred centuries B.C.E., who was taken from his home, enslaved, and brought to a foreign land, to become a leading literary light? How is it possible that the human stories he told back then and his invention of satire continue to influence us to this very day?

His higher power, to which he was connected, taught him how to do something he wasn't supposed to be able to do. You might even say that we all have the pursuit of happyness hardwired into us through our spiritual genetics, which can provide us with guidance no matter what we seek. The resources can be used to follow examples of what's humanly possible from the best to the worst. That's why when we say—*wow, if that person can do something supposedly impossible, I can, too!*—that statement is not just hopeful but backed up by someone else's past experience. So, too, we can look at someone else and say—*wow, if that person chose to do something I find reprehensible, I can choose not to do that.*

When choosing not to give in to forces of darkness, we naturally look for the alternative. In my case, I found spiritual connection in my mother's light. In spite of the ways that her dreams had been denied and deferred, the knowledge of her spirit in me empowered me not only to have dreams that she instilled in me, but also to exercise the power and the responsibility to make those dreams come true. Instead of simply inheriting spirit, *choosing* it makes it an active, living force. Thus, the conscious act of embracing light turns it on inside of you—as something alive, part of your soul, who you are and why you are.

Maybe this lesson resonates with conscious decisions you've made in the past to harness the light and the best of the energy of those around you. Or it's possible that you are now being given the opportunity to look back and notice your own spiritual choices. And if we believe that we have within our human genetics the wisdom of others who have come before us, that gives us an unlimited—and let me emphasize *unlimited*—reservoir of expertise that can be utilized for whatever we seek to pursue. It follows as well that we're all born with knowledge of the steps that have been taken by others before us and that will be taken by others after us.

As I've continued to research practical applications of spiritual genetics, I've been reading and discussing the subject with a range of spiritual thinkers. For example, Bishop Nathaniel Jarrett of the African Methodist Episcopal Zion Church referenced biblical passages that echo the premise of this lesson. He confirmed that indeed our Christian faith instructs us to believe that we are all born with a spirit that allows us to embrace God and light. No one is exempt.

Similarly, I understand from the teachings of Judaism that we are all born with the capacity to know God. Scripture tells us, after all, that we are each created in the image of the Divine and that we each have a divine soul—an indivisible essence that is inseparably bound to our creator. One of the most interesting discoveries that I made from reading the writings of rabbis and from talking to practicing Jews that I know is a story from Jewish lore about how the soul leaves the side of God reluctantly, carrying with it infinite and divine wisdom as it enters the body of a baby in the womb. But when the baby is born, the Angel Gabriel appears and touches the infant on the upper lip—the reason we all have that same indentation—which makes us forget all that we knew when we lived as one with God. It is said that our journey in life is to reclaim and rediscover all knowledge that our soul knew before we arrived here. How? Through life lessons, education, spiritual study, and good works in which lessons are learned and applied! Sound familiar?

Deepak Chopra has much to say about the ways that the science of genetics and human evolution is compatible with spirituality. As the president of the Alliance for a New Humanity (www.anhglobal.org)—a global nonprofit initiative that empowers individuals to become change agents—Dr. Chopra acknowledges that evolution has a spiritual as well as biological component, and that personal choice plays a pivotal role. One of the ways he suggests that we can connect to our higher powers for healing, growth, and empowerment is through meditation. For those who haven't meditated in any structured way before, the Alliance for a New Humanity website can provide you with step-by-step instructions. Basically, you need only sit quietly by yourself with your eyes closed and "pay attention to your heart." Then, Dr. Chopra says that you can begin to ask yourself "Who am I, what do I want, what are my unique talents, who are my heroes and heroines in history or mythology or religion, what's my life's purpose, what contribution do I wish to make to society?"

I've also turned to the teachings of Buddhism for insights on how to connect with the light within us. There is a funky saying that has a few applications for all of us: "If you meet the Buddha on the road to enlightenment, kill him." It's another way of saying that as long as you're following the Buddha, you ain't driving. Again, it's a reminder that as long as we hand the search for answers over to someone we think is wiser than us, we'll remain in the dark. The story behind that mantra, I've read, has to do with the dying words spoken by Shakyamuni, the historical Buddha, which were "Be a lamp unto yourselves." In other words, embrace *your* light. Or better still, be your own damn light!

While it is the best of our shared spiritual genetics that we can all aspire to embrace, I also am mindful of Dr. Angelou's admonition not to condemn or separate ourselves from folks who have chosen to submit to the dark—sometimes by default, sometimes because of ignorance or the lack of intention to evolve spiritually. What is our role, I wonder, when confronted by those individuals?

That's not an easy question for anyone. We can shrug and say, "Hey, I ain't my brother's keeper," and move on. Or can we? Perhaps, we can get out the garlic and perform an exorcism. Not my style! My option, taught to me by my higher power, is simply to show my light—and to remind that person that we are connected.

Through your spiritual genetics, anywhere and everywhere, you can let your light be a beacon for others.

My last advisory for this lesson is to start simply and powerfully from a place of love—as you contemplate ways that you can say yes to that which you hold high and no to that which you don't care to embrace in our human spiritual gene pool. Let the image or memory of someone you love, or someone you see as strong and wise, be reflected in you. Let their very best shine forth from your soul. Start and lead with love, and passion, and see where that goes.

LESSON #39
Breaking Generational Cycles

KEYWORD: *Healing*

If the knowledge that we're all human beings reminds us that nothing human should be alien to us, as Terence the playwright wrote, how can we use that awareness in breaking generational cycles? Let me simplify that by asking the question that comes up frequently: "How can we confront our own darkness?"

Few questions weigh as heavily on all of us. Some of the most heartbreaking letters that I read come from parents who pray desperately to be healed from the same negative cycles they saw their parents battle and are watching their children do the same. I am referring not only to the generational cycle of men who abandon their children, but also to the continuing trends that are putting more and more of our youngest citizens into foster care and the juvenile justice system. I'm talking about the generational cycles of poverty, domestic violence, addiction, crime, sexual assault, homelessness, illiteracy, and incarceration. I'm also talking about general cycles of bigotry, mental illness, obesity, dependency, and teenagers becoming parents before they've learned how to take care of themselves. And no less insidious are generational cycles of disrespect for others, a disregard for our planet, and a dismissal of our responsibilities to rise together or fall apart.

It may not be too large a stretch, if you look at various branches of your family tree, to expect that you may find some of those same destructive patterns. You may have chosen not to allow those behaviors to influence you. It's possible that you made that choice on a subconscious or preconscious level. You may also have not chosen and are now at the mercy of a cycle that controls you in ways you don't even know.

We know, of course, from medical and scientific experts that the likelihood that you may develop such concerns as substance abuse, mental illness, or obesity does increase when those issues are evident in parents and other predecessors. We also hear the debates over nature versus nurture when it comes to heredity, family upbringing, and social environment in relation to the cause of certain generational cycles. My point isn't to argue with experts but to say that instead of only looking at the disease model that asks "what went wrong?" when we look for possibilities for healing, we should also spend more time asking "what went right?" when cycles aren't replicated.

I've come to believe that we make decisions throughout our lives that determine who we become and why. It goes back to the saying that you take the cards you were dealt and play them, sometimes as they lay. This is to suggest that at some point, maybe even before you can remember using those cards, a game plan was chosen, and these patterns and cycles were established, while the form, shape, and depth of your soul were cast. Decisions were made, right or wrong, as to whether or not you would pursue your highest potential. Determinations were set not just as to right or wrong but as to how far you believed you could go. When confronting external factors, choices were made. Three consequences may have then resulted: the soul decides to (a) emerge and rise, (b) be beaten into the darkness, or (c) maintain the status quo. Your soul's version of Win, Lose or Draw!

It may surprise you—after all that's been said about the darkness that my stepfather, Freddie Triplett, represented—to hear that I'm now thankful for the card dealt to me by his presence in my life. He helped me understand this lesson about how generational cycles can be broken. Because he was the way he was, I witnessed firsthand the worst examples of human behavior—a display that prompted my choice to become who I am: everything that he was not.

I also chose not to perpetuate the generational cycle passed on from my biological father in providing the Y chromosome to multiple children borne by different women. My intent was to be the weak link in that chain, to break the cycle in my lineage. Frankly, I don't think anyone on that side of my family even knows how many lives he created. Notice that I didn't say "fathered." When I finally made my way at age twenty-eight to meet him down in Louisiana the first time, I took an important step in healing my long-standing case of the no-daddy blues, as I have since called it. And I wasn't alone. My newfound siblings shared the joke with me that every four years, just like the Olympics, somebody shows up looking for the daddy they never knew! We all resemble each other so much, my siblings told me all you had to do was take a look at 'em and say "C'mon in." The experience only reinforced my resolve to be a steadfast, hands-on father, actively involved in the lives of my children.

In adulthood, I could look back and recognize the spiritual part of the choice that I made in early childhood to not be that man who spread his seed around and then didn't spend time helping his offspring grow. At five or six years old, I learned something about healing myself in that process. Instead of feeling powerless, I could declare that I would never threaten or terrorize my children—as I'd experienced at the hands of my stepfather. As a five-year-old I didn't know anything about commitment, parental responsibility, or the potential scarring that abandonment can cause. But I knew what a promise was and the promise to myself became part of my soul, who I am, all intertwined in my spiritual genetics.

As you look at aspects of your life that are impacted by negative influences that you've inherited, remember that the act of healing from generational cycles and familial patterns isn't about an overnight, miraculous cure. At a teachers' conference in Los Angeles, I had an interesting conversation with an educator who had come from a household not too different from mine in terms of what I call the "cycle of silence." She knew exactly what I mean in my description of the "don't ask, don't tell" policy that was enforced by everyone in the family about unpleasant personal matters of grave importance. Her story was that she was never told that the woman who raised her, who she thought was her mother, was, in fact, her aunt. After her mother figure died, someone mentioned it offhandedly, as if it didn't matter. Part of her inspiration to become a teacher was to work with kids and instill in them the right to ask questions and be given answers.

Breaking the cycle of silence hasn't been easy for me. My mother, wise as she was in almost every area, resisted my questions around painful subject matter by insisting that it was water under the bridge and talking about it wouldn't do any good. As a parent, I found myself shutting down about serious issues about my son and daughter. It occurred to me, however, that if I didn't do something to break the cycle of silence, the pattern was going to be dumped onto them and then their children. Even if it was hard to explain why their mother and I weren't together, saying nothing would have been unfair to them. What I had to let Chris Jr. and Jacintha know, finally, directly, and without blame, was that things hadn't worked out between their mom and me. We had been unsuccessful at living together the first time around with Christopher and, though we tried to reunite briefly, which led to us having Jacintha, that effort didn't last. And my kids knew that we'd tried. But I also didn't want them to be drawn into our disagreements or to have to hear more blame—at least not from me. My choice was to tell them all of this but then to make sure they had their own relationship with their mother that didn't come with my commentary, pro or con, about her. That was my new policy—they could ask and I could tell, as long as it didn't burden them.

None of the three of us like confrontations, but both my children today will not suffer in silence by keeping feelings inside. And I praise the Lord for that every day. That cycle has been broken.

When you accept that your generational cycle can be broken, and remind yourself that though it will be hard, you aren't the first to do so, you'll be ready for the challenge of taking a close look to see how it was instilled in you in the first place. You're then prepared for the big job of making the conscious determination to uninstill it. Your higher power can help. Such was the situation for my friend and colleague Victor, now a devoted father, husband, successful actor, and activist in the arena of violence prevention. Victor told me about the decision he made when he was very young that he would never become the "madman" that his father was. Victor described to me the abuse that took place "on the level of torture," which he, his siblings, his pets, and his mother experienced at the hands of his father. "No one had to tell me that it was wrong," he said. "I think that children aren't born bad. Violence is a learned behavior." When I asked what it was that helped him break the cycle, his first answer was, "I knew that God had a better plan for me. I knew my father wanted to beat the goodness out of me and I refused to have my spirit broken." As an adult, while he knew absolutely he would never hit a woman, before he became a father he developed anxiety over worry that he might carry some kind of genetic predisposition to hurt his own child. But that fear was put to rest when his son was born. "The moment I held my baby in my arms," he told me, "I knew that I could never do to him what had been done to me. I knew that I'd broken the cycle."

Victor's story leads me back to the properties of spiritual genetics, not just the awareness that God had a better plan for him but also that he made the choice—and took action—to embrace his own goodness. He chose healing rather than spiritual stagnation or degradation.

Stories of individuals like Victor who find ways to heal from negative influences remind us that just as our bodies have innate mechanisms for fighting off disease so, too, do our souls. This understanding has led me to conclude that our spiritual genetics endow us with an ancient blueprint for healing, growth, overcoming, and prevailing that is common to everyone.

In 1931, the father of modern analytical psychology, Carl Jung, came to a similar conclusion with Rowland, a most challenging patient of his. I heard about this story from a man at a book signing who commented, "Your description of spiritual genetics and breaking destructive patterns of behavior is very Jungian!"

Since I wasn't sure what he meant, I decided to do further research and found a fascinating account of the saga of Rowland that had been sent in a letter to Carl Jung in 1961 from a man by the name of William Wilson. In that letter, Wilson reminded Dr. Jung about Rowland's case and recounted how Rowland had been so severe an alcoholic that after more than a year of treatment, Jung finally confronted his patient. He told Rowland that he was hopeless and couldn't be saved until he decided to save himself. Jung believed that he had the tools within his "collective unconscious"—a reservoir of consciousness that all humanity can access—but he was disconnected from his ability to access those tools. Dr. Jung told his patient, "I can only recommend that you place yourself in the religious atmosphere of your own choice, that you recognize your own hopelessness, and that you cast yourself upon whatever God you think there is. The lightning of the transforming experience may then strike you."

Wilson described to Dr. Jung how Rowland had eventually sought spiritual settings and was able to stop drinking temporarily, but never without relapse. He finally made it to New York and at last found the right spiritual setting in addition to a supportive group of friends and peers. The combination was that very transformational lightning strike. Rowland discovered the validating truth we've known all along—*hey, it's not just me!* Not only was he successful at breaking the cycle of alcoholism that was generational and cultural, but he was able to tell his story to friends and therapists to give them an overview of the steps that had helped him to do so.

Through Rowland's contacts, information and inspiration arrived for two individuals who were on the brink of their own demise and who were able to apply this blueprint for themselves. One of them was William Wilson, also known as Bill W. He found the approach so effective, he wrote to Dr. Jung, that he decided to codify the approach into twelve steps. That same Bill W. was the founder of the support organization of Alcoholics Anonymous.

The broadest application of the power we all have to embrace healing rather than our own doom can be seen in the insight that Dr. Jung gave his patient in telling him that the tools for curing his addiction were within him—there in the caverns of his soul, in ancient form. To apply them, he needed an example from others who were struggling and suffering similarly. This leads me to admit that sometimes it's not enough to have someone who hasn't experienced what you have tell you, "Hey, you already have the means within you, why aren't you succeeding at breaking the cycle?" Sometimes, it's important to hear the test and the testimony from someone who has been there, done it, and healed. Of course, that is the AA model.

One more application I'd like to suggest for breaking any patterns of behavior that prevent you from embracing your light is to use the C-5 complex tool to give yourself a structure for healing. Are you *clear* and *concise* about your desire to end a pattern of destructive behavior or a generational cycle? Can you make your motivation as *compelling* as you will need it to be to pass this test? Can you summon your oceanic persistence to take those baby steps in a *committed, consistent* way in order for the transformational lightning to strike you once and for all? These are tall orders, so it helps to remember that healing doesn't occur overnight. We can certainly borrow the mantra to take it, whatever it is, one day at a time.

As hard as breaking generational cycles can be, you can take heart in the knowledge that someone else has taken this same journey before and so can you. Your healing will then be a blessing not only for yourself, but for everyone else as well.

LESSON #40
Your Divine Inheritance

KEYWORD: *Abundance*

There are stories we're all hearing lately about how the seemingly most trustworthy advisors, friends, and family members have bankrupt the life savings of loved ones. Now, these instances wouldn't be the first time that responsible and reasonable folks have put too much trust into others that maybe they shouldn't have. Then again, it does seem to have taken on extreme proportions in recent times.

A letter came to me with such a story from Miller, a married father of two, who had a long history of making and losing money. In one year, he had gone from having his own company with half a million dollars of revenue to being broke. It was the partner who had emptied the coffers when he wasn't looking. The next year he launched another company, which slowly but surely took off like wildfire and put him at the top of his game. Then came a downturn, one thing leading to another, and soon enough he was back at square one—only with debt, overhead, taxes, and employees.

At thirty-four years old, Miller started over, already with four separate entrepreneurial efforts cooking, all of which were promising. And yet, he wrote, "Every time I get some traction, I hit my limit—one that I've placed in my own way. What was it that told you that it wasn't too late? I'm dealing with terrible credit, insecurity, trust issues, and health concerns. Where can I find the tools to go to the next level?"

The first thing that jumped out at me in his e-mail was the fact that Miller had already identified his main obstacle as the limit he had put on himself. Maybe he wasn't aware of how powerful that admission was. At the same time, most of his focus was on what he couldn't attain or what had been taken from him. He wasn't focusing on his true "divine inheritance"—the God-given abilities that were already within him and which could be used to their utmost.

Perhaps the reason he wasn't focusing on this inheritance was because he was looking in the wrong place for resources rather than in his spiritual toolbox. Many of us, like Miller, don't look there often enough because we feel that we don't deserve the abundance that is due all of us in our pursuits of happyness. It's not math—as in "if you do x you'll get y"—or at least not in my view. My experience is that our blessings don't just arrive when we achieve our aspirations. They're given the moment our higher power lifts us up as we choose to set forth on any pursuit that is significant and worthy of our actions. So, it would then follow that we deserve to be blessed at the starting gate and every step of the way—not just at the finish line. Then again, our blessings might not be material or monetary.

You may be thinking right now that many earlier lessons could redirect him to a sense of worth and contribution. Building on those themes, this lesson adds a further layer as a reminder that each of us holds the deed to a vast divine inheritance that doesn't diminish like a bank account.

I suppose this was something that I'd always known theoretically, but it wasn't until reading a story told by Quincy Jones in his autobiography that I really understood the truth of it and the uses for that truth. Before I had the joy of getting to know him personally, I'd been fascinated to read of his ups and downs in pursuit of his award-winning careers as a musician, composer, producer, and global humanitarian.

My assumption had been that everything had sort of built effortlessly from the time that the young trumpet-playing phenomenon arrived on the music scene. Not exactly. By the late 1950s, after much early success, Quincy had finally started to make a name for himself and had set off on an extended European tour as a bandleader and tour organizer. While his focus was on his music and managing the demanding tour, money was not coming in as fast as it was going out. Meanwhile, he wasn't keeping an eye on his other financial interests in the United States or on those he had entrusted to do that. All of a sudden, he was informed that mismanagement back home had come close to wiping him out.

At the time that I read about his ordeal, though I wasn't in the same kind of dire straits, I'd been going through my own experience of regretting that I'd put certain of my affairs in the hands of those who didn't have my best interests in mind. It was definitely stressful enough that I immediately related to how Q dealt with his crisis.

First of all, he didn't allow the appearance of lack and limitation to throw a wrench into his knowledge of who he was and what he was meant to do in life. In fact, as he later told reporters, "We had the best jazz band on the planet!" Then why were they literally starving? Because, Q discovered, it turned out that he had more to learn and more to do to set the table so that he could eat. The lesson for him was, "There was *music,* and there was the music *business.* If I were to survive, I would have to learn the difference between the two."

Those were marketplace and mastery lessons he still had to learn. But what he had to know in his soul was the spiritual part of this lesson. Instead of giving in to an attitude that lack of money was going to be his undoing, he challenged that limitation and chose to believe, as he put it, that the financial losses were nothing compared with the divine inheritance that was on its way. He said as much in his memoir, and later to me directly, "I accepted that God had bigger dreams for me." Indeed, he celebrated the abundance of talent and opportunity he had already received, and he declared it to be only the beginning of what God and the universe had in store for him.

By choosing to believe that there was something even more special he was intended for, which was still to come, he allowed his true, unlimited inheritance to be revealed in ways that he could never have predicted. In the short run, once he decided to learn more about the music business, a relationship developed with Mercury Records that helped him through the next passage. After mastery of that pursuit as vice president of the label, he went on to become a leading, game-changing player in almost every aspect of the recording and entertainment industries.

The premise that God has bigger dreams and plans than even we can claim for ourselves is one we can choose to accept or not. It's up to us to say yes or no, and then, to be ready for receiving what we've selected.

A short while after reading Miller's e-mail, I wondered if the lesson of divine inheritance that had inspired me earlier on would be of interest to him. When I decided to follow up first, and see how he was doing, I was further inspired by his answer. Times were very tough. His circumstances had not dramatically improved. But something had changed. He had decided that he was going to focus on providing for the basic well-being of his family. For all those years, he had attached monetary status with his pursuit of being someone significant in the world. Now he was looking for other kinds of abundance to attach to his importance. Miller has always focused on "getting somewhere" and "making it," but he was doing something that he never had before; he e-mailed me, "I'm just being where I am and waiting for God to give me instructions."

Miller message leads me to a last advisory that I should add about the divine inheritance intended for us to do, be, and have is that all of this unfolds for us in divine time. It doesn't run on overnight FedEx or the schedule of our choosing. We can prepare for it, however, just as Miller has, by declaring ourselves ready for our instructions.

Divine time is when we've done our part, too, when all the steps have been taken, all of the prerequisites have been fulfilled, the anvil has been pounded, and the trail to the farthest star has been plotted. Welcome your inheritance. Then get out your boldest highlighter and underline this next sentence and speak it out loud wherever you are if you dare: "I am ready."

LESSON #41
God's in the Details

KEYWORD: *Reverence*

It's a good thing that I've got a sharp, visual memory, because whenever I see a beautiful, moving sight, the idea of whipping out a camera or cell phone to take a shot just seems to cheapen the experience for me.

Later on, of course, I regret sometimes not having some way to preserve the memory. Nonetheless, a very basic yet potent spiritual lesson for me has been to find reverence in living the moments of my life without a special lens. Real, raw, touching, funny. That's how I show reverence to God—just by admiring his handiwork. It doesn't have to be a sensational sunset or a perfect orchid or a view from the edge of the Grand Canyon.

And I'd love to say that I've had an encounter with a burning bush or two, but the closest that I can remember to getting a sign from heaven was the time that I noticed roses growing in the Oakland ghetto—a story that I tell in other settings—which led me to find my first place to rent after homelessness. Maybe it wasn't a divine sign, but those roses flourishing in the neighborhood where they weren't supposed to be able to grow were miraculous. It was one of those details that had God written all over it.

A dear friend and colleague told me the story about how she gave her father a ride to the bank on what must have been the worst day of his life. He'd been going through marital problems and had just been told that he had an inoperable brain tumor. Forty-six years old. But when she saw her dad emerge from the bank he was smiling from ear to ear, almost skipping. What had happened? The pretty bank teller had flirted with him. Was that it? God was in those details.

Reverence for those details doesn't require us to do anything special. "Wow" works. Applause is nice. You know I'm partial to doing the alligator dance and throwing the confetti, too.

I've also applied this lesson as a reminder that prayer doesn't have to be complicated. My mother used to say that the best words in the English language are *please* and *thank you.* Dr. Angelou added to that two more helpful words, *I'm sorry.* All of those words are great ways to start prayers.

God by any name we want to call him does listen—especially when we listen to what has been called that small still voice within us that comes from the light of our spiritual genetics. My favorite prayer is that of simple gratitude. I've also learned from this lesson that when in doubt about what I'm supposed to be doing next, there's nothing wrong with seeking guidance by saying to my higher power—"Thy will, not my will."

It can be a stretch to find ways of feeling reverent in the midst of crises like the turbulence we've seen on Wall Street and in our economy over the past couple of years. The downturn didn't take a major toll on my company—partly because by staying small, it's much easier to be flexible and resilient enough to adapt to rougher waters. In times of economic peril, the larger battleship financial institutions sometimes have a much harder time making a U-turn when they're heading straight for the glacier. Another advantage for us was that we had not gotten involved in the business of giving out cheap loans—the linchpin of the subprime mortgage crisis. It was never a good idea but it was very profitable for shareholders, so what do you do? Sell what they're buying, right?

The fact that my beloved alma mater, Bear Stearns, was one of the first casualties in early 2008 was so painful to me. Ironically, it came in the midst of banner good news on a day when my team at the office and I became participants in an offering with Visa, the largest IPO in the history of Wall Street. At a time when all the troops at every stop on the street were scrambling like lab rats to either get in on the deal, or to jump off the ships that were sinking—making every call, pulling every string, pushing every button, kissing every ring—I was thrilled that we'd clinched the deal. But that didn't keep me from feeling heartsick about the announcement that Bear Stearns was being taken over by J. P. Morgan Chase & Company.

My thoughts were with the individuals who were family to me and who were having to face the greatest crisis of what had otherwise been a proud and prosperous odyssey. The partners and employees had collectively lost billions, and even though the financial loss didn't directly affect me, it was like watching my hometown being battered by a category 5 hurricane and there was nothing that I could do to stop it.

The person most in my mind was my old boss and mentor, Ace Greenberg. A couple of months before the takeover, when I'd visited the midtown Manhattan Bear Stearns headquarters, I had found Ace in his familiar spot on the trading floor. Little had changed. Though he was no longer steering the ship, he was the same tenacious, hardworking visionary under whose stewardship the company had grown from just over a thousand employees to almost fourteen thousand. That wasn't the first time we had been in contact after he had fired me back in early 1987—which had seemed like the worst crisis of my career but had been the best thing that could have happened to me. As the years went on, every time I saw Ace, without saying it in so many words, he indicated how proud he was that I had taken the best of the values that had been his bottom line in growing Bear Stearns to the height of its success—passion, discipline, character, contribution.

On that last day I visited him on the floor, I couldn't help but smile in admiration at what an unapologetic character he is. Famous for being a fanatical bridge player and superb amateur magician, Ace was also a well-known master of company memo writing—on everything from the importance of quickly transferred calls (and his threat to give private lessons to those who flunked spot checks), to the need to avoid arrogance or complacency in good times, and the need not to hide from clients in bad times. Ace was so intent on everyone, partners and associates, being easy to locate when out of the office that he once wrote in a memo, "I have contacted Marlin Perkins of the St. Louis Zoo and the next person that I have trouble finding will be fitted with a radio collar. Please impress our policy on the people who work with and under you. The collars are bulky and not very attractive."

Probably the most well known of Ace's memos had been issued right around the period of my arrival at Bear Stearns in the mid-1980s. Ace wrote:

When mortals go through a prosperous period, it seems to be human nature for expenses to balloon. We are going to try to be the exception. I have just informed the purchasing department that they should no longer purchase paper clips. All of us receive documents every day with paper clips on them. If we save these paper clips, not only will we have enough for our own use, but we will also, in a short time, be awash in the little critters. Periodically, we will collect excess paper clips and sell them.

Seeing Ace in action on the floor before the takeover, I had taken the opportunity to express my gratitude to him and could barely conceal my happyness when he looked me straight in the eye and let me know that he wasn't surprised in the least that I'd "done good."

When news broke two months later that such an important part of my history had come to an end, I felt compelled to call Ace. Most of my team thought that wasn't necessary. Surely he would know I was thinking of him, they said, and maybe it would be better to wait until the dust settled. As a compromise, I decided to pick up the phone and just leave a message with Mr. Greenberg's assistant. But she insisted on putting me right through to him, transferring the call immediately.

When I greeted him, before I could say something encouraging, Ace cut me off, saying, "Chris, you get some good breaks, you catch some bad breaks in life—you just have to move forward. You know about this." After taking a beat, he characteristically added, "Chris, by the way, can you lend me five dollars?" and then broke into his biggest belly laugh!

After we hung up, I made sure to send Ace not five, but *six* single dollar bills, along with a note to make sure he saved the paper clip that I'd enclosed as well—for the next leg of the journey that was about to begin.

When you think of all that I had gained from the opportunity to learn and work in a field of my choice, six dollars and a paper clip was a pretty incredible deal for me, wouldn't you agree? That's a moment for reverence. There's God in those details, too.

As a tag to that story, I have to add that the overnight loan I extended to Ace was returned just as promptly with a note from him. He explained that he couldn't accept the money because "I don't want my creditors to find out." He gave me one more laugh for that day, in the midst of the ongoing crisis, between whatever else there that we call balance and a blessing. It is not an accident that the signed photo I have of Ace Greenberg sits between pictures of my mother and Nelson Mandela.

All that's required for reverence is the choice to pay attention to the details. When you spot someone on the street begging, you don't have to do anything or give that person a nickel. But see them. Please see them. They've got God in their souls, too. You don't have to be God, by the way, and rescue that person. But if you want to help, next time you start to leave a restaurant with half your plate still full—why not have it wrapped up to go, and hand it to the next hungry person who crosses your path? Or if you prefer, show your reverence by going home and writing a check to an organization that has a track record in helping root out the causes of homelessness that propel the cycle. That is reverence.

When everything in the world appears to be spinning out of control and it can seem that too many of us are ignoring the great challenges of our times, and that we've lost connection to our souls, each of us needs to look for God in the details to get us back on track.

The solutions we need, individually and collectively, may not be visible to us yet. With reverence, we may pursue them, humbly, creatively, courageously. And, while we're at it, we may choose to give praise and be joyful that we can.

LESSON #42
Passing the Torch, Raising the Bar
KEYWORD: *Growth*

As you most likely have experienced for yourself, there are certain rites of passage for everyone—weddings, funerals, births, graduations, birthdays, and other observances or rituals—that stand out as peak moments of spiritual connection not only to one another but to all who have come before us and all who will come after us. These events frequently yield some of our most cherished memories and can serve almost as culminations of every lesson we have learned up until that point.

I'd like to share such an experience with you, knowing as I do that parts of it may summon memories for you of important rites of passage in your life. The occasion was Mother's Day 2008, the proudest day of my life. In the weeks and months leading up to that day, a few different events had been in the works for a while. In less than four years, thanks to tenacity, planning, passion, and laser-beam-like focus, my daughter, Jacintha, Jay for short, was set to graduate from her dream school—Hampton University in Hampton, Virginia.

Over the course of many visits to the campus of this revered institution of higher learning, a historically African American college—nestled in a picturesque town along a beautiful waterfront setting—I often thought of how Jay's journey was carrying forward the dream of Bettye Jean Gardner. And so now that graduation day was approaching, the finality of it coming to fruition filled me with incredible nostalgia.

The other milestone was that on the same morning before the graduation ceremonies were to start, I met my first grandchild. That's right, Christopher Jr., that little baby boy who'd lived with me through our time in the wilderness, had become the father of the most beautiful, precious girl—who I held in my arms that morning in wonder, knowing that one day she would look up at her father and say, "Poppa, you're a good poppa." Of course, those were the words that two-and-a-half-year-old Chris Jr. had spoken to me not long after we moved into our first place after homelessness and things were still tough. That was all I needed to hear to go forward.

If you're a parent or a grandparent, you'll probably relate to the wild mix of emotions that I was having on that day. Likewise, if you're a teacher, a mentor, or a champion for someone whom you've watched grow in every way over the years, you'll also know what a blessing that is. And if parenthood isn't yet on your horizon, I can assure you that the most valuable lessons you can learn—spiritual and otherwise—may well be taught by the children whose lives you care for.

You can imagine the emotions that were churned up for me that day, made more intense by the fact that I'd been called upon to deliver the commencement address. As I approached the podium and gazed out at what had to be more than ten thousand people on hand to celebrate the 2008 graduating Onyx Class, that moment was my rite of passage. This was, at last, proof that I'd kept the promise made to myself at five or six years old to become the father that I'd never had. The choice to pursue a path of growth by embracing the light of my spiritual genetics had led me to this moment. Now it was time not only to pass the torch to the next generation but also to start where I was—with new possibilities and further stars to seek. But before that, it was time to honor the rite of passage of the graduates whose day this truly was.

I'll share some of the thoughts with you that I spoke about that day, just as you take this opportunity to imagine the rite of passage from where you were only yesterday to where you'll be tomorrow.

My speech began with a confession, as I acknowledged, "It has been my privilege to address bodies as broad and diverse as the United Nations, major Fortune 500 companies, and community organizations all over the world. But this moment, this day, this celebration, is absolutely the greatest event that I have ever been privileged to participate in."

As I scanned the crowd, hoping to direct my comments to my daughter in her cap and gown, I continued, "And I say that for one very selfish reason. Today my child walks across this stage and will become the first person in the history of my immediate family to graduate from college since we got off a slave ship four hundred years ago. So, for us, it has been four hundred years to Hampton."

Of course, I knew from the murmur in the crowd that I wasn't alone in this experience of seeing a child or grandchild become the first in the family to graduate. It dawned on me that spiritual genetics was once again at work, tapping the dreams and prayers of ancestors from all walks of life who sought freedom, opportunity, and education for their families and future generations.

My message to the graduates began with my promise to show my appreciation by giving the shortest commencement address in history. Continuing, I said, "I would like to share a few things that hopefully you will consider as you cross this stage and step into the rest of your life. I gave a lot of thought to what could be of meaning and relevance to you at this, the beginning of your pursuit of career, life, and happyness. I decided not to spend my time here with you to discuss current economic trends and conditions, what could or could not happen politically, nor what corporations are considering the near-term response to both of the aforementioned. I would like to take this time with you to encourage you to dream a bigger dream, to dream, dare, and do." And then I had to add, "Seek to become world class at whatever it is that turns you on," to which a roar of applause followed, much to my surprise. Sometimes the most obvious truths say it all.

After sharing with them several of the life lessons that have been mainstays for me, I finally spotted Jacintha and spoke directly to her, saying to everyone else as well, "I would like to close my remarks with a brief nod to my child." Though I couldn't see her face for the blur of tears that I was fighting back, I told her, "There are no words to express the joy that you have brought not just to me but to our entire historical and extended family. Some folks that you knew, some folks that unfortunately you didn't get to know better, and some folks you only heard of. Because today when you walk across this stage you will become the first person in the history of our family, since we got off a slave ship four hundred years ago to graduate from college."

Again, applause and cheers followed. I talked to my daughter but I was speaking for everyone in noting that four hundred years to Hampton was a metaphor for our collective journey, four hundred years of blood, sweat, and tears, and of oceanic persistence. "When you cross this stage today," I continued telling Jay, "be mindful of all the folks who came before you, who made this day possible. For the last four years you did the work, you had the ball, you handled your business. But never forget the folks who came earlier."

I reminded her of her grandma, my mother, who couldn't pronounce my daughter's name and insisted on calling her Cindy. I reminded her of her great-uncles, and how Uncle Bro, Momma's oldest brother, had broken down in tears when he showed me the road he and my mother had to walk to get to school. "Uncle Bro cried grown-man tears as he recalled how little white children riding by on horseback or in wagons would spit on him and call them 'nigger' simply because they wanted to go to school."

I also wanted her and everyone in attendance to be mindful of Uncle Joe Cook, a man who wasn't really a blood relative at all, and someone whom Jay had never met. But within our spiritual genetics, he was part of our human family, a man "who was left with a pronounced limp for the rest of his life after he walked all the way from Mississippi to Milwaukee—because he heard he could go to school there."

Then I returned again to Bettye Jean Gardner, who most certainly at that moment was watching all of this from heaven, dancing with her wings on. With Jacintha's plans to go on to graduate school in Italy to study design, this wasn't Momma's crowning glory for the dreams that had been instilled in me, but a passing of the torch to Jay and all in attendance. My mother's message to the graduating 2008 class of Hampton University and all of us is that not only do we have the opportunity but indeed the responsibility and the power to realize our dreams and, furthermore, to always pursue happyness. We have that power because in the wiring of our spiritual genetics, we are designed for growth. We are designed to learn our lessons and to go on to prevail.

And finally, I summed up my life as a parent, on behalf of those of us who invest in the dreams of others, by bragging about my baby girl, now a college graduate, and how much she had taught me. I had to put it this way: "Men don't know what love is until they have a daughter. When Jacintha was eight years old she climbed on my lap and said she was never going to grow up, that she would always stay my little girl forever. When she was thirteen she told me she didn't need me to hold her hand to cross the street and last night she took my arm as we went to dinner to celebrate her graduation." I think in that moment I saw thousands of fathers wipe away their man tears, so I added, "We love our sons, I love my son, but every man in here will tell you that when that little girl looks up at you and says 'Daddy' . . . the world stops."

And there in that audience were many single parents who had to be both momma and daddy, as there are the world over, and it makes not one bit of difference when we come to these moments to collectively feel the gratitude and pride for where we have arrived. Our children are our greatest blessing.

For this privilege of parenthood, I ended with great praise and great thanks, starting with words spoken at my mother's funeral, when all I could do was to stand at her casket and say, "Thank you, Momma." Again to Jacintha I said, "Right now I thank God for letting you be my daughter and I thank you for letting me be your father." Last but not least, I thanked the graduating class of Hampton University, echoing my earlier words that the only takeaway I hoped they wouldn't forget was my mantra: "Always Pursue Happyness."

The cheers, whoops, and hollers for the theme song that you can never sing enough were better than if I had been Miles Davis and Muhammad Ali at the peak of their careers. But I had to add a final thought, "The absolutely last thing that I want to say to my children is that we all know that never again for our family will it be four hundred years to Hampton."

The lesson that I learned about pride and happyness at my daughter's graduation and the birth of my son's first child, my granddaughter, is one that I want to leave with you, that I hope finds a place in your heart for safekeeping. On that day, I celebrated the miracle of being simply a stepping-stone in the journeys of my children, and others. Not without plenty of tears, as I've duly reported.

Thus, I came to the end of one journey and left there after hours of dancing the alligator and throwing confetti, aware that I was about to start the next journey—destination not yet defined. All the life lessons in sum and the choices made to put them to use had brought me to this new departure point. And I realized, quite clearly, that the most important lesson of all was the one coming up around the bend, the one I had yet to learn.

So there you are, take this lesson and apply it in good health, wherever you choose to go, whatever you dare to dream and do. Godspeed, go make yourself proud.

Six / The Good Old Everyday

Finish each day and be done with it. You have done what
you could. Some blunders and absurdities no doubt crept in;
forget them as soon as you can. Tomorrow is a new day;
begin it well and serenely and with too high a spirit
to be encumbered with your old nonsense.

—Ralph Waldo Emerson
Poet, essayist, pursuer of happyness

An Introduction to Lessons #43 and #44—Ordinary Lessons for Happyness

Well, as we come to our last stop on this ride, I have just a few more life lessons to share that come from the absolutely most obvious treasure trove. This is the world of everyday life, where all of us who are ordinary normal folks inhabit a classroom that really can teach us everything we need to be able to savor the happyness we have pursued.

The ordinary lessons that are learned in the everyday classroom, as I understand them, have nothing to do with smarts, how you think, whether you've mastered nuclear physics, or you've been blessed with blazing intellect or even an abundance of common sense. The lessons we're here to explore are those we learn with our hearts.

Sometimes I think of these as "turn-the-corner" lessons, surprises that you come across in the least likely places when you've decided to go right rather than left. They're welcoming joys that greet you when you've turned the corner after a struggle. They're often the quiet moments that create pleasure and teach you to revel in an experience rather than rushing off to where you're supposed to be. They're the spontaneous conversations you have with the cashier in the supermarket—once a stranger, now your new best friend. They're the small-world coincidences; for example, when you're in a foreign country and all of a sudden your neighbor from back home walks by.

When I started to select a handful of e-mails, letters, and questions that best illustrated the lessons that will conclude our conversation—at least for now—the stack took over my desk! I couldn't limit my selection to one, two, three, or more, even when I closed my eyes and chose at random. Every time I did that, something else turned up that added texture, dimension, and feeling to the picture of how we embrace the happyness we've pursued all along the way.

Instead of giving you the examples from others, I decided to share the message that was given to me when I received a beautiful piece of artwork as a gift. The portrait was of a little boy looking up to a man standing next to him. The caption read "Would the child that you were respect the man that you've become?"

Perhaps you can relate that question to where you are now. In many ways, it ties together all the lessons for pursuit and gives us a real measure for how we know when we've truly arrived. When you can answer yes to that question, it's hard to beat on the euphoria Richter scale.

These last two lessons are mainly here to reinforce that experience of joy, which is truly our divine inheritance, and to remind ourselves of the classic idea that it's not the destination but the journey that counts—as my wise children, Christopher Jr. and Jacintha, have taught me. Lessons #43 and #44, in which we'll focus on happyness in terms of "the journey versus the destination," discuss the following:

> #43 The resource of **appreciation** is evergreen, as long as we choose to use it daily.

#44 As this final lesson is here to remind us, the freedom to
pursue our dreams brings with it the **responsibility** to do so.

Since we'll be parting ways before too long, I'm going to be sending
you off with some new and improved maps that you may find very
empowering—especially because you'll be creating them. Paper and
pen for making notes are optional. Passion is not.

Like I said at the start, it's on you. Pop that clutch one more time,
give it some gas, and let's roll.

LESSON #43
Don't Postpone Joy

KEYWORD: *Appreciation*

Are you ready?

Here is your first assignment: *Do one thing today for yourself that
makes you happy.*

"But I can't!" "My schedule won't allow it." "I can't afford to."

Need I continue with any more excuses?

Well, if you're driving, you really *can* choose to do one thing, prefer-
ably something that you've been putting off for a rainy or better day;
just do it. If you need some ideas, I'm happy to share with you some of
the items on my list. Every now and then, a stop at the nearest soul
food home cooking restaurant gives me joy. And you know how I feel
about having my shoes shined or shining them myself. Pure joy is putting my feet up and hanging out with my kids. Yes, all right, I love
taking my baby out for a spin in the fancy automobile that sits in my
garage and otherwise collects dust. It tickles me to no end to drive it
barefoot with just my big toe on the gas pedal! I love "retail therapy"!
Whenever I land in a new locale, the first treat that I can give to myself
is to go window shopping on the main thoroughfare. Then I'm right at
home. And when I return to my actual home and prepare to leave again,
either/or, I take joy in unpacking or packing. Bags to riches, after all!

So put something down on a piece of paper that you can do today. You got this, you know you do.

Next assignment: *Do one thing for yourself that makes you happy every day. Put it at the top of your daily to-do list.*

This lesson is self-explanatory, as you can see. *Don't postpone joy.* If you haven't felt joy in a long time and aren't feeling it at all, let alone postponing it, your breakthrough might be right around that corner you haven't been exploring lately. Go see what's there. You may be pleasantly surprised.

I had a surprise waiting for me back in the middle of 2007 when a business trip to San Diego gave me the opportunity to spend some time with my mentor and friend Gary Shemano. After the conference was over, we decided we'd drive back to San Francisco together; on the way Gary surprised me by announcing that we were going to stop off so that he could introduce me to his mentor, a master entrepreneur. No memorable words of advice were spoken but to stand in the presence of greatness is a feeling you never forget.

Perhaps you've had such an experience. If not, there may be someone's hand in your own community that you'd like to shake—without agenda or need for anything other than the human connection. You do honor to yourself when you honor the accomplishments of someone who has set the bar for everyone else, just as you honor those for whom you've set the bar.

Gary was as jazzed as I was that he could arrange the meeting. It had been something like twenty-three years since he had shown up at the brokerage firm where I'd first worked and recruited me to Bear Stearns, later telling me that it was initiative and passion that had impressed him. Gary had not only given me that incredible launch after teaching me everything that he knew, but he had never stopped cheering me on and taking personal pride in my journey.

Gary's intensity, drive, and brilliance were partly drawn from the spiritual genetics he embraced from his father. In San Francisco in the early days, when Gary's dad was pursuing his American dream, he had been a champion of the working-class folks whom nobody else would open doors for. Gary had taken that light which shone in his father and lived by it every day. Apparently, other genetics were working well in his favor, too. He was as dapper and vital as ever, not slowing down in the least—even though he assured me that he was focused much more on family, golf, and life. He was still intense.

When it was time to hit the road, we went to throw our luggage in the back of his black Mercedes 500SL. Realizing that we were almost on empty, we headed to the nearest gas station to fill up. While standing there at the station, I noticed that his four-year-old car was so pristine, polished to almost blinding perfection, it looked brand new. This was a giveaway that Gary was as meticulous as ever.

"Are you sure you've really mellowed?" I asked.

Gary insisted that compared with his past intensity, he was practically serene.

As he started to pump the gas, I looked around at the gorgeous, sunny California day and had to laugh when something unusual struck my eye. The convertible roof on Gary's car looked like it had just been unwrapped from the factory.

"Gary," I asked, "you ever take this top down and enjoy this car?"

"No," he shrugged.

Then I asked him something else. "Do you ever listen to anything other than these radio rant talk shows?"

"No."

The time had come for me to teach a lesson to my mentor. "Look," I said, "fill the tank, move over, I'm driving." Before taking over at the wheel, I added, "Hey man, how do you put the top down anyway?"

Gary looked shocked, as he pushed a button and rolled back the roof for the first time ever. Sheepishly, he walked around to the passenger side and sat down, looking over at me like—what the hell? "Gary, man, you need to learn how to enjoy life" was all I said to him, as I pushed some buttons on his sound system to find options for cruising music.

With the tunes on, we screeched out of the gas station and onto the freeway, pedal to the metal. Top down, music blasting, soaring up to the Bay Area at about 80 mph, we sang, laughed, talked, and whooped it up all the way there—truly loving, savoring, and appreciating the moment.

Gary admitted that it was totally a new experience for him and a learning one at that. Proof positive—tigers can indeed change their stripes. Over the course of our drive, we also caught up on some of the characters we had known. More than a few times when one of us asked about whatever happened to so-and-so, it turned out that person was no longer alive. There were a lot of fast-lane movers and shakers who'd been doing great one day and then keeled over the next. They left behind dreams unpursued, roads not traveled, joy postponed.

When we arrived at our destination, we high-fived each other and went our separate ways, promising to remember not to postpone joy and also to appreciate every opportunity life brings.

The irony is that we are coming to this lesson much later than lots of folks, perhaps including you. Or maybe, like me and Gary Shemano, you've spent too much time pursuing what's next and not enough appreciating what's now.

The reality of being "multimedia" as I've become, at my own peril, is that my schedule is clocked to the point that I know where I'm going to be every day for the next eighteen months—sometimes down to the scheduling of each meal. That's a far cry from not knowing where the next meal was going to come from. And it's definitely something I appreciate. Then again, it's overwhelming to look at a schedule like that. You can miss all of now by constantly having to check to see where you have to go next. That is why I am so thankful for having learned to appreciate, be, enjoy, and experience the now and the where of the present.

Often when I am out on the road, conversation may lag and the question arises as to what city is next on the agenda. My consistent response is, "It doesn't matter. All that matters is that right now, I am right here with you." People appreciate this answer and what's more, it sends a reminder to my heart to soak up the energy of where I am—to be *present* in the present, to be *here now* in the here and now.

Your next assignment, then, is to take a minute—sixty seconds—to be where you are now and experience the joy of it. Appreciate it. If nothing joyful comes to the surface, reach back into the past for the memory of your happyest moment that you can conjure up and let it be your touchstone.

My happyest moment takes me back to the age of seven, when one Milwaukee winter day after school, I came in the house, took off my coat, and heard Moms call me from the kitchen, "Chrissy Paul!" The calling of my nickname Chrissy Paul was usually the prelude to "put your coat back on and go to the store." Only this time, Momma went on to say, "Come here, I got a surprise for you!" And I went around the corner down the hall and into the kitchen and there was Uncle Henry—returned from his travels connected to his army service, there to see me.

To some this might seem like a bright spot on a gloomy patch. But for a little boy with the "no-daddy blues"—which is what you get when your stepfather constantly reminds you that you're not worthy of being claimed by the man who fathered you—it was everything. And in my memory, because Uncle Henry passed away so soon—only a year later—the surprise of having him show up was the ultimate gift. This was Henry Gardner, the inspiration of coolness, with the dazzling grin, impeccable goatee, and the sharpest-dressed person I'd ever seen. Uncle Henry was the same jazz lover who'd introduced me to the music of a cat named Miles Davis and who let me know with every gesture he ever showed me that I was loved. He was my guy.

The moment when I saw who it was, I ran straight toward him and he caught me in his arms, picked me up, and threw me high in the air—and that feeling never left me. That was the happyest day of my life. As far as sheer joy, ain't been nothing close to that since.

Not that there haven't been other amazingly happy moments and peak experiences. But nothing to rival that. The only thing to rival it would be if he walked in my door right now. One day when I was at the airport I spotted a dude who looked exactly like Uncle Henry, a TSA officer. It was uncanny. The goatee, the grin, the style—everything! In fact, the first time I saw this guy, I ran over and hugged him. Freaked him out! He gave me a stern look that said it all: you know you can't touch the government.

Uncle Henry showing up to surprise me for no other reason than that he loved me—wow, that was my happyest day. He knew my situation, and when it came to going out of his way to make my day, he didn't postpone joy either.

That leads me to make a last advisory for how you can utilize this lesson. Perhaps there's someone you know right now who could use and really appreciate some joy. You know there's a friend or relative, coworker, associate, or even an old rival, who would probably appreciate a surprise. Just show up. Be Uncle Henry for someone whose situation you understand. Go ahead and put that on your list, too—and then go make it happen.

LESSON #44
Claim Ownership of Your Dreams
KEYWORD: *Responsibility*

It is not by random selection that I've chosen this lesson and its assignment as the last to share with you. The theme that the pursuit of happyness is more than a right or a privilege, but is in fact a responsibility, is one we've touched on throughout the lessons explored all along. Now is the moment of uttermost truth. Are you in? One hundred percent?

Any milquetoasty "well, all right, yes, I guess so" ain't gonna cut it! If you're not revving your own rocket engines right about now, it's time for leadership—that is, your own. You're the boss. You're the woman. You're the man. If you haven't yet become the boss of your life, perhaps you should ask yourself why not. You may want to ask yourself what you've got to lose. There is a cost, absolutely, when you decide to be in charge of your own unlimited possibilities. The freedom to choose your destiny does indeed come with a price—responsibility. Much earlier, in our first lesson, we saw that a dream is only a dream without a plan. But neither a dream nor a plan, nor concerted action, will empower you to go the distance without full-throttled responsibility.

B. B. King put it best when he said, "Paid the price to control the dice, paid the cost to be the boss."

I've learned this lesson in so many everyday, ordinary settings. The letters, e-mails, and questions that I receive are all testimony to the importance of claiming ownership of our dreams. I've shared only a tiny fraction of them with you, but I hope they've reminded you of your possibilities and unlimited potential.

That said, as we established from the very beginning, the most powerful way to claim ownership of your dream, right up front, is to ask the questions that belong to you. The answers can produce a wealth of guidance, but ownership of your dreams, I believe, starts with your questions. Most of them begin with familiar words: *what, where, why, how, who* and *what for,* and definitely *when.*

The question now is from me to you. Are you ready for graduation from these lessons so that you can truly pursue your highest aspirations and *Start Where You Are,* like never before?

If you're still thinking about it, please feel free to dog-ear pages, write notes, and choose which resources are most relevant to where you are and the particulars of your pursuit of happyness. For those of you ready to blast off to your own moon landing, I will recommend highlights from each chapter that should be in your victory toolkit. First, I expect that you've found or chosen to *find your button* and it's absolutely turned on with rocket-blasting passion. Second, as you go forward with your plan of pursuit, I'm confident that you have unearthed the gold from your past and *value all experience* as your foundation of education. Third, I imagine you know that marketplace success is forged by hitting the anvil of hard work and from your willingness to *learn the ropes* of your pursuit. Fourth, I applaud your bold vision to *seek your farthest star,* bringing with you the mastery you've already attained as you step forward into your empowerment zone. Fifth, I know that you have begun to understand the universe's unlimited reservoir of help that is yours for the asking when you *connect to your higher power* and embrace the light of your spiritual genetics. And, finally, sixth, I salute your ultimate decision to *claim ownership of your dreams* as you commit to *ALWAYS PURSUE HAPPYNESS.*

Now that you have finished your course work, it's time for you to go and apply everything that you've learned or that you will continue to learn from your own life lessons. The point of this last life lesson— *Claim ownership of your dreams*—is to illustrate that the responsibility to do that is yours. Only you can determine your willingness to accept the good this universe can give you when you reach out your arms for it.

The subject of responsibility came up in an amazing close encounter that I enjoyed as I turned the corner one evening at festivities that I was honored to attend in South Africa, when I spotted none other than the icon, Sidney Poitier. If you know anything about his story, you may find it as fascinating as I do that he grew up on a tiny primitive island in the Bahamas without running water or electricity, yet today he is one of the most learned, enlightened human beings you could ever meet. He arrived in America at sixteen years old and had to teach himself to read and write, lived homeless at his start, worked as a dishwasher, and only stumbled onto an audition for actors because the theater happened to be close to a room he was renting at the time. His first audition was so terrible, the man in charge threw him out bodily and told him to stop wasting other people's time and to just go back to his job as a dishwasher. Sidney couldn't believe that the man knew what his job even was! Then and there, he made up his mind to seek the distant star and become an actor. It had never crossed his mind, but because someone told him "you can't"—well, you know what happened next. From becoming one of the most important actors in history, he turned to directing and producing, to global philanthropy, and then to becoming one of the most acclaimed, top-selling authors of recent years.

When I spoke to Sir Poitier—so known from *To Sir with Love* and from having been knighted by the Queen of England—his eyes were full of light and curiosity on the subject of spiritual genetics. With a working knowledge of what most astrophysicists know and suspect about the origins of the universe, he challenged me to go further than our connection to our human ancestors—to connect our genetics to the beginning of time. If, as some believe, everything began with the big bang of a grain of sand—God in that form—we could each have that very power within us! "But whatever you do, Chris," he said to me in all seriousness, "ask the big questions. The hour is late. Our planet needs all of us to ask the big questions."

With that powerful advice that we all need to take responsibility for the future of our planet and for our own futures, I leave you to do your homework and begin to write your acceptance speech for the attainment of your pursuit of happyness. You can thank whoever was part of making it happen in your life and you can spike the ball for yourself—it's all up to you.

And one last postscript I want to add is that responsibility, like joy, should also not be postponed.

Finale—Takeaways
Get 'Em and Go

Following are some pocket-sized reminders of the life lessons I've shared with you and their applications, with some extras that you might have missed or that I've thrown in for good measure.

Overture: C'mon In

+ The value of life lessons left on the shelf is lost. Take them down, examine them, take the guidance they provide, and apply as needed.

One / Start Where You Are—*Universal Lessons for Pursuit*

+ There is nothing you most need for starting than resources that are already yours—asking to be acknowledged and put to use immediately for any pursuit you can name.

+ Start by letting go of excuses that block your road, and begin to recognize your safety net of capacities and your trust fund of assets that are distinctly yours.

+ Seize the gift of where you are to start your pursuit of happyness—that's why they call it the present!

Lesson #1—Without a Plan, a Dream Is Just a Dream (the C-5 Complex)

+ *Pursuit*
+ It's always best to be in pursuit, as opposed to being pursued.
+ Plan your pursuit with intention *and* action: Clear, Concise, Compelling, Committed, and Consistent.

Lesson #2—We All Have the Power of Choice

+ *Empowerment*
+ Choose to shake off the limitation of lowered expectations.
+ Give yourself permission to call BS to any limits on your potential.
+ Know that where you are is by choice and not chance.

Lesson #3—The Cavalry Ain't Coming

+ *Attitude*
+ Your own attitude is the only thing you can truly control.
+ Acknowledge you're where you are because you drove here.

Lesson #4—Start with What You've Got in Your Hand

+ *Ingenuity*
+ If you do something with nothing, you can do anything.
+ With ingenuity, you make anything yours—giving it your fingerprint.

Lesson #5—Baby Steps Count, Too, as Long as You Go Forward

+ *Purpose*
+ However you take them, all steps count, as long as you take them on purpose.
+ We're all specks in the universe, but the dynamic changes when we become purposeful, directed specks.

Lesson #6—Stop Digging Your Potatoes

+ *Instigation*
+ Choose to believe your best years are still to come.
+ Enough hesitating, ready or not, tell yourself to jump—and remember that no one has to dig it but you!

Lesson #7—What Would the Champ Do?

+ *Inspiration*
+ Inspiration is the very breath of life. You can draw from the victories of your heroes to see what's possible.
+ If the Champ's still fighting, you can, too.

Lesson #8—Say "Peace Be Still"

+ *Perspective*
+ Embrace your abilities to change the channel or to stand your ground in crisis.
+ In stillness, gain perspective by seeing it with all your senses.

Lesson #9—Even Lewis and Clark Had a Map

+ *Research and Development*
+ There are no crazy ideas. J. K. Rowling started with a crazy idea and followed other maps, until she could throw them away and draft her own.
+ The best two questions for R&D are "what do you do?" and "how do you do that?"

Lesson #10—Find Your Button

+ *Passion*
+ There's no Plan B for passion! Besides, Plan B sucks.
+ If right now, you can't wait for the sun to come up so you can do your thing, you're doing the wrong thing.

Two / The Thorny and Golden Past—*Personal Lessons Drawn from the Past*

+ Those who can't remember the past are doomed to repeat it.
+ When asked if I would change one thing from my past, my answer is a resounding no. That includes the good, the bad, the ugly.
+ The future and the present are rooted in the past, thorny as it is. It is golden.

Lesson #11—Who's Afraid of the Big, Bad Yesterday?

+ *Freedom*
+ Freedom is priceless and the freedom to access the lessons of the past doubly so.
+ It's all right to approach yesterday with abandon or with caution; getting there is all that matters.

Lesson #12—In Your Library of Resources, Value All Experience

+ *Self-awareness*
+ The answer to whatever you seek to know about yourself now has its roots in the past.
+ It's never too late to revisit your personal Library of Resources. Besides, you've already got the card; and the place, once opened, never closes.
+ In the archives of your past, value all experience.

Lesson #13—Draw the Line of Your Life

+ *Discovery*
+ We learn very young that discovery is the reason we wake up every day.
+ The three truths the past teaches you: (1) you were meant to be here in this life, to learn, love, and be loved, (2) you are the hero of a meaningful story that is yours alone, and (3) everything and everyone are in your life for a reason.

Lesson #14—Whose Child Are You?
+ *Identity*
+ If your identity has been marred by a false message sent to you in the past, you can reject it as untrue anytime you so choose.
+ You are a child of the universe, loved and intended to be here, a person of worth and substance in this life.

Lesson #15—Check Out Your Own Version of Genesis
+ *Forgiveness*
+ We make peace with our past, through forgiveness, when we make the choice to first understand it. While we choose to forgive, we don't have to forget.
+ We can hold on to belief in unlimited potential that we had in the Garden.

Lesson #16—Who's Who in Your 'Hood?
+ *Trust*
+ Your original cast of characters taught you about trust, which shapes who you are today and tomorrow.
+ When you learn whom to trust and whom not to trust, you can still appreciate all the players in your story.

Lesson #17—The Red or the Yellow Bike?
+ *Motivation*
+ What is your why?
+ What is your version of the red or the yellow bike?

Lesson #18—Sometimes You Gotta Give Up Christmas
+ *Independence*
+ Everybody has their own version of a rotten Christmas; sometimes you gotta let it go.
+ Independence is enabled by engaging your three As—the capacities that help you to *know yourself* (authority), *be yourself* (authenticity), and *choose for yourself* (autonomy).

Lesson #19—No Test, No Testimony

+ *Courage*
+ Courage is taking the next step in the dark.
+ Be your own Moses and lead on.

Three / Hitting the Anvil—*Marketplace Lessons for Success*

+ When in pursuit of the means for attaining success, we've got ourselves an embarrassment of riches. We can borrow what's already known from other people's success!
+ And we can also use what we already know from our own experiences and life lessons learned while hitting the anvil of any past and current pursuits.

Lesson #20—The Law of Hard Work Is No Secret

+ *Initiative*
+ If not now, when?
+ If not you, who?

Lesson #21—Core Strengths Forged on Your Anvil

+ *Confidence*
+ Do you know what your anvil is? Cultivate and lead from your strengths.
+ If you don't believe it, then why should I?

Lesson #22—Wizards Begin as Blacksmiths

+ *Transferable Skills*
+ All the steps of knowledge can be transferred.
+ It is okay to fail—the knowledge is transportable. It is not okay to quit (which is also transportable, unfortunately).

Lesson #23—Are You Bold Enough to Go Back to Basics?

+ *Resilience*
+ The marketplace rarely turns a blind eye to boldness, even when you have to go back to the basics.
+ There is a direct correlation between boldness and happyness.
+ Make sure your version of your best blue suit is pressed and ready to wear.

Lesson #24—Supply and Demand Ain't Rocket Science

+ *Marketing*
+ Everybody's selling something.
+ Sell what they're buying and go to where they are.
+ Never be intimidated to approach someone with buying power, as long as you have something of interest to them.

Lesson #25—Truth Is a Hit

+ *Authenticity*
+ Nothing can defy the laws of supply and demand like the truth.
+ When you create something that is original, make sure you mark and brand your assets to protect them. Remember the cube!

Lesson #26—Learn the Ropes First, Then Conquer Rome

+ *Discipline/Character*
+ Talent is dazzling, but without discipline and character, the ride is destined to be short-lived.
+ Learn the ropes of becoming a world-class human being, then conquer Rome.

Lesson #27—Who's Who at the Office and in Your Spheres of Influence?

+ *Networking*
+ Make friends before you need friends.

+ Marketplace relationships build on trust and the recognition of mutual successes.
+ Bonus: Sometimes the juice ain't worth the squeeze.

Lesson #28—It Takes as Much Energy to Bag an Elephant as It Does a Mouse

+ *Focus*
+ Create a big-game mentality for yourself and everyone around you.
+ The bigger the field, the more you need to focus on making your world smaller—tight, keep it tight.

Lesson #29—Share the Wealth

+ *Community*
+ Share the wealth of your experience, your expertise, your time, and your goods and services.
+ Practice cooperatition—everybody wins when everybody wins.
+ Community begins at home, at the office, and in the neighborhood and extends globally.

Four / Your Empowerment Zone—*Life-Changing Lessons for Mastery*

+ When do you know that you've been hitting the anvil enough that you're ready for mastery? When life-changing lessons come along to prove it.
+ The quest to become world class at something is universal—it's not just you or me!

Lesson #30—Seek the Farthest Star

+ *Risk*
+ It is our nature to seek further than we logically can.
+ Risk is why we're here instead of under a glacier with the dinosaurs.

Lesson #31—Seeing Ghosts, Reading Signs

+ *Reinvention*
+ When reinventing yourself, see ghosts of opportunity and read the signs to prepare yourself for the challenges.
+ You can defy the Gypsy curse and go to the big time if you let the process play itself out; be prepared to write your own ending.

Lesson #32—Opportunities, Like Pancakes, Are Best Served Hot, but Sometimes You Gotta Set the Table Before You Can Eat

+ *Timing*
+ When you're in the empowerment zone, timing is a balancing act.
+ Be prepared to take advantage of the right timing, and don't forget fundamentals.

Lesson #33—Stay Open, but Don't Wing It

+ *Adaptation/Survival of the Fittest*
+ Change or be changed.
+ If you've lost your mojo, it won't come back if you're not open to new input, but stay grounded in who you are and what you believe.

Lesson #34—Mo' Money, Mo' Options, Mo' Problems

+ *Balance*
+ Instead of working hard for the money, see it working for you as a means to an end.
+ Money ain't the cavalry you've been waiting on to cure your problems—it's only one resource.

Lesson #35—Money Is the Least Significant Component of Wealth

+ *Worth*
+ End your dependence on money as a measure of your worth and your belief that get-rich-quick schemes lead to wealth. There are no retired drug dealers!

+ Replace the word *wealthy* with the word *resourceful*. Now take
  stock.
+ Become your own banker by counting your true assets on your
  personal balance sheet.

Lesson #36—Conscious Capitalism: A Personal and Global Primer

+ *Contribution*
+ The first step of conscious capitalism is to create value for yourself and your shareholders that you have identified as such.
+ The second step of conscious capitalism is to add value to the
  world.

Lesson #37—Make Your Dream Bigger Than Yourself

+ *Vision*
+ Never underestimate the power of vision, even when you're looking through the tiniest window—as long as you see with the eyes
  of your soul.
+ Be about the business of taking on causes that go beyond yourself. Grow your vision and your dream.

Five / Spiritual Genetics—*Spiritual Lessons for Connecting to Your Higher Power*

+ God by any name is in every single human being.
+ Unlike your mother's nose or other inherited physical traits that
  you can't choose, we have options as to which of our spiritual
  genetics we embrace within ourselves.
+ The best of our spiritual genetics from our entire human history
  are within us to be accessed.

Lesson #38—Embrace the Best of Your Spiritual Genetics
+ *Enlightenment*
+ Terence, the Roman playwright, reminds us, "I am human, and nothing that is human is alien to me."
+ In valuing all human experience that is part of your spiritual genetics, choose the light, reject the dark.
+ Be unto yourself a lamp.

Lesson #39—Breaking Generational Cycles
+ *Healing*
+ Healing is a natural capacity of our soul.
+ Lasting healing begins with the conscious choice to break the cycle—by embracing the positive steps that have been used before and taking strength from your higher power.

Lesson #40—Your Divine Inheritance
+ *Abundance*
+ The experience of lack and limitation is real, but avoid its destructive power by accepting the greater purpose that God and the universe intend for you.
+ Sometimes you may need to let the game come to you in Divine time. Trust in the abundance that's on its way.
+ And as for abundance, there's such a thing as too much if you can't appreciate it; that is, with certain exceptions—peace, fun, and sex!

Lesson #41—God's in the Details
+ *Reverence*
+ There is no one right or wrong way to honor God's handiwork, as long as you don't ignore it.

Lesson #42—Passing the Torch, Raising the Bar
+ *Growth*
+ We are spiritually and genetically predisposed to pursue growth and fulfillment for ourselves and our loved ones.

+ The most empowering, transformational lesson you can learn about growth is the one you learn next.
+ Growth and happyness are yours to create. If I've created mine for me, who else but you will create yours?

Six / The Good Old Everyday—*Ordinary Lessons for Happyness*

+ Pursuit without resulting happyness is the epitome of living interruptus.
+ The everyday world lets our hearts teach us how to savor what we've pursued all along.
+ Let the everyday surprise you with a lesson you didn't even pursue.

Lesson #43—Don't Postpone Joy

+ *Appreciation*
+ Do something for yourself today that you've been putting off.
+ Appreciation may only be of the opportunity to pursue happyness, or it may be of the memory of your happyest day. Don't postpone that appreciation either!

Lesson #44—Claim Ownership of Your Dreams

+ *Responsibility*
+ The freedom to choose the pursuit of happyness and to dream, dare, and do brings with it the responsibility, not the right or the privilege, to do so.
+ Accepting responsibility is accepting that your dreams really can come true.

Acknowledgments

Thank you!!! My mom always taught me that the most power-ful words in the English language are "please" and "thank you."

First, I would like to thank the millions of people around the world who embraced the story of *The Pursuit of Happyness* and the tens of thousands who felt compelled to reach out to me in order to share how *Pursuit* touched, moved, and changed them. It was, in fact, those people—via e-mail, phone calls, snail mail, and people coming up to me on trains, planes, into my office, and at the airports—that shared their connection to the book and inspired *Start Where You Are*. I always say *Pursuit* is the story of US! It was the questions of the tens of thousands that birthed *Start Where You Are*.

Thank you, Mim, my voice, you know me so well you finish my sentences. Thank you for your tireless work and commitment. Eli, thank you for sharing your mom; and Victor, thank you for the love you give Mim—it affects her work, you know.

Rachel Nagler, my publicist and conscience, soon to be a mother yourself, you are indispensable to all things *Pursuit*. Jen Gates, aka JGate, who will never doubt me again, thank you always for all that you do above and beyond the call of agenting. Jane Rosenman, we thank you for helping bring clarity and focus to our big ideas.

Thank you Dawn Davis, our editor, who barely had time to catch her breath after *Pursuit* to have a second child and begin working on *Start Where You Are*. Dawn remains one of the few folks who will tell me "no" and I care! Ha! Gratitude goes to the entire team at Amistad/HarperCollins, especially Bryan Christian and Christina Morgan, aka Shaker Heights. All have been instrumental in the process of giving birth to "the Book."

Big props to the entire team at Gardner Rich LLC, Christopher Gardner, Inc., and Gardner Rich Asset Management Group for continuing to dream. As for that one person who has made not only this book a reality but juggles every pursuit I've undertaken, that is the president of my companies, Collene Carlson, thank you for your loyalty, vision, and hard work. Thanks to Tina Sanders, who makes the impossible possible every day, and to Mike Dolan, my personal FBI agent. Salvadore Guerrero, there is a lesson in the book that best describes my value of you and your efforts. Mark Clayman, thank you for your ongoing enthusiasm and ideas.

Thank you to my children, Christopher and Jacintha, and especially the newest member of our family, my first grandchild, Brooke, who I call Honey Bear. For those of you who read *Pursuit*, you will recall my being haunted by the ghosts of Christmas past for many years. This past year marked a turning point when I saw my granddaughter take her first steps on Christmas Day. That was the greatest Christmas present ever. That ghosts can now leave me.

And, H., thanks for sharing your soul with me.